YORKSHIRE
FISHERFOLK

'It's amazing what a lot there is in an old man's head when somebody else starts him talking and puts questions to him ... . I considered the whole course of my life, and the things that had meant most to me were the first to come back to memory.'

Tomás ó Crohan, The Islandman *(1929)*

'It is probable that any human being attempting to describe the life of another will only approximate to representing that life as it appears to the person described. A good deal of guessing will always remain to be done, and at the end we may not know whether we have guessed aright – whether we have understood or misunderstood. But it is always worth-while to try to understand; we shall learn more, at any rate, in that way, than if we are content only to guess.'

Lady Bell, At the Works *(1907)*

YORKSHIRE FISHERFOLK

*A social history of the
Yorkshire inshore fishing community*

PETER FRANK

Phillimore

2002

Published by
PHILLIMORE & CO. LTD
Shopwyke Manor Barn, Chichester, West Sussex

© Peter Frank, 2002

ISBN 1 86077 207 2

Printed and bound in Great Britain by
THE CROMWELL PRESS
Trowbridge, Wiltshire

CONTENTS

For Mary
(without whose unstinting support
this book could not have been written),
Jonathan, Nicholas and Rachel,
with love and gratitude

LIST OF ILLUSTRATIONS

Acknowledgements

I am extremely grateful to those individuals who so readily loaned photographic materials and gave their permission for them to be reproduced. These include Mrs Thelma Paylor of Whitby and David Wharton, also of Whitby (especially for the sequence of photographs taken by Mr Hector Handyside of J. & J. Harrison of Amble, Northumberland, showing the building of his coble); and Mrs Jean Moralee of Staithes. Some of those who loaned photographs are no longer alive, but I wish to record my appreciation posthumously to the late Hugh Lambert Smith, William Wright, John Thompson, Edward Verrill and Dora M. Walker. Scarborough Museums and Scarborough Public Library both granted permission to reproduce photographs in their collections, as did Bridlington Public Library and Whitby Lifeboat Museum.

I appreciate, too, being allowed access to the Munby Collection by the Master and Fellows of Trinity College, Cambridge, together with permission to reproduce several photographs therefrom. Both the Science Museum, London, and the National Maritime Museum, Greenwich, supplied illustrations of, respectively, a Yorkshire coble and a Yorkshire lugger. As mentioned in the text, three plates derive from illustrations to an article by the late Leo Walmsley that appeared in *The National Geographic Magazine*.

In the early years of the 20th century, Whitby was regularly visited by a photographer from Bath, Greystone Bird. Some of his work came into the possession of Whitby Photographic Society and it was through the good offices of a member, the late Kenneth Adamson, and with the kind permission of the Society, that I was not only able to inspect this collection, but also to reproduce a number of images from it.

As mentioned in the Preface, I cannot overstate my gratitude to W. (Bill) Eglon Shaw of the Sutcliffe Gallery, Whitby, who generously gave me full access to the entire Sutcliffe collection, as well as permission to reproduce five images from it. Plates 1, 52, 84, 92 and 104 are photographs by Frank Meadow Sutcliffe Hon. FRPS (1853-1941) and are copyright The Sutcliffe Gallery, Whitby, YO21 3BA by agreement with Whitby Literary and Philosophical Society, Whitby Museum. (For further information tel: 01947 602239 or visit the web site on www.sutcliffe-gallery.co.uk.)

Many of the illustrations in the book come from my personal collection of, mainly, old picture postcards that has been assembled over the past thirty years. Amongst these are images that were photographed in the early part of the last century by local photographers-cum-postcard publishers. These include W. Fisher, who first set up his studio in Filey in 1857, and J. T. Ross, who appears to have been active in and around Whitby from about 1902 until not long after the end of the First World War.

Three illustrations derive from original paintings by J.R. Bagshawe (1870-1909) that were reproduced as postcards by Raphael Tuck and Sons in the early years of the last century in Tuck's 'Toilers of the Sea' series, while a fourth is taken from the posthumously published J.R. Bagshawe, *The Wooden Ships of Whitby*, 1933.

Finally, if I have failed to acknowledge any source, or, indeed, should I have inadvertently infringed copyright, the fault is unintentional and the responsibility entirely mine. It goes without saying that any such omission would be rectified in any subsequent edition.

P.F.

PREFACE

WHITBY is where I was born, and there it was that I spent my childhood, youth and early maturity. I have much to be thankful to Whitby for. It is a close community; sometimes narrow-minded and cloying, but warm, supportive and friendly most of the time. It is set on a superb coastline and backed by high moorlands and beautiful dales; a wonderful environment in which to grow up. I was fortunate, too, in having a good primary and secondary education. In particular, those wartime years in the firm, kindly charge of the late W.A. Burton at the Mount Boys' Junior School have had a profound influence upon my outlook on life.

Gradually, and fostered in their different ways by my mother and father, I began to realise that I owed a considerable debt to Whitby. That realisation became ever more acute after leaving the town. So, in a way, the present study is an attempt in some small part to discharge that debt, to put back into the community which sustained me so well in those formative years a little of what I have so liberally taken out. But why particularly a study of fisherfolk?

In the early 1970s, I chanced to attend a talk given by George Ewart Evans. Mr Evans's subject was the disappearance of the horse-based rural society in the face of the ubiquitous internal combustion engine. He warned that vast bodies of knowledge, traditionally transmitted orally from generation to generation, were rapidly being lost, and that to a great degree the loss was irrecoverable. As he says in his *The Horse in the Furrow*, a study of horses and horsemen in East Anglia, 'In their lifetime they have seen, not merely the passing of a few generations, but the passing of an era'.[1]

Stimulated by Mr Evans's remarks and enthused by his superb books which derive in substantial part from his pioneering work in oral history, it gradually dawned on me that the motorisation of fishing craft pre-dated the 'tractorisation' of agriculture in Britain. My next visit to Whitby confirmed what I had begun to suspect: the traditional fisherfolk community had undergone considerable change, even in my own limited memory. Gone were the sailing-cobles which had served Yorkshire fisherfolk since Saxon times. Almost disappeared were the traditional long-lines. Men no longer 'jazzed' for salmon or 'blashed' for sea-trout; and as ways of catching fish had fallen into disuse so too had much of the fisherman's vocabulary. Nor was it easy to discern a fishing community as such. True, certain family names still recurred

— Storr, Leadley, Winspear, Verrill, Cole — but increasingly fisherfolk were dispersing amongst the local community in general as car-ownership extended residential limits ever further away from the harbourside.

None of these changes was necessarily retrograde. Often they reflected growing affluence and economic security; or, as in the case of motorisation of fishing craft, greater margins of safety. Yet it was clear, too, that together with undoubted benefits there had been losses. Work though less arduous, was more routine and involved fewer skills. Much specialised knowledge had been replaced by new knowledge of a more universal kind. For example, the knowledge needed to sail a boat had been replaced by the knowledge needed to drive a boat.

I realised also on that visit to Whitby that personalities who in one's childhood had seemed to be everlasting were no longer there. In panic almost, I bought a tape-recorder and began a frantic attempt to record as much information as possible. A disastrous interview and a faulty machine prompted a more circumspect approach. People, I realised, are not 'sources' to be opened up and dipped into at random, as if they were books or a bundle of documents. I began again, this time explaining carefully what I was about. The response was heart-warming. Everyone I approached, courteously, uninhibitedly, willingly agreed to share their recollections. Thus, it was my privilege to talk with men and women who gave up fragments of their experience to posterity. Many have since reached their span. There was Tommy White, the last surviving Whitby fisherman to have sailed in a Yorkshire herring plosher. It was Tommy who was remembered as having tramped from Cardiff to Whitby after being paid off his ship, rather than spend a large part of his hard-earned money on an expensive train fare. Then there was Maud Hind, whose recollections figure so prominently in what follows. And James Cole: his memory went back to the 1880s when, as a boy, he first fished the off-ground in a Staithes yawl alongside his father and grandfather. Nor shall I ever forget the quiet dignity and immense knowledge of the late John William Storry. To these, and to all those whose names are listed below, I am truly grateful.

To gather oral evidence while it was still accessible was imperative, but at the same time I began to read as much background material as possible. The library of Whitby Literary and Philosophical Society proved to contain rich materials for this kind of study, and I am much obliged to the Society and its officers for their generous assistance. In the same way, the staff of Whitby Public Library was invariably helpful, as were the librarians at the University of Essex, Colchester. Official government publications, especially the Sea Fisheries Reports of 1865 and 1879, were indispensable, and I received prompt assistance on several occasions from the staff of the State Papers Room of the British Library, London. Greatly appreciated, too, is the permission of the Master and Fellows of Trinity College, Cambridge, to publish material from the Munby manuscripts.

As background to all this were numerous informal conversations in pubs and clubs, visits to museums and art galleries, and several trips off to sea to observe the fishing at first hand. In this latter respect, I thank Skipper Matthew Hutchinson and Skipper Louis Breckon, and their crews, for their kindness in having me aboard, and for their patience in answering my many questions.

For obvious reasons, the present study cannot pretend to be exhaustive. But it does attempt to rescue as much technical knowledge as possible about the fishing which might otherwise have been lost. Moreover, it tries to place this knowledge of lore and skills within its historical, economic and social framework. The geographical focus is Whitby and its neighbouring coastal villages. However, no part of the Yorkshire coast is excluded and Flamborough, Filey, Scarborough and Redcar figure prominently in certain chapters.

Documentary evidence dates from the Elizabethan period onwards, but the main chronological focus is from about 1860 to 1914. Much of the oral evidence concerns the first two decades of the 20th century, a time of rapid social and technological change. Economic hardship for working people generally and for fisherfolk in particular was widespread. The social gulf was deep. Even W. MacQueen-Pope, the eulogiser of the middle classes, acknowledged that,

> In the Victorian and Edwardian days there was a section of the nation possessed of a tremendous measure of the wealth of the world. They were few. At the other end of the pole there were people who lived from hand to mouth, who feared unemployment, who existed under shocking conditions and worked under worse, and who found it almost impossible, often quite impossible, to feed and clothe themselves and their children adequately.[2]

It is with this point in mind that the first two chapters set out the economic history of the coastal communities. Central to the analysis of the fortunes of the inshore fishing industry are the interaction between fishing and other types of employment, and the repercussions that technological innovations had upon the fishing directly, and indirectly through their effects upon the market.

Subsequent chapters deal with the geology and geography of the Yorkshire coast, for these, it is argued, are the chief determinants both of the location of settlements and of fisherfolk's homes and of the type of craft employed in the fishery.

The main body of the study is concerned with the fishing seasons – the boats, gear and methods of fishing; while a later chapter attempts to record the rôle of women (although it is doubtful that it is possible to do full justice to the part women played in the home and in the fishing economy generally).

Fisherfolk had a second, casual economy. Because they were so much at the mercy of the weather, it was impossible for them to rely upon anything approximating to a regular income; and so, as described in Chapter Ten, they had to find other ways to make ends meet.

Finally, two aspects of community are briefly considered, religion and politics, for it is these that both bring fisherfolk into focus against the background of society at large and emphasise the degree of their separateness. The Afterword consists of but a few impressionistic contrasts to highlight the changes that have occurred in the inshore fishery in recent years.

In the talk to which I have referred already, George Ewart Evans stressed the usefulness of material objects as a means to get people talking unselfconsciously. He described how he would often take along some small implement to ask an elderly person to identify or explain its use. This, he said, was an excellent way to put people at ease, since it enabled them confidently and expertly to instruct the enquirer.

Artefacts to do with the fishing were not readily available, but it occurred to me that photographs might be an acceptable substitute. They were. Initial reaction to being shown an old photograph was to identify the characters in it. This was often of great interest to me personally, but of only marginal utility so far as the wider study was concerned. However, such discussions did very effectively conduce relaxed conversation, and in that respect alone the exercise was well worthwhile. There were other benefits, too.

Often it was possible to discern items of gear in the backgrounds of photographs. Specific questions were asked about these. There was naming of parts. Uses were described. Sometimes more photographs were produced, but this time by the person being interviewed. Invariably permission was readily given to have copies made.

It was singularly fortunate that Whitby was the town photographed by Frank Meadow Sutcliffe.[3] Bill Eglon Shaw, proprietor of the Sutcliffe Gallery, gladly gave me permission to examine the complete archive and this was of inestimable value in the early phase of research. Gradually, my own collection of old photographs grew. Museums, friends, private collectors, local postcard dealers all enabled me to assemble an extensive visual record of the life of fisherfolk in the late 19th and early 20th centuries. Especially generous in lending me photographs out of their private collections were the late Hugh Lambert Smith and Whitby Amateur Photographic Society, David Wharton, Mrs Thelma Paylor, Mrs Jean Moralee and Ms Liz Shipley. David Cleveland, himself an enthusiastic recorder of East Anglian maritime history, was ever willing to make photographic copies for me.

Early photographic equipment was bulky and heavy, shutter speeds were slow. Consequently, there is a dearth of interior domestic shots, and pictures of fishermen at their work at sea are also extremely rare. To some degree, however, these shortcomings are repaired by the work of certain local artists, some of national repute. Notable among these was J.R. Bagshawe (1870-1909). He lived and worked at Whitby and Staithes, and, unlike most of his contemporaries, he actually went to sea with the fishermen where he sketched and made drafts from life. Bagshawe's paintings have great artistic merit. They are valuable to the social historian, too, in that they combine absolutely authentic detail and lifelike atmosphere.

Most of the research for this study and the bulk of the writing of it were done in the 1970s and early 1980s. Once completed, professional concerns of a very different kind drew my attention away from it: it was a time of profound historic change in the Soviet Union and my work as professor of Russian politics at the University of Essex and as commentator on Russian affairs for ITN's Channel Four News unfortunately left little time for social history. Still, my wife and children (now grown up) kept urging me to have the study published: I had a moral duty, they argued, to keep faith with all those people – most of them now long dead – who so generously shared their knowledge and memories with me. So, what is offered here is a token of gratitude to the town of Whitby and a tribute to the men and women who down the ages fished off the Yorkshire coast.

PETER FRANK
Colchester, 2002

COD

Sources of Oral Testimony

Robert Allan
Martha Ellen Boddington (née Richardson)
Louis Breckon
Gordon Clarkson
William Esplin (Bill) Clarkson
James Grimes Cole
Marion Cole (née Allan)
Anthony Goodall
George Frampton
Alice Maud Hind (née Harland)
Albert Hunter
John (Jack) Hunter
Jane Elizabeth (Jinny) Hutchinson
Matthew Hutchinson
Jane Jameson
Ann Lowis (née Welham)
Robert Marson
Laurence Murfield
James Noble
Robert William ('Mitchhouse') Richardson
Robert Storm
John William ('Woodpeg') Storry
William (Bill) Sutherland
Edward Verrill
John Verrill
Dora M. Walker
Jeffrey Waters
Thomas (Tommy) White
Harold Winspear
Matthew Winspear
Ned Wright

One

THE FORTUNES OF A
NORTH COUNTRY PORT

1 *Whitby: a study by Frank Meadow Sutcliffe, c.1898.*

WHITBY was 'a great fischar Toune' when Leland visited it in 1536. Nearly three centuries later, in 1816, it was found that out of a population of 10,203 only nine were fishermen. At about the same time it was remarked: 'The domestic fisheries of Whitby are on a very circumscribed scale'. Yet by 1893, 120 men and boys were fishing out of the port, the number increasing to about 150 by 1908.[1]

If fishing was Whitby's staple industry in the 16th century it was no longer so by the early 18th, for, as Defoe noted as he passed through on his tour, 'they build very good ships for the coal trade, and many of them too, which makes the town rich'.[2] A little later John Thisleton, the local barber-poet, declaimed:

> What a place is Whitby grown!
> Once but a poor fisher town.[3]

Growth had indeed been rapid – from 3,000 inhabitants in 1700 to an estimated 8,500 by 1779, the year when Charlton (Whitby's first modern historian) observed: 'Whitby has long been noted for building good ships for the merchants service and coal trade, but never was in so much fame on that account as at present'.[4] The Rev. George Young (the port's other notable historian) in 1817 echoed Charlton's opinion when, 'on the united testimony of respectable strangers from various parts', he insisted that, 'in strength, beauty and symmetry, our vessels are equalled by few, and, I may venture to say, excelled by none'.[5] But less than a century later, in 1902, the last ocean-going ship to be built at Whitby was launched, to be followed by much social distress in the town.

The pattern, it seems, was that, as alternative employments became available during periods of prosperity, fishing as an occupation declined. Conversely, when the local economy slumped, men resorted to fishing as their chief means of subsistence. But although this pattern is clearly discernible in the case of Whitby, the historical development of the coastal villages of Staithes, Runswick and Robin Hood's Bay was slightly different. There, changes in the structure of the national fishing industry had profound consequences over and above local economic factors.

The reasons for Whitby's rise to pre-eminence as a ship-building port are not entirely clear. Up to about 1680 the Netherlands had dominated European sea-borne trade. In addition to progressive commercial methods, Dutch supremacy was founded upon the *fluit*, or flyboat, 'a light, slight, but practicable shell employed to contain and float a ponderous and clumsy cargo'.[6] In other words, the flyboat was a craft that had the capacity to carry big loads using relatively small crews, thus saving considerably on costs. However, between 1680 and 1720 supremacy in shipbuilding shifted from Holland to the north-east coast of England.

Professor Ralph Davis has shown[7] how up to about 1680 English ship-wrights had been conservative in their designs, techniques and commercial practices, preferring to continue to build ships modelled on the East Indiaman: heavily armed, carrying a great area of sail, and thus requiring a big crew in proportion to the ship's loading capacity. This conservatism might have been broken down more rapidly had not the Anglo-Dutch wars brought many flyboats into English ownership as prizes. The Third Dutch War ended, however, in 1674, and as the last decade of the 17th century approached the captured flyboats were wearing out. Also, after 1662, the Navigation Acts prohibited the purchase of foreign vessels, and this, too, emphasised the need for English shipwrights to display greater initiative.

Meanwhile, London continued to concentrate on building warships and vessels for the East India and Levant trades, while the formerly important East Anglian centres, such as Ipswich, which had suffered most under the impact of the Dutch prizes, went into an irreversible decline. The void, it turned out, was to be filled by the ports of the North East. Here is Davis's account of what happened:[8]

> There is no direct evidence about shipbuilding in the critical periods from about 1680 to 1720, when the flyboats were wearing out and the English were compelled to build their own coal, timber and flax carriers. Four things are certain, however: that shipbuilding on the north-east coast was of small importance during most of the seventeenth century; that by the early eighteenth century considerable numbers of ships were being built somewhere in England for greater stowage and cheap operation; that by the middle of the eighteenth century Whitby and Scarborough ships had a reputation for just such qualities; and that when the registration of ships began in 1787, the north-east coast from Newcastle to Hull was by far the largest seat of the shipbuilding industry, and had obviously been so for a long time. I take this as indicating – in the absence of positive evidence – that the north-east coast was the place where sprang to life, in the decades around 1700, the new industry with the future in its hands, the building of English ships which could adequately replace the vanishing Dutch flyboats.

Some mystery remains, then, as to *why* it was that the north-country ports rose to such prominence. In the case of Whitby specifically, the contemporary

2 *Whitby stands at the mouth of the Esk, the only river to flow into the North Sea between Humber and Tees. Its harbour is protected by massive sandstone piers. In the 18th and 19th centuries Whitby was a major shipbuilding and ship-owning port. This photograph (c.1909) shows Scottish herring boats becalmed in the lower harbour.*

historian Lionel Charlton offers a solution. It was due, he said, to the alum trade.

For centuries England's principal export had been woollen cloth. Until the advent of synthetic substitutes in the 19th century the substances used to dye the cloth were very unstable and needed to be 'fixed' in order to hold the colour. The fixative (or mordant) used was alum. Up to about the year 1595 most of the alum for the woollen textile industry came from Italy, where the popes had a virtual monopoly in this commodity. But at about that date Sir Thomas Chaloner, realising that the Cleveland shales contained alum, established works at Guisborough. The new industry was soon extended to the Whitby district and important alum works were opened at Sandsend, Saltwick, in the valley of the River Esk, and elsewhere in the vicinity.

The manufacture of alum demanded huge quantities of fuel. The hewn rock was laid upon a bed of brushwood and the pile was set on fire. Successive layers of brushwood and shale were heaped up until a height of 90 to 100 feet was reached and a length and breadth of from 150 to 200 feet. These piles burned slowly for several months, and then the residue was steeped in pits filled with water. The resultant solution was drawn off and eventually placed in huge pans. A process of boiling and evaporation followed and the concentrated liquor was finally left to crystallise into pure alum.

It has been calculated that it required at least three tons of coal to produce one ton of alum. In 1661 1,100 tons of alum were made at the Mulgrave works alone, and in the year 1633-4 2,450 London chaldrons of coal were imported into Whitby specifically 'for his Majestie allome works' (a London chaldron at that time has been estimated at about 27 hundredweights). In addition, shipments of kelp and urine were brought in as ingredients in the refining process. All these heavy and bulky commodities came by sea. Whitby then, as now, was isolated to the landward; and in any case communication other than by sea in the 17th and early 18th centuries was atrocious, even for the ordinary traveller, let alone for heavy loads.[9]

To return to Charlton. Writing in 1779, he was in no doubt but that it was the need to satisfy the demand for fuel that set Whitby along the path to unprecedented prosperity.

> For the making this allum it was necessary that large quantities of coals should be procured, an article till then but little known on our part of the coast. These were not any ways to be so readily had as by shipping from Newcastle or Sunderland; and it being found very expensive to bring ships for that purpose from distant parts of the nation, a design was formed to have vessels always in readiness on some convenient part of the coast, whence they might put to sea in moderate weather. Here Whitby seemed to claim precedence of all other places, not only as it contained a harbour, but also had in it a number of fishermen, who having been long enured to the sea, might easily be rendered good sailors. Fired with the prospect of gain, and encouraged by the allum owners, some of these fishermen purchased two or three vessels of small burden, about the year 1615, with which they undertook to furnish the allum-works yearly with a certain quantity of coals; and having found out the way by sea to Newcastle and Sunderland, after the allum was made and fit to be carried to market, with a little assistance from pilots, they next ventured themselves and ships as far as London, whither nobody belonging to Whitby before that time had ever gone without first making their wills, it being looked upon as an attempt so very dangerous, that it was equal chance whether or no they ever returned. When they arrived there, and had disposed of their allum, fish, butter, and such other commodities as they carried with them, they returned home again freighted with merchandise for Whitby, which was there always sold and disposed of to a considerable advantage.
>
> After gaining a little experience in this trade, and considering that their ships were not to lie unemployed when the allum-works were supplied with

coals, their owners by degrees found out the way also to other ports, where they carried coals, and such other articles as they found would there redound to their advantage; thus by little and little was the coasting navigation introduced and established at Whitby. The profits which arose from the ships they had of course incited others also to adventure their property at sea: more vessels were purchased; and in twenty or thirty years time, by a resort of several ship-carpenters to the place, the inhabitants themselves were enabled to build new ships at the port of Whitby, with the oak timber that was then very plentiful and very cheap in its neighbourhood, so that commerce kept gradually increasing.

Charlton's analysis may seem to be somewhat conjectural in places, but, in the absence of evidence to the contrary, it is difficult to refute his main point: that alum provided the stimulus needed for the successful growth of the Whitby shipping industry.

By 1779 the port was building up to twenty-five ships annually, worth, in all, about £80,000. Another ten or twelve thousand pounds a year came from ship repairing. Some three hundred carpenters belonged to the town, and a hundred apprentices. Ancillary trades offered yet more employment, there being, for example, up to eight hundred spinners and 'a very considerable number' of weavers producing 5,000 yards of canvas weekly. About a thousand men were at sea.

Wars were beneficial to Whitby's trade, and the American War of Independence stimulated a great demand for transports, for which the roomy collier-brigs were ideally suited. Out of the 251 ships registered at the port, the majority 'are always employed in the coal trade; but, since the unhappy disturbances arose in America, seventy or eighty of them are in the transport service'. Another fifteen or twenty ships were engaged in the Baltic trade (carrying mainly flax, pitch and deals), while fourteen or fifteen went whaling to Greenland. A few each year sailed to the White Sea, the Mediterranean, France and Holland; and an occasional vessel traded with the West Indies.[10]

The wars with France (1793-1815) placed an even bigger premium on Whitby ships, and the local economy flourished. From an estimated 8,500 in 1779 the population of the town had increased to over ten thousand in 1816 (and this at a time when no English city, apart from London, had attained 100,000). A census carried out by Dr Young provides a detailed impression of the diversity of trades and occupations in Whitby in the early part of the 19th century. There were by then 403 carpenters, of whom some 150 were sea-going, and

besides, 29 boatbuilders, 17 block and mast makers, 34 sawyers, 64 ropers, 12 riggers, and 40 sailmakers. There are 104 weavers, and 39 flax-dressers;

3 *The* Star of Hope *(257 WY), pictured here at Whitby, was a Staithes mule. Her master when she was first registered in 1897 was Ralph Cole. Weighing 11 tons (compared with the two and a half to three tons of the average-sized coble), she was 37½ feet long on the keel (42 feet overall) and had a crew of four.*

In the foreground is Elizabeth Freeman *(127 WY). Big cobles like this one, although virtually identical in design and construction to smaller cobles, were known as 'ploshers' on the northern stretch of the Yorkshire coast and as 'splashers' at Filey. They were used exclusively for netting herring and were laid up in winter. Henry Freeman, the lifeboat hero and survivor of the 1861 disaster, was owner and master of this particular plosher. When in June 1870 he landed the first herring of the season at Whitby they sold for 1s. 10d. a hundred.*

most of whom belong to the manufactories (where steam-powered looms had been installed). There are also many other tradesmen whose employment depends in a great measure on the shipbuilding and manufactures: ... joiners, 79; painters, 26; coopers, 20; blacksmiths, including founders, 56.

Most of Whitby's food at this time was supplied by the small farmers of the surrounding moors and dales who sold their produce at the weekly market, but other retail trade in 1816 was in the hands of 52 grocers (some of whom were ship-chandlers), 37 butchers (many of whom supplied meat to the ships), and 30 drapers. There were, too, 161 shoemakers (including clogmakers), 69 tailors (including staymakers), 69 masons and bricklayers, three plasterers, nine glaziers, 22 tinsmiths and braziers, nine hatters, seven saddlers, seven watchmakers, 26 bakers, 12 brewers, 18 hairdressers, 22 tanners and curriers, five tallow-chandlers, 37 cabinet makers and upholsterers, three wheelwrights and tanners, and 132 labourers.

Apart from shipbuilding, the town's staple industry, and the various trades ancillary to it, the statistics reflect also Whitby's growing affluence. Of the masons, bricklayers, plasterers and glaziers, the cabinet-makers and upholsterers, many must have been employed in building and embellishing the fine mansions which the yard-owners and shipping interest were having built on the fringes of the town. The shops, too, reflect a combination of everyday and luxury services; for, in addition to those mentioned already, there were six hardware shops and six slop-shops, and six toy-shops and seven jewellers' shops. Beverages were in good supply, there being 16 dealers in wine; 56 in spirits; and 65 in ale and porter. The 72 dealers in tea were outnumbered only by those who dealt in tobacco, of which there were eighty-three.

Other employments mentioned by Young include banking, insurance, the Excise, the post office and the stamp office. However, into this picture of bustling industry, trade and commerce intrudes a sombre detail: in December 1816 the number of paupers in the workhouse rose to 173, although it is probable that these were chiefly the aged, the infirm and the very young, since, as yet, there appears to have been no shortage of work for the able-bodied.

Whitby seems to have shared the nationwide distress brought on by the return to peace-time conditions after 1815, although, by 1828, she was still ranked as the seventh port in England in terms of registered tonnage, owning 280 vessels of 46,086 tons gross (only London, Newcastle, Liverpool, Sunderland, Hull and Whitehaven exceeding this amount).[11] Towards the end of the 1820s, however, a further recession set in. Demand for shipping declined. Nationally it was a time of radical social and political unrest, and the years from 1836 to 1842 have been described as 'the grimmest period in the history of the 19th century'.[12] Whitby appears to have experienced this slump somewhat in advance of the rest of the country (1831 being an exceptionally bad year for the town) and to have recovered somewhat earlier. The reason for this recovery, perhaps, was that Whitby was one of the first places to enjoy railway communication.

A six-mile stretch of horse-operated tramway was opened between Whitby and the village of Grosmont up the Esk valley in 1835, and by the following

FACING PAGE:

4 *Like parents, like children ... Generations of Whitby boys and girls have fished for pennocks from these steps at Coffee House End.*

year the line had been extended another 15 miles inland as far as Pickering. George Stephenson had surveyed the route for this railway, and it was in Whitby in 1834 that he became friendly with George Hudson. Hudson seems to have acquired a lasting affection for the town at about this time, and he it was who was instrumental in persuading the board of the York and North Midland Railway to buy out the Whitby-Pickering line in 1844 and link it subsequently with the new York-Scarborough route. At the same time, steam locomotion took the place of horses.[13] These developments were to have far-reaching consequences.

First, in anticipation no doubt of the benefits to be derived from speedy landward communication, the Whitby Herring Company had been formed in 1833 (several of the shareholders were investors, too, in the railway). It was this development, in conjunction with the general economic recession and its attendant unemployment, which unquestionably supplied the impetus leading to Whitby's restoration as a fishing station. 'Since the formation of railways', wrote a local observer in 1860,[14] 'the quantity of fish sent into the interior has considerably increased, and consequently an impulse has been given to its capture'. However, the bulk of the herring was still being caught by visiting boats from the neighbouring Yorkshire ports and from Yarmouth, only seven or eight vessels at this time being from Whitby itself.

The second consequence of the advent of railway communication was an upswing in exports shipped out of Whitby. Hitherto these had consisted chiefly of alum and a quantity of agricultural produce, especially butter and hams, from the surrounding area. But in 1834 the Whitby Stone Company was formed: 'It owes its origin to the railway, which laid open, and rendered accessible, rich quarries of stone …'.[15] The stone (known variously as sandstone, freestone, or, when shaped, blockstone) was shipped from Whitby, principally for the London market, where it was used in the construction of public buildings and other municipal works.

Simultaneously, ironstone was being mined at Grosmont and elsewhere in the Esk valley, and in 1836 the first cargo of ore was exported by sea to Tyneside. A decade later, 'The whole of the iron-works in the neighbourhood of Newcastle, as well as those of Messrs. Bolckow and Vaughan on the Tees, were now supplied with what Cleveland ironstone they required almost entirely from the Grosmont district, and the vale of Esk was looked upon at this period as the most favourable locality for cheaply and extensively working this deposit.'[16] The movement of iron-ore was entirely by sea through the port of Whitby.

The third benefit conferred by the railway was the development of Whitby as a resort. As early as 1718 her 'Air salubrious and the Sea just by' had been celebrated in verse, the poet asserting that 'Tunbridge and Epsom shou'd to WHITBY yield'.[17] But it was to be another 70 years before the roads had been put into a sufficiently good state of repair to maintain a regular stage coach; and the first one, in 1788 to York, charged a single fare of 14 shillings inside or eight shillings outside. The hazards of the journey and the cost of conveyance were enough to deter all but the most determined traveller. Nor did the proprietors of the Whitby-Grosmont railway have passenger traffic in mind when they embarked upon that enterprise. But when, in addition to transporting minerals, six thousand people made the journey during the first three months of operation, the company saw the business to be had from tourism and announced that coaches were to be available for hire by parties – thus, the first excursions ever![18]

Despite such favourable auguries the company failed to make a profit, and, as remarked earlier, sold out to the York and North Midland in 1846; whereupon George Hudson set about developing Whitby as a resort on a most ambitious scale. Land was purchased on the West Cliff and an extensive building programme began. The Great Exhibition in 1851 revealed the possibilities of travel by rail for pleasure and recreation, and, as the Industrial Revolution began to distribute its benefits a little more liberally, an increasing number of people found themselves with sufficient leisure and money to visit the seaside. For those with more ample means, the *Royal Hotel* in 1858 was charging 9s. a day with private rooms, or 7s. 6d. a day using the public rooms.[19] For the less affluent, there were day excursions by rail from industrial West Yorkshire, and the occasional trip to the seaside with its fresh air, donkey rides on the sands, and new sights to be savoured must have afforded a welcome respite from smoke-laden Bradford, Leeds and Sheffield for those artisans with a shilling or two in their pockets.

There was one other important local industry (indeed, it was unique to Whitby) which arose during the 19th century, and that was the manufacture of jet. From about 1830 small quantities of jet had been wrought into attractive jewellery, and when some examples were displayed at the Great Exhibition demand for jet ornament increased rapidly as a consequence. The death of the Duke of Wellington in the following year, 1852, caused a wave of mourning to sweep fashionable circles, and when Prince Albert died, in 1862, Queen Victoria's predilection for jet resulted in widespread emulation. By the end of the decade a thousand men and boys were engaged in the manufacture of Whitby jet.

The events of the second half of the 19th century constitute the story of Whitby's decline. Following several disastrous voyages and with the price of oil dropping to an uneconomic level, whaling from the port had already come

5 *Tin Ghaut, Whitby (c.1900) — yards and courts were very picturesque; but women had to work hard to keep things spick and span.*

to an end in 1827. The next casualty was the sea-borne export of ironstone. In 1850 rich deposits of iron ore were discovered in the Cleveland Hills some ten miles from Middlesbrough: 'From the 1,000 tons of ironstone expected from Eston each week, when the first blast furnace was blown in 1851, the tonnage quickly reached 3,000 daily: in ten years' time there were over forty furnaces in the district and production of pig-iron amounted to 500,000 tons annually.'[20] The workings at Grosmont closed immediately; and although they were to start up again (indeed, two blast furnaces were erected which produced 30,000 tons of pig-iron annually), the bulk of shipment was by rail. Contracts for the export of ore by sea to Tyneside were hampered by 'the wretched condition of the harbour at Whitby, which is so much silted up with mud and other debris, that no ship of any size can leave the port with a full cargo'.[21] This complaint, made in 1861, was a portent of similar problems yet to come.

In 1867 the last cargo of alum left Sandsend by sea, and the industry which had supplied the original stimulus to the development of Whitby as a major shipbuilding centre came to an end. Ways had been found to extract alum cheaply from coal, and this, together with the discovery of stable synthetic dyes, rendered the local produce uneconomic. Technological innovation was partly responsible, too, for the demise of the Whitby jet trade.

The fashion for Whitby jet persisted until 1874, when 1,400 men were employed in its manufacture. But its popularity encouraged the use of substitutes such as glass and vulcanite, and the natural product suffered. More importantly, tastes changed. Women were tiring of an ornament so closely identified with death and mourning, and sales declined rapidly. From the peak of 1,400 in 1874, the numbers employed in the manufacture of Whitby jet fell to under three hundred ten years later, causing much distress in the town.[22]

Shipbuilding was slower to adapt to technological change than many other basic industries. As Dr Hobsbawm has pointed out, until the mid-1830s annual construction of steamships in Britain rarely exceeded 3,000 tons. In the decade 1835-45 it ran, roughly, at an annual level of 10,000 tons. Even in 1855, when 81,000 tons were built, there were still ten times that amount in sailing tonnage; and not until the 1880s was more steam than sail tonnage built in Britain.[23] In this respect, the Whitby shipbuilders proved to be commendably responsive to change.

About 1866 sailing vessels belonging to Whitby had reached a peak in terms of numbers and tonnage: 411 vessels registered 74,859 tons.[24] But steamship development was by now proceeding apace and winning an ever-increasing share of the coal-trade. The number of sailing vessels under construction declined inexorably; between 1866 and 1870 only three were built at Whitby's principal shipyard. The watershed was reached in 1871. In

February the last wooden sailing ship (the barque *Monkshaven*, 371 tons) was launched; in June the *Whitehall* (1,100 tons) left the slips, the first iron-hulled, screw-propelled steamer to be built at Whitby.

Nineteen steamers were launched in the five years from 1871, the biggest being 2,300 tons, with an average of 1,357 tons (see Table I). However, the halcyon days were to come in the decade 1876-85 when 53 ships were built: a particularly good record, given that these were depression years for Britain. But in 1885 itself no ships at all were built at Whitby. The slump had caught up; and after 1889, when seven ships were launched, uninterrupted decline set in.[25]

Table I   Ships built at Whitehall Shipyard, Whitby, 1851-1902

Years	Ships launched	Gross tonnage of largest	Average gross tonnage
		Sailing Ships	
1851-5	6	345	221
1856-60	5	268	214
1861-5	5	445	335
1866-70	3	414	401
		Screw Steamers	
1871-5	19	2,300	1,357
1876-80	28	3,000	1,627
1881-5	25	3,100 (2)	1,870
1886-90	19	3,600	3,139
1891-5	11	4,200 (5)	3,915
1896-1900	9	5,675	5,072
1901-2	3	5,700 (2)	5,087

Source: H.B. Browne, *Chapters of Whitby History 1823-1946*

The shipbuilders had tried, with some success, to adapt to and keep pace with modern developments; first iron steamers, and then, from 1887, steel. But Britain, with its huge Empire and extensive overseas trade, required ever bigger vessels. Whitby had the skilled labour force, it had capital, and also the will to keep abreast of new technology. In the end, however, geography defeated her. From the outset, iron, and later steel, plate had had to be brought in from the Tees, and the finished hulls had had to be towed back to the Tees to have their engines fitted. In other words, Whitby lacked an industrial base to sustain modern shipbuilding in the long term. Also, the physical geography of the harbour itself proved to be an insurmountable obstacle. The shipyard was located in the upper harbour and to reach the open sea meant manoeuvring engineless hulls through the narrow bridge that joined the east and west sides of the town. The *Whitehall* had a 28½ ft beam and there was little difficulty in getting her through the 45 ft-wide waterway; but when the *Emma* (4,160 tons) was launched in 1898, with a beam of 44 ft, she had only six inches clearance on each side. Moreover, it was becoming increasingly difficult to maintain a sufficient depth of water in the harbour to float out even the unladen hulls.

The end came on 10 April 1902 when the SS *Broomfield* left the slipway: she was the last ocean-going vessel to be built at Whitby. Much local capital remained invested in shipping and a substantial tonnage was still registered at the port; but the era of ship-construction was over. The melancholy epitaph was written in 1908 by the chronicler of Whitby shipping: 'Our harbour has a deserted appearance, whilst our steamers trade to and from all parts of the world'.[26] In the aftermath, there was an exodus of skilled workers, mainly to Teesside, where they were absorbed into the yards at Middlesbrough and Hartlepool. For the unskilled men there were few opportunities in 1902. Many remained unemployed; others went fishing. Early Edwardian Whitby had a desolate, demoralised air about it: the locust years had arrived.

Two

'HARROWING THE SEA'

7 *Cobles on the scaur, Robin Hood's Bay.*

STAITHES in 1817 was by far the biggest fishing station on the Yorkshire coast. Out of 28 five-men boats,* 14 belonged to Staithes, six to Runswick, five to Robin Hood's Bay, and three to Scarborough. At the same time, there were between 250 and 300 smaller cobles, of which 70 belonged to Staithes, 35 to Runswick and 35 to Robin Hood's Bay.[1] The picture was much the same thirty years later. Runswick, with a population of 383, was 'entirely inhabited by fishermen'; and, wrote Ord in 1846:

> The fishery of Staithes – especially in cod, haddocks, and herring – is very important, being the main branch of commerce and chief support of the place. Upwards of eighty boats, large and small, are in constant requisition during the season, the larger being manned by seven fishermen, the smaller four each, the remainder requiring only three hands. Upwards of three hundred men are engaged in this hazardous service, aided by numbers of women, who assist in collecting bait, mending the gear, and other necessary employments.[2]

From the mid-19th century onwards, however, the primacy of fishing in these coastal villages was challenged, and a pattern similar to that of Whitby developed. That is to say, the introduction of new employments begins to decrease the proportion of men engaged in fishing. In the 1850s, ironstone deposits were opened up in the country behind Staithes and Runswick, and, with the sinking of the Grinkle mines, an artificial harbour was built by the proprietor midway between the two villages and named Port Mulgrave. By 1860, 'numbers [of fishermen] also are now ... employed in working and shipping the iron',[3] and by about 1883 many Staithes fishermen had forsaken the sea altogether 'and turned to the mines for a secure livelihood'.[4] At Runswick, at the turn of the century, 'half the menfolk made their living from the sea, while the others were miners working at the Grinkle ironstone mines which were about four miles away in the Boulby Hills'.[5]

At Robin Hood's Bay there were no new land-based industries to offer competition, yet fishing on any substantial scale ceased here first. The conventional explanation of this is that men increasingly turned to seafaring, and that there was much local investment in shipping. This was true; but so did many Runswick and Staithes men go into the merchant marine, without its being detrimental to the fishing. Also, why should investment in shipping

---

* For a discussion of the different types of boat, see Chapter Four.

be, apparently, so much greater at Robin Hood's Bay than elsewhere? The answer is entirely speculative.

When duties on imported articles of consumption were high, smuggling on the Yorkshire coast was epidemic. Staithes had a reputation for such activity, but Robin Hood's Bay was particularly notorious, and preventive officers were stationed at both these places in the early part of the 19th century. With the introduction of Free Trade and the lowering or removal of excise dues, it is possible that the fishermen of Robin Hood's Bay preferred to invest their gains in shares in shipping or go to sea themselves in preference to subsisting entirely on the risky and arduous occupation of fishing. In any event, fishing died out and no one knew, or was prepared to say, why. In 1870, a Mr Farsyde of Robin Hood's Bay, moving a resolution to promote a railway between Scarborough and Whitby, said that 'he could very well remember when there was a very large fishing trade carried on, but all of a sudden it disappeared and no-one appeared to know how or why'.[6] However, neither the end of smuggling (if that was indeed the reason), nor the establishment of ironstone mines in East Cleveland accounts entirely for the demise of fishing as the chief occupation in the Yorkshire coastal villages. For, in addition to changes in the infrastructure of the regional economy, important developments were taking place in the national fishing industry, and these were to have profound effects upon the inshore communities.

The widespread introduction of trawling in the 19th century had a revolutionary impact upon the fishing industry in Britain. Traditionally, most fish had been caught using either lines or drift nets. Cod, haddock, ling, plaice and other species which live on or near the sea-bed were taken either by hand-lines, or by long-lines strung out along the sea bottom. Nets, hanging like deep curtains below the surface were used to catch fish that swim near the top of the sea – herrings, mackerel, pilchards, and sprats. There were some local variations, such as stow nets: huge bag-shaped nets streaming in the tide from anchored boats into which sprats and young herrings swam and were trapped. These were employed mainly in the Solent, the Wash and the Thames estuary. In general, however, before the advent of trawling, fish caught themselves, either by taking a baited hook, or by unwittingly swimming into a net and becoming enmeshed in it. Using these methods, a degree of selection was involved: certain baits used in certain places caught certain kinds of fish; drift nets shot at a particular time of year off a particular stretch of coast caught herring. The trawl net was less discriminating, and it could be manipulated, thus giving man vastly superior advantage over his quarry. If to this is added steam-power, which, in the shape of railways, first created and opened up a truly *national* market for fish, and then, later, made possible the screw-propelled trawler, it becomes clear that fishing underwent several fundamental changes within a relatively short space of time.

There is some dispute as to whether trawling as a method of fishing originated at Barking on the Thames, or at Brixham. Its earliest sustained use seems to have been at the Devon port, beginning in the latter part of the 18th century. Initially, the Brixham men worked the local ground, a stretch about twenty miles long and from three to eight miles off-shore, extending past Torbay towards Portland. As the number of vessels increased and the local grounds became depleted, the Devon men ventured further afield. As early as 1818 they were fishing out of Dublin, and a few years later were on the Channel grounds off Ramsgate, many of the men settling there with their families.[7]

The introduction of trawling into the North Sea seems to have come about somewhat haphazardly, but the story can be pieced together from evidence given to the Sea Fisheries Commission in 1878 by two Grimsby smack-owners, Frederick Campbell and John Gidley. Fifty years earlier, Campbell had been one of the crew of the Revenue cruiser *Greyhound*, operating in the southern part of the North Sea. On board were some men who had been used to trawling in the Channel, and they persuaded the commander to get a trawl-net. The trawl was let go, but when they got it on board again there were only two fish in the net, so they gave up, 'because there was no fish to catch in the North Sea'. However, shortly after that, William Soad, from Ramsgate, started trawling inshore and made a good living from it. Later, three trawlers worked off the Lincolnshire coast, but, doing badly, they moved further north to Scarborough. Gidley was one of the men who left Ramsgate to go north to Scarborough; he 'just made a living'. In 1833 he, and others, moved from Scarborough to Hull, where, five years before that – according to Campbell – there had been no fishing vessels at all, and only one at Grimsby.[8]

The remarkable development of the Humber ports was due to the accidental discovery, in 1843 or thereabouts, of Silver Pits. At the southern end of the Dogger Bank, and due east of Flamborough, was a deeper area marked on the Admiralty chart 'Outer Silver Pit'. One exceptionally severe winter trawling was tried there on chance: 'soles were found during that very cold season in almost incredible numbers; the nets were hauled up bristling with fish trying to escape through the meshes, and such enormous catches were made as the most experienced fishermen had never before thought possible'.[9] Thereafter, the development of Hull as a fishing station was rapid. From 40 trawlers in 1845 (and these coming mainly from Brixham and Ramsgate) the number grew to 270 by 1863, and by 1877 440 smacks were registered there. The growth of Grimsby at that time was even more

8 *North Landing, Flamborough.*

spectacular. In 1859 the Manchester, Sheffield and Lincolnshire railway was extended to the port, thus guaranteeing a populous market for Grimsby-caught fish. The year before, five trawler-smacks had moved across the Humber from Hull, and these had increased to 70 in 1863. By 1877, 505 fishing vessels were registered at Grimsby, the great majority of them trawlers. The effect of railway communication can be seen, too, in the quantities of fish sent away from Grimsby by rail: in 1859, the year the railway first reached the port, 4,742 tons were carried, and this figure had almost doubled by 1863; but by 1877 it had leapt to 44,376 tons.[10]

Such impressive growth rates were attributable, of course, partly to the greater number of vessels employed in the fishing, and also to the discovery of new grounds. But the central factor was undoubtedly the introduction of trawling as an entirely new mode of catching fish.

The device used was the beam-trawl, which took its name from the beam of wood (usually elm) designed to keep the mouth of the net open. The length of the beam varied from 36 ft to 50 ft, while the triangular, purse-shaped net bag was up to 100 ft long. The beam itself ran over the sea-bed on stirrup-shaped runners (known variously as shoes, heads, or irons) which had the effect of keeping the beam itself about three feet above the ground and

9 *A paddle tug towing a sailing brig on the Tees at Middlesbrough, c.1890. The steel works typify Middlesbrough's staple industry, while in the background the ore-bearing Cleveland Hills are just visible.*

Ecclesiastical records show that for at least a thousand years communities of fisherfolk have maintained a continuous existence along the Yorkshire coast. But whenever fishing has faced competition from alternative employments, fishing has invariably lost. As shipbuilding at Scarborough and Whitby boomed in the 18th and early 19th centuries, fishing declined at those ports. Ironstone mining in Cleveland proved attractive to the fishermen of Runswick and Staithes, while elsewhere 'pleasure boating', at least during the holiday season, was less arduous and more lucrative. Fishing flourished at Redcar as early as Elizabethan times, but with the meteoric rise to industrial prominence of Middlesbrough in the 19th century, both as a steel-making town and as a port, fishermen at Coatham and Redcar at the mouth of the Tees turned increasingly to piloting shipping as their principal source of income.

allowing the lower part of the mouth of the net to billow out behind it thus forming a 'bosom'. This lower edge was attached to the ground rope, usually an old hawser covered (or rounded) with thinner rope to prevent it from chafing and to make it heavier. When the trawl was in motion, 'the fish which may be disturbed by [the ground rope] have therefore no chance of escape at either the sides or back of the net, and as the outlet under the beam is a long way past them, and is steadily moving on, their fate is sooner or later decided by their passing over the ground rope and finding their way into the funnel-shaped end of the net, from which a small valve of netting prevents their return'.[11] In other words, this method of fishing involved not even the most rudimentary selection of the type or size of fish caught: anything in the way of the trawl was swept into the bag, and it was this feature which constituted the core of the traditional inshore fishermen's complaints against trawling.

The outcry was so great that, in 1863, the Government felt obliged to set up a Royal Commission to investigate the charges that were being made, namely, that trawling was destroying spawn and fry, with a consequent depletion of fish stocks; and that the trawl-smacks were interfering with the gear of the

10 *Tees pilot cobles on Redcar beach. Fishermen raced each other in them to get alongside ships bound for Middlesbrough to guide them through the shoals of rock at the approaches to the river. As there was no harbour at Redcar, cobles had to be launched off the beach directly into the breakers; hence the wheeled undercarriages, doubly necessary if the tide was out.*

inshore fishermen, so that, taken together, the livelihoods of traditional inshore fishing communities were being imperilled.

The worst affected stretch of coastline in England was that between Berwick and the Humber, and when the Commissioners visited Staithes on 30 September 1863 the story they heard was essentially the same as that told by the men in the Northumberland villages to the north and at Filey and Flamborough further south. James Fell, a fisherman at Staithes for forty years, reported that the line fishing had diminished greatly over the previous decade or two:

> I don't think there is one fourth or one fifth the catch now compared with what was the catch ten or fifteen years ago … . I have been going for a week and I have brought 700 or 800 cod ashore, a ton of halibut, and a great number of skate and haddocks … . Now we can hardly get any fish on the same ground close to the Dogger. The smacks are there now, and they have so trawled over the ground that they have ruined everything about there, where we used to get the most fish … . If we did happen to be fishing there the trawlers came amongst us and would take all our lines away. There were so many there that we could not keep clear of them.

11 *Pilot cobles were painted black and the name of their port was prominent on the bow. Redcar fishing boats were registered* MH, *Middlesbrough, whereas pilots bore the legend* TEES. *This photograph belongs to Mrs Clay of Redcar. It shows her father, Captain Watson Dixon, and the little boy with the dog is her brother. The boat is named after another brother who, at the age of nine, was washed overboard and drowned. The Watson Dixons were Tees pilots for five generations, claimed Mrs Clay, who was born in 1895. Most pilot cobles were 'double enders' (pointed at both bow and stern), but the* Frank *had a traditional square, sloping stern.*

These are selected passages of James Fell's evidence, but the gist is the same throughout. It is clear, too, that the line-fishermen were concerned with quality, and not just with the quantity of fish caught, as this extract from one Commissioner's interrogation of Robert Verrill shows:

Are your lines much the same that they were 20 years ago? – No, they are a great deal superior.

Are they longer? – They are larger and finer and the hooks are better adapted for catching fish.

Do they use the same kind of bait? – Yes, exactly. I can attribute the falling off to nothing but the small fish being destroyed before they come to perfection.

What destroys the small fish? – The trawler.

Have you ever seen the [trawl] nets drawn up? – Yes, and I have seen the small fish shot overboard.

Have you been alongside the trawler when the nets were drawn up? – Yes, I have been alongside, but not on board.

What have you seen come up in the trawl net? – I have seen large quantities of small fish, haddock, codlings, which are young cod, and such like. I have seen the trawl taken aboard on the deck, and have watched them pick the soles, and then throw all the other overboard. All that was thrown overboard was quite destroyed … .

Was it because they were small or because they were mangled that they were thrown away? – Because they were small.

They were too small to be useful to take to market? – Yes.

Did you notice whether they were injured by the trawl? — Yes, they had been lying there while they got dead. Now I have taken them off the hook alive as 'wick' as they ever were. I have put them down into the water again, and I have never seen but one lie on the top of the water until it died, and birds, such as gulls, came and took it away.

The next witness, Burton Verrill, was asked by Professor Huxley, the other Commissioner, whether he thought anything short of banning trawling would be of any advantage. 'I would abolish them altogether', replied Verrill, 'if I was in the Government.' Not surprisingly, the Commissioners were not impressed by his proposed solution; nor, apparently, were they sympathetic towards the complaints of the line-fishermen in general, for their advice to the Government when they presented their Report was that the supply of fish had increased, that the method of fishing involved no waste of young fish that could be prevented without interfering with the fisheries as a whole, that spawn was not destroyed by the nets, and that all fishery restrictions should be removed except such as were desirable for protecting and keeping order among the fishermen. All these recommendations were accepted by the Government and embodied in the Sea Fisheries Act, 1868.[12]

The next major watershed in the development of trawling came in 1877. For some time steam paddle-tugs had been used at the north-east ports in calm weather to tow sailing colliers down the Wear and Tyne and out to sea where they could pick up a breeze. Occasionally, tugs were hired by fishing smacks for the same purpose, and it occurred to skippers to put their trawls down as they were being towed. It was William Purdy of North Shields, master of the paddle-tug *Messenger*, who, in November 1877, took what in retrospect seems to be the obvious step of attaching a trawl net to the tug itself. The experiment was successful, and very soon over forty steam-paddlers were engaged in trawl-fishing. It was, after all, an opportune moment: the national economy was depressed, trade was slack, and the number of sailing colliers was declining rapidly in the face of competition from steamships, which rarely needed the services of a tug. In such conditions, the economics of operating a tug as a fishing vessel seemed very attractive, as John Lawson, owner of the *Patriot*, was quick to realise.

The *Patriot*, worth about £2,000, was the most expensive paddle-tug engaged in trawling. Her earnings from fishing between November 1877 and July 1878 were £12 to £56 gross a week. Ordinary running expenses (for coal, oil, and tallow) were £5 a week, with the balance divided equally, one half going to the crew and the other to the owner. Also, in terms of fish landed at North Shields, whereas 300 tons came from line-fishermen over a period of 11 months, the trawlers sold 900 tons in nine months. As Lawson remarked at the time, 'the steam trawlers have so increased the take of fish that the lines no longer pay. It is a question of competition'.[13]

Respect for competition had been the paramount factor in determining the Commissioners' recommendations in 1868. Now, ten years later, as a

---

12 *Trawler smacks in Scarborough harbour. Trawling is a comparatively recent innovation. It reached Scarborough round about the 1820s, but with the discovery of the rich fishing ground known as the Silver Pit in 1843 the centre of gravity of the trawling industry shifted to the Humber ports of Hull and Grimsby. Still, Scarborough continued to be a trawling station; although there was a great deal of conflict between the smacks and the inshore coble men, who claimed that the trawl nets damaged their gear and destroyed spawn and young fish. 'The smacks now are a great dread to the Scarborough [inshore] men,' John Robson, a coble fisherman for nearly fifty years, told a Royal Commission in 1878. 'They cut the drift nets. The drift-net fishermen are now terrified to go out.'*

second Royal Commission was hearing evidence, the same arguments were being deployed by the trawling interest. Traditional inshore-fishermen were probably as wedded to the principle of free enterprise as any other group at that time; but William Lisle, a line-fisherman from Cullercoats in Northumberland, put a somewhat different perspective. He was, he said, 'in favour of free trade, but not in favour of allowing one class of men to injure another class'.[14] Perhaps unwittingly, Lisle had hit upon the basic *social* distinction between trawlermen and line-fishermen, that of class.

Line-fishermen do not fit conveniently into any of the conventional sociological patterns of class analysis. On the one hand, they were manifestly workers (they made and mended gear, sailed and rowed boats, did not employ labour, and so on); but, on the other hand, they were capitalists, if only in the minimal sense that each owned his own gear (and some also held a share in the boat). From the outset, line-fishermen sensed that the trawlermen were not of their own kind. As John Dawson, a line-fisherman out of Newbiggin for 50 years, was quick to remark: 'All classes work on these trawlers. They are not fishermen, and are paid wages for the work.'[15] The essence of the social and economic change wrought by trawling is contained in those two short sentences. Trawling had created a fishing *industry*, with its own socio-economic pyramid – a small group of owners (capitalists) at the top, and a large number of workers (wage-earning proletarians) at the bottom. It had its own national market, brought about by railways, telegraphic communication, the use of ice, and, later, of refrigeration. Against this kind of highly organised and powerful set of interests, the small scattered fishing communities, using traditional methods (partly out of preference and partly because of lack of capital), and operating on a communal basis within essentially local or regional economies, stood little chance in a situation of 'free' competition.

The complaints against trawling made to the Royal Commission in 1878-9 were largely the same as those made fifteen years earlier: that it destroyed spawn and fry, and damaged or interfered with the inshore men's gear. By now the line-fishermen were clearly becoming desperate, and there were many echoes of Burton Verrill's call to abolish the trawlers altogether. John Duke of Flamborough maintained that they ruined the fishing ground by destroying the food, killing the brood, and taking spawning fish. He would make it illegal for any boat to carry a trawl. John Robson, a coble fisherman for 49 years, reported: 'The smacks now are a great dread to the Scarborough men. They cut the drift nets. The drift-net fishermen are now terrified to go out.' Samuel Stockdale, a Filey fishmonger and fisherman, produced samples of plaice, dabs and soles caught in a trawl and laid them out before the Commissioners, saying, 'These fish are too small to be caught'. John Bunyan, a Whitby fisherman, said that he could make more money with half a share when he first started fishing than he could with a share and a half now. At Staithes, John Turttles,* 85 years old and connected with fishing since he was 10, urged the prohibition of trawling altogether. William Grimes was worried mainly about the steam trawlers which he would have done away with:

> They can creep in where sailing smacks cannot come. There is smooth ground here about a mile from the shore on which these steamers can work … . No trawl should be allowed to come there. There should be the same law on the Dogger; the same law everywhere. The fish would then be better, and all the fishermen would have a fair chance.[16]

The line-fishermen might as well have saved their breath. The Commissioners, by sustained questioning, elicited the information that the populations of the inshore communities had risen, that the numbers of boats had increased, and that the gross value of catches had also gone up. What they did not attempt to do, however, was to seek explanations for these increases in terms of changes within the local economy, nor did they attempt to assess the incomes of individual households deriving from fishing to see whether the overall increases were reflected in improvements in the fisherfolk's standard of living. As for the conservation-type arguments, the Commissioners (who, it should be emphasised, had very little proven scientific knowledge at their disposal, such was the state of marine biology at that time) seemed to be much more receptive to the views of the trawling interest. The kinds of opinion they heard were: 'this fishing is as productive now as it was twenty years ago', and 'the trawl net stirs up the ground and does good' (Samuel Randal, Scarborough trawlerman). 'When trawling for soles on the Dogger Bank, found the bank in May, June, and July swarming with millions of little soles, an inch or so long. They get jammed in the ground rope like seaweed, but they are never caught in the meshes of the net.' — Henry Wyrill, fish merchant, Scarborough. 'The trawlers increase the trade by opening the ground and the food for the fish to consume. The trawl also distributes the spawn.' — Joseph Gravels, paddle-trawler skipper, North Shields. 'Trawl fishing does not interfere with the spawn and the fry'; and: 'Thinks that the trawl cultivates the sea just as the harrow does the land.' — John Sims, President of the Smackowners' Insurance Association, Hull. The Commissioners were especially impressed by this last argument, reproducing it in their Report.[17] (Incredibly, the same point was being made a century later in defence of modern beam trawling for soles in the English Channel by Belgian vessels. 'Who is he trying to kid with his suggestion that beam trawling, just like farm machinery,

---

* Almost certainly, this should be 'Trattles' (a common Staithes name at that time).

cultivates the sea-bed?' retorted a Newhaven fisherman, who went on: 'It's all very well talking of "tilling" the grounds, but can Mr Claeys [a Belgian trawler-owner] assure us on replenishing the stocks; we are not farmers able to plant seeds, following the "tilling", all we are left with is wanton destruction in the wake of the beamers.'[18]

But the two considerations that weighed most heavily with the Commissioners were the contribution that increased landings of fish, as a nutritious and relatively cheap food, were making to the national well-being; and the large amount of capital, private and municipal, invested in the trawling industry.[19]

As early as 1838, a writer in *The Penny Magazine* perceived the potential offered by the railways to the development of fisheries: they 'cannot fail to bring fish into new channels of consumption'. He went on:

> The railways which are now constructing in various parts of the country will place the fisherman in connection with a population sufficiently great to render his gains more certain and regular … . More money will come into

13 *At Staithes, whenever storm threatened, the cobles had to be manhandled up onto the staith itself out of harm's way. This was a communal task and everyone readily lent a hand. Oars for Staithes cobles were made especially strong, as they were used as skids when moving the boats up the steep beach in an emergency.*

his hands. At present the fluctuating value of his industry keeps the fisherman poor. He cannot accumulate capital, and is therefore too much dependent upon the casualties of a day, a week, or a season.[20]

Had the pattern of fishing remained as it was in 1838, this rosy future might have been realised. Of course, there *were* examples of 'rags to riches'; cases where the experienced, thrifty skipper bought a second boat, paid off the mortgage, invested in more vessels, until eventually he became the owner of a substantial fleet. But such men were few, and many more boat owners finished up employed on someone else's smack, working for a wage and a small share in the net profit. Moreover, many of the men and boys who made up the crews of the trawler fleets operating out of the Humber ports in the second half of the 19th century were recruited from the orphanages, reformatories, and workhouses of the inland industrial cities.[21] Their work at sea bore little resemblance to that of traditional fishermen; very few skills were needed, and their working conditions were appalling (not to mention their moral condition, which prompted the foundation of the Royal National Mission to Deep-Sea Fishermen in the early 1880s).[22]

In 1878, a single trawl-net was worth £70 to £80.[23] In contrast, as late as 1900, a 21-ft, three-man Yorkshire coble could be bought at the rate of £1 a foot;[24] while, in 1878, a complete set of six long-lines (including buoys, tow lines and anchors), sufficient for a coble's three-man crew, was costed at £11 11s. 6d.[25] In the same year, 400 smacks carrying 2,000 hands were fishing out of Hull; and 'taking into account the people indirectly interested, there must be 20,000 persons in Hull dependent on the fishery'.[26] With paddle-trawlers valued at up to £2,000 each, and with municipalities expending large sums of money on landing facilities (North Shields had just spent £26,000 to promote the fish trade), it was obvious that the small communities of traditional fishermen could not find the capital necessary to compete with the new trawling stations. Many coastal villages still lacked railway communication, and places such as Cullercoats, Newbiggin and Craister, in Northumberland, and Staithes, Runswick, Filey and Flamborough, on the Yorkshire coast, were devoid of proper harbours, the boats being launched off open beaches.

The other consideration which the Commissioners had in mind in 1879, when they recommended the maintenance of the *status quo*, was the undoubted benefit to be derived from the wider and cheaper supply of fish. The line-fishermen were, of course, correct when they argued that line-caught fish were of superior quality and reached the consumer in better condition than trawled fish (and the trawlermen's opinions to the contrary were, to say the least, disingenuous). But for many poorer classes in the big industrial conurbations fish was a new article in their diet, and they lacked the discrimination to distinguish between the two types. In any case, consumption of fish by such people was determined primarily by cost, not quality, and trawled fish was cheap.

From the late 1870s the traditional inshore fishermen were left to cope with trawlers and new market conditions as best they could. At the same time, the trawling industry itself was beginning to make the transition from sail to steam. Although it was not until 1877 that the master of the paddle-tug *Messenger* had first experimented with trawling, steam's potential had already been recognised. In August 1873 the yacht *Dewdrop*, a sailing boat with an auxiliary steam engine, had visited Scarborough, provoking the comment from the local newspaper that '[it] opens the question, as it has done elsewhere, of the desirability of applying steam as a locomotive agency to our fishing craft'. By the end of 1880, up to twenty steam trawlers were working off Scarborough, and the port 'presented a livelier appearance than it has done for many years past'.[27] As the neighbouring *Whitby Gazette* later commented, 'the steamers bid fair to shortly obtain a monopoly of the trade'.[28] In fact, several decades were to elapse before sail disappeared entirely from the Yorkshire fisheries, but on the trawling side of the industry the days left to sail were few. Their performance in 1880, when a single boat's overnight catch had sold for as much as £80, prompted Edmund, the Scarborough boat-builder, to lay down the keel of a new fishing vessel, to be fitted with a screw propeller. Once again, technological innovation benefited the fishing industry. The screw gave greater manoeuvrability, and also removed the necessity for paddle casings, bulky encumbrances which could so easily interfere with the handling of gear. The last Scarborough paddle-trawler was wrecked only in 1910, but its heyday was already long past.[29]

More or less coincidental with the introduction of screw-trawlers was the advent of a new type of trawl. Again, the precise origin of the 'otter-trawl' is uncertain, but an early pioneer of its use was Skipper Normandale of the Scarborough screw-trawler *Otter*, and, as Godfrey suggests (*Yorkshire Fishing Fleets*, p.31), this may be how the new trawl came to get its name. In any event, the heavy, dangerous, cumbersome beam was abandoned and replaced by 'otter boards', which, meeting the resistance of the water, sheered outwards thus keeping the mouth of the net open. Rollers took the place of shoes, while the upper edge of the net was buoyed with corks. The bridles remained, as on the beam trawl, and so did the single warp leading to the boat. However, the risk of being brought broadside-on to the sea should the net snag on the bottom soon resulted in the use of twin warps; although, as Godfrey points out, 'this brought further problems, leading to the development of a winch with two separate drums, which revolved independently'.[30]

From about 1880 onwards, then, the fishing industry was rapidly assuming its present-day character. Around Britain's coastline there were still thousands of small craft propelled by sail and oar; but in the Irish Sea, the Channel, and the North Sea fleets of steam-powered trawlers were operating. In 1891 the first steam screw-trawler fished off Iceland and the era of modern distant-water fishing had begun.

14 *A naturalist visiting Runswick (shown here c.1905) described the village as being 'a singular rookery of cottages, built with only walking space between them, one above another, in the cliff side'. Ornithological imagery is repeated when he adds: 'Last winter, 1874-5, two houses were destroyed by a sudden fall of the cliff, one being literally turned inside out and the furniture thrown out of the windows … . The fishermen have no fear: they look on their misfortunes as matters of course, and cling to the face of the treacherous cliff like a colony of martins.'* (George Roberts, Topography and Natural History of Lofthouse, *1882*)

To return to the North Yorkshire coast: the mid-1880s were hard years for Whitby. The shore-based economy was suffering from the general depression, as was indirectly the fishing (already hit by steam-trawling). Worse still, the jet trade was in rapid decline, and whereas ten years earlier 1,400 men had been employed, with 'an ordinary artisan' earning £3 or £4 a week, now only 300 men still had jobs and 'a man has to work very hard to realise, by way of payment for his industry, 25s. for the same period'. In 1883 eight ships had been launched from the shipyard; the following year only four; and the year after that, none at all. In little more than twelve months the number of workers employed at the yard fell from 800 to 'but a handful'. The *Whitby Gazette* reported: 'The iron shipbuilding trade at Whitby is stagnant, and large numbers of men, such as labourers &c., who belong to no society at all, and of course obtain no relief from any union or association, are hungering and starving in the streets.' Many local men in the merchant navy were also out of work: Harrowing's (a Whitby shipping company) had 11 of its 12 steamers laid up in January 1885. For the fishermen, 1884 had produced a prolific herring season, but the quality of the catch was not good, 'and the prices realised were very poor and in many cases unremunerative'. In the winter of 1884-5:

15 & 16 *Runswick, c.1905.*

The deep sea fishing, too, was a comparative failure. All the large boats sailed for the deep fishing ground in the autumn, for the returns for their enterprise were not at all adequate to justify them in prosecuting the industry for the time originally intended and at a very early period in the winter the whole of the boats laid up, and it is reported that with one or two solitary exceptions they are in debt. In Whitby alone, 20 large boats laid up[*] and their crews numbering on the aggregate well on to 200 men and boys, returned to their village homes and engaged in line fishing. Neither has this part of the fishing industry been so successful as was hoped for. The fishermen complain of the scarcity of fish. Year by year the quantity of fish usually caught by the line is diminishing and the cause of the scarcity is not far to seek. The trawlers, week by week, trail their ugly engines over the favourite fishing grounds within a short distance of the land, raking up immature fish, disturbing the spawn, and maiming, mauling, and killing that which if legitimately caught would be of the highest service for edible purposes ...[31]

Whitby's lowly position as a fishing station at this time, 1885, is reflected in her ranking in a list of east-coast ports (see Table II).

Table II

Number of fishing vessels (15 tons and over) registered at 15 of the principal ports on the east coast of England, 1884-5

Port	1884		1885	
		(posn in parentheses)		
Berwick	117	(7)	124	(5)
Newcastle	1	(15)	7	(14)
North Shields	25	(9)	61	(9)
South Shields	10	(13)	15	(12)
Sunderland	9	(14)	24	(10)
Hartlepool	12	(12)	4	(15)
Whitby	24	(10)	23	(11)
Scarborough	122	(6)	117	(6)
Hull	472	(3)	452	(3)
Grimsby	636	(1)	684	(1)
Yarmouth	625	(2)	589	(2)
Lowestoft	462	(4)	425	(4)
Harwich	16	(11)	14	(13)
Colchester	86	(8)	88	(8)
London	138	(5)	113	(7)

Source: Adapted from data in *Whitby Gazette*, 14 March 1885

Whitby came 11th out of 16 ports (1885): but her real position was even worse. The first seven ports in the table together possessed 2,504 boats;

---

[*] The boats belonged, in fact, to Staithes, but were laid up at Whitby in the upper harbour.

17 *Filey's broad, sandy bay made it a favourite holiday resort for young families. This sunny scene with the bathing machines, and the pierrots performing before an audience every one of whom is wearing a hat, is evocative of innocent, leisurely days at the turn of the century. But, breaking the horizon offshore, is a Filey yawl whose crew would toil the whole year round, in winter for cod, ling and haddock, and in summer from Shields to Yarmouth following the shoals of herring.*

whereas the remaining eight ports (of which Whitby was the fourth) had only 236 boats among them. Whitby's position was to worsen. By 1893, she had only 10 first-class boats (averaging 37.7 tons each), and nine of these belonged in fact to Staithes.[32]

Another factor contributing to Whitby's lowly rank was the state of the harbour. 'Will no one bestir themselves' asked a correspondent to the *Whitby Gazette* plaintively in 1885, 'that even a poor little smack may get into her harbour at every tide?'[33] Apparently, no one would; least of all the Trustees, whose meetings at that time were either slanging matches or inquorate. So bad was the harbour that 'vast deposits of sand and mud still impede the channel, making it sometimes impossible for fishing boats to reach the quays and discharge their cargoes'.[34] By 1900 a deplorable situation had been reached. In January, the *Whitby Gazette* reported that: 'Large quantities of mud and sand were washed out of Whitby harbour by a fresh* during Saturday night. A good groin [*sic*] to hinder it from coming back again, would be the best

---

* 'fresh' – flood of fresh water down the Esk caused by rainfall on the river's upper reaches. Known also as a 'spate'.

thing the Harbour Trustees could do. But why make suggestions to this benighted, impecunious body?' In March, the Dock End (the usual landing place for herrings), was described as 'a stinking cess pool, and a very great eyesore'. That summer the herring fishing at Seahouses was 'successful'; Hartlepool had had a 'splendid season'; Scarborough was 'doing well'; but 'Whitby has had a wretched season'. The reason, according to the local newspaper, was because: 'The herring industry at Whitby has been almost completely killed by the unenterprising Harbour Board, who do not have the courage to speculate in the hire or purchase of a tug-boat [to tow the sailing drifters out to sea].' At the end of September, when the harbour was normally crowded with craft from Scotland, East Anglia, and Penzance, the citizens of Whitby stood on the cliff top and watched 'a continual stream of Scotch fishing boats, at distances varying from a mile and a half apart, passing Whitby … apparently going south for the herring fishery'.[35]

The Harbour Board was chiefly made up of members of the shipping interest and local shop-keepers or small businessmen. Once shipbuilding ceased in 1902, what little incentive there had been to keep the harbour in good repair disappeared for the shipowners; while, as ever, the shopkeepers' concern was to hold down the rates. In 1904, when Aflalo was touring the fishing ports of England and Wales, he wrote: 'When I was at Whitby, a tidal harbour that must need unremitting dredging to keep it in order, I found that the only dredger belonging to the Harbour Trustees was away on hire.'[36]

So it was in the early part of the 20th century that, just as national and local factors had combined to reduce Whitby to a very depressed economic condition generally, so did developments in the national fishing industry tend to depress the fishery. Since then, Whitby has recovered some lost ground, but at Staithes, Runswick and other coastal villages fishing as a full-time occupation has declined steeply. In 1909, a local observer wrote of Staithes: 'The lads are all going to the mines and inland to the big towns, for the line fishing is poor indeed … .'[37] By the outbreak of the First World War, the last of the Staithes yawls* had stopped fishing, and a tradition which can be traced back, through documentary sources, nearly 1,300 years came to an end.

The demise of Runswick has been sensitively chronicled by J.S. Johnson, who, born in 1911, spent his boyhood and youth there. Ironstone mining had already attracted many men away from the sea, while others found it more profitable to go pleasure-boating during the summer holiday season. In 1933 only four cobles were still fishing, and by 1945 the number had fallen to two. It became increasingly difficult to find enough men to launch the boats, and when, in March 1950, one of the crew of the *Radiant Morn* dropped dead as

---

* 'yawls' – successors to the five-men boats (see Chapter Four).

the boat was going off, 'there was no one to take his place, so the coble was laid up and eventually sold'. Three months later, as the remaining coble, *True Vine*, was being launched, exactly the same thing happened – George Taylor collapsed and died. So ended centuries of fishing at Runswick. The fishermen's homes were bought up as weekend cottages and 'at the present time [1973] there are only twenty natives living in the bay and eleven of these are over sixty, and two over eighty'.[38]

Fishing has never quite died out completely at Staithes, otherwise the pattern is much the same as at Runswick. As cobles were motorised in the 1920s, and with the introduction of the larger keelboats (see Chapter Four), several Staithes fishing families (Coles, Theakers, Verrills) migrated to Whitby with its market and protected harbour. To the south, the same was happening. The Mainprize family, for example, moved from Filey to Scarborough; while the Dukes (originally from Flamborough) and the Storms came to Whitby from Robin Hood's Bay.

At Whitby, the Urban District Council assumed responsibility for the harbour. Extensions to the piers, to act as breakwaters, were completed in 1914, and later an efficient grab-dredger was purchased, with a consequent improvement in the depth of water in the channel. In 1931 there were 105 fishermen at Whitby,[39] a figure which remained constant up to the outbreak of the Second World War. Then, all but the old men and boys were called up on active service. Post-war improvements include a new fish quay, ice-house and market, and further deepening of the channel. By the mid-1970s there were 16 keelboats and 12 cobles working out of Whitby, involving about a hundred full-time fishermen. Four cobles fished out of Staithes, one at Runswick, but none at Robin Hood's Bay. Only one of the Whitby keelboats was engaged in the traditional line-fishing; the others were all trawling.[40] Today keelboats are bigger, but fewer, and long-lining has virtually ceased.

HADDOCK

Three

HAVENS AND HOMES

18 *Staithes, c.1905.*

IN THE NORTH the Yorkshire coast is bounded by the River Tees, and in the south by the Humber. High cliffs for much of its extent, at the extremities it is low-lying and sandy, as between Spurn Point and Bridlington. There, the sea gnaws away at the land, only to throw up its spoil at some different place. So, today, Hornsea church is not half a mile inland, whereas an old inscription recites:

> Hornsea steeple, when I built thee
> Thou wast ten miles off Burlington,
> Ten miles off Beverly, and ten miles off the sea.

North of Burlington (now more commonly known as Bridlington) sand and clay give way to chalk, and the broad sweep of the bay is checked by the sheltering bulk of Flamborough Head. Beyond, the Wolds end abruptly in sheer cliffs at Bempton and Speeton until, once more, the coast dips and curves to form Filey Bay with its sandy foreshore and protective Brigg.

The old mariners' rhyme sounds a warning about these rocky headlands:

> Flamborough Head as you pass by,
> Filey Brigg you must not come nigh,
> Scarborough Castle stands over the sea,
> And Whitby rocks lie northerly.

After Scarborough, however, the rocks are no longer chalk, but sandstone and brittle shale; while inland the cultivated Wolds give way to bleak, heather-clad moors, intersected here and there by wooded ravines whose becks discharge their peaty waters into the North Sea. Another, more subtle, change occurs, too. Headlands are called *nab* or *ness*, inlets and bays are *wykes*, and numerous place-names end in *–by*; unmistakable evidence of Viking settlement over a thousand years ago.

Whitby – ancient Streonshalh – was an obvious prize for the Danish invaders; for, as well as the booty to be seized from its Anglo-Saxon abbey, the town stood on the Esk, an unpretentious river, yet the only estuary between Humber and Tees.

Northwards from Whitby extend precipitous cliffs rising to 660 feet at Boulby, the highest in England, before petering out beyond Saltburn into the sand dunes of Redcar and South Gare at the mouth of the Tees. It is an inhospitable coast, safe enough when the winds blow offshore, but treacherous in northerly and easterly gales.

19 & 20 *Except at its extremities, towards Tees and Humber, the Yorkshire coast is rocky. Fishing communities sprang up wherever there was shelter from the stormy, northerly winds. Cowbar Nab affords Staithes meagre protection and, until breakwaters were built in the 1920s, rough seas battered the village whenever there was an onshore gale.*

That the first settlers along this shore were seafarers there can be little doubt, since the very locations of villages bespeak a concern for shelter from the storm and, so far as it could be ensured, a safe haven for the boats. Staithes, Runswick, Robin Hood's Bay and Scarborough all hug the northern end of their bays to huddle in the lee of the headlands.

Fresh water was another prime consideration and several fishing settlements grew up where becks or rivers entered the sea. Also, given a choice, a sandy shore was preferred to rock, as it made landing somewhat less hazardous.

Even the village of Flamborough, high on its headland, fulfils two of these three criteria. In the absence of a beck, dew ponds and wells served as a source of fresh water; and the village itself was built roughly equidistant from North and South Landings, so that the fishermen had a sheltered approach to shore in all but an easterly gale.

Apart from at Flamborough, houses were situated as close as possible to the waterside, Staithes being an extreme example. One reason was that the original settlers built on a narrow strip of land, Seaton Garth, having claimed squatters' rights. Looking back in 1924, an old man wrote:

> I can remember several of these old type of cottages. They were generally only one storey high, and some had an attic under the thatch. To enter you generally had to go down one or two steps. The walls were from two to three feet thick, and composed of mud, clay and rough stones. I have heard some old people say that their grandparents told them – that takes us back about two hundred and fifty years – that when they were young it was the usual thing, when two people were going to get married, for the whole community to join together to build them a house … . Long after they began to build them of more substantial material they still relied upon the voluntary help of their friends and neighbours to do all the carrying, for without this mutual assistance it would not have been possible for the poorer people to have obtained a house … . The only pay they got was an invitation to the covering-in supper.[1]

These earliest houses at Staithes stood only a little above normal high-water mark, and in rough weather were prone to flooding. In one terrible storm a mother and child retreated upstairs and were saved from drowning only by the efforts of neighbours who broke through the roof from the house above.[2]

FACING PAGE:

21 *To the north of Scarborough the cliffs are of sandstone and shale, while to the south the Yorkshire wolds terminate in sheer faces of chalk. After Flamborough Head the land declines until it eventually peters out in a spit of shingle, Spurn Point, at the mouth of the Humber. In the days of sail, mariners had a rhyme to guide them along the rockbound stretch of coast (see page 40).*

22 *Fisherfolk built their houses as near as possible to where their boats were moored; sometimes, as in this case at Staithes, virtually at the water's edge. This photograph although poor in technical quality is rich in detail. These were two of the very oldest cottages in Staithes, built, tradition has it, on a narrow strip of land between the foot of the cliff and the shore itself by claiming squatter's rights. Sandstone was gathered from the beach, and the community would build the house for a newly wed couple. The shutters on the lower windows were to keep out sea spray during storms, while the living room of the house on the right, being below ground level, often suffered inundation. On the cliff side are barking coppers where lines and nets were steeped in a solution of 'cutch' (a kind of tannin) to preserve them. Herring nets are spread over a mast to dry behind the girl, who is carrying floats for the nets. The floats were made by the fishermen themselves from animal bladders got from the butcher's. These were cured then tarred and painted before being inflated to make them buoyant. Also drying on the spars behind the bunch of bladders to the left of the girl is split, salted fish (probably saithe, known locally as 'blackjack'). In the 18th century Staithes had a great trade in this stockfish, exporting it as far away as the Mediterranean; but by the time this photograph was taken, about the turn of the century, it was used mainly for home consumption in winter.*

However, the usual reason for fisherfolk's living close by the waterfront was so that they could be constantly near to their boats, the principal wherewithal of their livelihood. Only at Whitby, Scarborough and Bridlington were proper harbours built, and at villages where launching was off open beaches boats had to be manhandled up onto dry land out of reach of the waves if a storm arose. Anyone waking during the night at Staithes or Runswick and noticing a change in the weather would rush down the street shouting 'Turn out! Cobles!'

At Whitby the fishing community lived in the narrow streets by the harbour: on Sandside and Tate Hill, in Henrietta Street, and in upper Church Street

23 *Staithes, c.1905 — families were large and fisherfolk's homes were often overcrowded.*

around the Market Place (on the east side of the River Esk), and in Haggersgate and on Burtree Cragg (on the west side).

In the main, these were among the most ancient streets in Whitby, and many of the buildings themselves were very old. Whereas now a good few have been 'restored' and converted into 'desirable' second homes for week-ending yachtsmen and other city dwellers, at least until after the end of the Second World War many lacked the basic, modern, sanitary amenities of bath, flush lavatory, and internal piped water supply. A great many, too, were tenement buildings erected in the second half of the 18th century to accommodate the influx of labour to work in the shipyards and graving docks. By 1870 these hastily constructed, speculative properties were in a sorry state: 'They [the fisherfolk] live, for the most part, in a place called the "Cragg", at the back of the harbour, in wretched, old, tumble-down tenements, built many years ago in the cliff-side, for which they pay three or four pounds a year.'[3] In January 1900, part of the cliff gave way. Two dwellings occupied by fishing families, and estimated to have been two hundred years old, were demolished: 'The houses stood with their backs towards the side of the cliff, and some two feet distant to it.' There were four fatalities, including a mother and her infant child.[4]

Runswick was particularly prone to such disasters, Dr Young reporting that, 'As portions of the cliff are occasionally shooting, houses are often rent and dislocated, others wholly demolished, and instances are said to have occurred of houses slipping down entire, together with their bases, and taking up a fresh position below'. On one occasion, apart from a single house, the entire village slipped into the sea, and only the circumstance that most of the inhabitants were that night at a wake prevented great loss of life.[5]

By 1846 Runswick, with a population of 383, was 'entirely inhabited by fishermen' who dwelt in what the historian J.W. Ord was pleased to call 'huts'.[6] Later, in 1874, a naturalist from the West Riding, on a rambling tour of Cleveland, wrote with appropriate choice of simile that: 'The fishing village

---

FACING PAGE:

24 *Galleried fisherman's house, Wilson's Yard, Church Street, Whitby. This was the home of Thomas and Florence Hutchinson and their eight children: five girls and three boys. Their middle daughter Jinny (born shortly after this photograph was taken, in 1905) remembers that her parents and the youngest daughter slept in the room on the right. To the left was the kitchen cum living room. Above were two attics: the boys slept in one, girls in the other. The room on the left beneath the gallery was where her father stored his fishing gear (note the coble oar and tiller leaning against the wall). The small shed on the right was the privy. In order to give a little more space, the door to the cottage opened outwards onto the gallery. Florence Hutchinson is resting a fish basket on the 'oven end' which jutted into the yard from a neighbouring baker's shop. Many women prepared meals in a dripping tin and then paid the baker a penny to have them cooked in his oven. A favourite dish was 'cuttings pie': three pennyworth of bits of meat and offal ('cuttings'), with vegetables and gravy, topped with a suet crust.*

25 *On the opposite, west, side of the River Esk many families lived on the Cragg in, as a London journal put it in 1870, 'wretched, old, tumble-down tenements, built many years ago in the cliff-side, for which they pay three or four pounds a year'. In January 1900 part of the cliff gave way and two dwellings occupied by fishing families did indeed tumble down. The four fatalities included a mother and her infant child. The picture shows the aftermath.*

of Runswick is a singular rookery of cottages, built with only walking space between them, one above another, in the cliff side.' The fishermen he added, 'cling to the face of the treacherous cliff like a colony of martins'.[7]

Runswick, Staithes and Flamborough were predominantly fishing villages, but elsewhere, as at Whitby, the fisherfolk were only part of a larger population. Even so, clustered about the waterfront, they constituted a distinct and distinctive group. At Scarborough many fishing families dwelt in Quay Street; while Filey's Queen Street, as one former resident put it, was 'the quarter where the fishermen lived'. Indeed, 'quarter' is precisely the correct word to describe what amounted almost to a cultural, as well as physical, segregation. 'Filey in our day', recalled Ned Wright (born round about 1890),

> was a 'tale of two cities'. The dividing line was the church with the clock in the tower. When we were kids we used to leave school on a night, perhaps you would get your tea and were just going out, and Mother would shout. And when you were back she wanted something doing. Well, you rushed and you did it and then off you went. And the first thing that you were asked when you went back home at night was 'Now, then. Where have you been?' 'We've been down new Filey.' You see, yon side was old Filey and the other was new Filey, and the answer you got when you told her was 'What's thoo want down there? There's nowt down there for thoo, keep thisel' at this side'. And you'd maybe get a clout for going.

To many of the painters, writers and photographers who, from the 1880s onwards, flocked to the Yorkshire coast the jumble of houses, red pantiled

26 *The Cragg, Whitby (c.1905). Old and 'wretched' the houses on the Cragg may have been, but opinion is unanimous that there was a very close community spirit amongst the inhabitants. 'Everyone helped one another' is a frequent recollection. Neighbours assisted at births, and were 'bidden' to attend funerals; while for weddings the flagstones for the entire length of the Cragg were sanded.*

roofs one atop another, and the maze of courts, ghauts, steps and yards of the fishing *quartiers* were merely picturesque, although some had a proper appreciation of the problems of living in such cramped and often overcrowded dwellings.

In his novel *Three Fevers*, Leo Walmsley (1892-1966) has left a detailed impression of the interior of a fisherman's cottage in his native Robin Hood's Bay:

> Even in broad daylight the room was dark, for it had only two small windows ... . Against the north wall stood a mahogany veneer sideboard with a scrolled back, whose top was only a foot from the ceiling, and the space left was occupied by a coloured picture of Grace Darling in a gilt frame. East and west of this were bright representations of two steamboats ... one with Vesuvius in eruption for its background ... . The sideboard had a cloth with an embroidered fringe. It bore a collection of china: three pairs of vases (very precisely 'paired'), a china bust of Lord Haig, and one of Lord Jellicoe to match, a china model of Burnharbour Priory [Whitby Abbey], and one of the Eddystone Lighthouse, with a thermometer in front. Above the fireplace on the south wall was a varnished oak overmantel ... . There was a vari-coloured rag mat in front of the fire.[8]

The accuracy of Walmsley's description may be judged by comparing it with that of a recent writer, J.S. Johnson, who, remembering his childhood and youth spent at Runswick, likens living-rooms to 'miniature museums':

> The walls were covered with pictures and paintings of ancestors, and lots of other articles which the family had accumulated over the years. On the mantel-piece were pot ornaments, around the fireplace and on top of the drawers one could hardly find enough space to place a box of matches, because of the number of small and large brass pieces all gleaming [and] making a wonderful sight, but oh! the work it must have entailed.[9]

Most fishermen's houses, says Johnson, were really very small cottages, with one main room downstairs. Upstairs there were usually two small bedrooms, and, above these, an attic reached by a ladder, where the boys of the family slept. Interiors were dark:

> As most of these cottages were built on the steep hillside, they consequently only had windows which looked out towards the bay, and many of these were very small. Being built in these positions and having open coal fireplaces many of them smoked when the wind was in a certain quarter, further adding to the family's discomfort. One or two I often went into during the day were so dark I just had to stand still when I first entered until my eyes became accustomed to the gloomy darkness.[10]

27 & 28 *Photography's technical limitations at the time (c.1907) mean that visual impressions of the interiors of fisherfolk's homes are rare; but these drawings of a cottage at Scarborough, said to be 'from life', are fairly detailed. Note the stone-flagged floors.*

In the tenement dwellings at Whitby and Scarborough many fishing families lived on the first floor, and this increased greatly the burden of housework for the women.

An inkling of what life was like is afforded by oral evidence. Alice Maud Hind (*née* Harland) was born in Whitby on the Cragg in 1896. Her father, Robert Harland, was a fisherman and successively bow-man, second coxswain and then coxswain of the Whitby lifeboat. Her mother, Jane Forden was her maiden name, was a fisherman's daughter. Jane and Robert Harland had 10 children. Maud, the oldest of the girls, described the family home:

> *We went up two flights of stairs and there was a small kitchen; and there was a big room, and we had one bed-place. And every one of us was born in that house barring my youngest brother. We had to carry the water up two flights of stairs. We had to take everything down two flights of stairs. All had to be carried up and down. The privy was downstairs, and we had a wash-house with a copper. No bedrooms – just one big room with two beds and a bed-place.*

That Maud Hind's description is typical is confirmed by the present writer's own recollections dating back to the early 1940s; but more reliable still is the testimony of a Non-Conformist minister who, in the 1880s, carried on much pastoral work among fisherfolk on the Cragg: 'Narrow and steep the staircases in the lowly homes; the rooms, tiny cabins and the bed-place a cupboard in the wall, doors shutting it from sight during the day.'[11]

Despite the gloom and overcrowding, most fisherfolk's homes were cosy and clean, 'the general impression one got was that of warmth and comfort' wrote Walmsley,[12] while Nellie Erichsen described a home in Staithes 'whose outside is so bare and exposed, [but] is very snug within'.[13] On the other hand, Frank Meadow Sutcliffe (1853-1941), the distinguished pioneer photographer, mentions how, in 1905, he visited the home of an elderly Whitby fisherman who was crippled with rheumatism: 'The walls of his cottage were simply running down with water. His sea boots [at that time made of leather], which he had not been able to put on for some months, were green and white with fungoid growth.'[14] Much, however, depended upon individual circumstances. When in January 1865 Munby, the diarist, visited two houses in Quay Street, Scarborough he was confronted by greatly contrasting scenes. At one he found 'a neat houseplace, sanded floor, bright fire, tea set, china ornaments'; whereas at the other he climbed dark, old stairs to a small first-floor room occupied by father, mother, daughter and young son, the room 'poor and shabby: nearly filled by two bedsteads'.[15]

Lack of space was exacerbated by lack of facilities. At Runswick, for example, there was no piped water in the village, all water having to be drawn

29 *Leo Walmsley took this photograph to illustrate an article which he had published in* The National Geographic Magazine *in 1933. A year earlier his novel about the fisherfolk of his native Robin Hood's Bay had appeared.* Three Fevers *describes the line fishing, potting for crabs and lobsters and salmoning in authentic detail.*

and carried from two natural springs, and only about 1950 were the last cottages connected to the main water supply. Electricity did not reach Runswick until the early 1930s. Toilet facilities were practically non-existent, as Johnson recollects:

> There were no toilets for fishermen, only earthen closets for women which were emptied by the men. The main toilet for these men was under the lifeboat slip: handy for them as they went down to their boats. One had to be careful where one put one's feet if walking under the slip, and the smell sometimes was awful especially if there had not been a rough sea for a while and the weather had been warm, not to mention the flies.
>
> All fishing villages were the same from what I can gather. I know at Staithes there was a place there called Sky Shitings; this was where the men emptied the buckets over the cliff …[16]

A preoccupation for men and women alike was the kitchen fire, and much time and energy were spent on gathering fuel. At Whitby *beck sticks* carried down the Esk were gathered on Tate Hill Sands, and all along the coast women and girls searched high-water mark for driftwood: 'They've gone on the scaurs, early morning, and maybe they haven't had a drink or a bite', Maud Hind recollected her mother telling her. Sometimes a ship would run aground and coal from the cargo or bunkers would be washed up. When this happened everyone set to to salvage what they could for winter fuel. The entry in Staithes School's log book for 3 February 1886 is typical of many such: 'Most

30 *Recollections of fishermen's cottages at Runswick suggest that they were dark, overcrowded, yet warm and cosy. Water had to be fetched from springs, and toilet arrangements presented a problem. For women and children there were earth closets, whereas the men, it is remembered, 'just used the world at large' (a favourite spot being beneath the lifeboat slipway).*

wretched attendance this morning probably owing to a ship having been wrecked under the cliff near Staithes, laden with coals, children being occupied by their parents in gathering them up.'[17] Little wonder the fire was so important, for it provided not only warmth but also the means to cook, clean, wash and launder. As several elderly fisherfolk remarked, 'So long as you had a good fire you were all right'.

Finally, it cannot be overemphasised that fisherfolk's homes were work-places as well as dwellings. As is described in a later chapter, there it was that much of the gear was made, mussels and limpets were shelled, and lines cleaned and baited. At the centre of this domestic economy was the woman, at the very least a co-partner in the fishing enterprise, and also chiefly responsible for all those many tasks which society's prevailing norms decreed to be hers. Fishermen did not have an easy life; but few, one imagines, would have changed places with their partners. Their horizons were broader, resting principally on the sea and, most particularly, on their boats, which, together with the womenfolk, were an indispensable element in their lives.

Four

FISHING CRAFT

31 *The yawl* True Love *at Whitby,* c.*1908.*

THE 'SCAURS' which fringe much of the Yorkshire coast are platforms of rock stretching from the foot of the cliffs down to, and beyond, low-water mark. The rock is blue-grey shale, slippery, and fissured with water-filled gullies and pools. Boulders of sandstone litter the scaur, and long fingers of hard rock, submerged at high tide, jut out from the shore. These are called 'steels'. If one imagines the keys of a piano, then the black keys might be likened to steels, and the white ones to the relatively deep-water channels in between. When approaching land, the fishermen, with the aid of marks on the shore and a nice sense of the turbulence or smoothness of the sea under the boat, had to navigate their craft down the channels of deep water, through the breaking surf, and up onto the steeply shelving beach. Moreover, if conditions were too bad to land they had to try to remain at sea until the storm blew itself out; or, more likely, run for a port where the configuration of the coast gave some protection. To meet these rugged demands a special type of craft was needed, and, over many hundreds of years, there evolved the 'coble'.*

To launch off unprotected beaches into rollers and breakers sweeping in from the open sea, the bow of a boat had to be deep and sharp to cleave the waves. The need to be afloat seconds after launching made a keel redundant, yet, as a substitute when sailing, a long rudder projecting well below the boat's bottom was imperative. Similarly, when coming in to land, a boat had on the one hand to fend off the breaking surf and, on the other, to maintain maximum stability so as not to capsize: hence the coble's square, sloping stern and the practice of landing stern first. And, of course, to withstand the buffeting of launching and landing in these conditions, not to mention the wear and tear caused by the fishing itself, the boat had to be very strong in its materials and construction, while at the same time have a degree of 'give': too much rigidity would result in the vessel's breaking up. An Elizabethan document illustrates these points vividly:

> ... You next come to Redcarre, a poor fysher-towne, where, at a lowe water, you may discover many rockes within half a mile distante from the shore, some in front, and some on either hand lie in circle-wise, having certaine inletts for the boates called *cobbles* to passe in and out. Truly itt may be sayde of these poor men, that they are lavish of theyre lives, who will hazard 20

---

* In Yorkshire pronounced with a short 'o', cobble. On the Durham and Northumberland coasts the 'o' is long.

or 40 myles into the seas in a small troughe so thinne that the glimse of the sunne may be seen through ytt ... the boat ytself is built of wainscott, for shape exceedinge all modeles for shippinge; twoe men will easily carrye ytt on land betweene them; yett are they so secure in them at sea, that some in a storm have lyved aboarde three dayes. Their greatest danger is nearest home, where the waves breake dangerouslye; but they acquainted with these seas, espieyne a broken wave reddy to overtake them, suddenly oppose the prowe or sharp ende of theyre boat unto yt, and, mountynge to the tope, descend down as yt were unto a valley, hoveringe until they espye a whole wave come rowlinge, which they observe commonly to be an odde one; whereupon mountinge with their cobble, as it were upon a great furious horse, they rowe with might and mayne, and together with that wave drive themselves on lande.[1]

Until the advent of the internal combustion engine and its adaptation for use in fishing boats during the 20th century, it remained the case that human 'might and mayne' were the only means of mastering that 'great furious horse', the sea. John William Storry's recollections are remarkably similar to the Elizabethan account:

> I was once in a coble with old Mr Murfield – he was a Sailors' Home man – and we were at sea, coming home [to Whitby] from Robin Hood's Bay. And the steamers what's going ti north, we could just see the mast tops and the funnels; we couldn't see the hulls. And we were in a small coble. We landed in Joe's Nab ... Black Nab is its proper name, on the chart ... . It was all wind, nor'-west wind, gale: it was a gale. The lifeboat was coming after us, the rowing boat was coming through the Rock. We were trying to get to nor'ard of the Nab, but she wouldn't steer: the mast kept jumping out of t'step. Every time we went to steer the mast jumped out, and we were afraid of it going through the side and putting us in the water. So we lowered the sail and we backed up into Saltwick Hole stern first. We backed up, and we fetched Joe's Nab.

Even at Whitby with its deep-water harbour entering in a coble bow first could be risky, especially if a sea was breaking on the Bar (a ledge of submerged rock lying across the entrance):

> If you were pulling [rowing] up to the harbour, watching the breakers on Skate Heads, we used to watch there for a smooth.* When it was a smooth there, we used to row in. But when it was breaking out there, inside the Buoy, we used to lay until there was a smooth out there. See, we didn't come in any way: you had to watch a smooth in. And we had to pull two hundred yards in to the old pier ends. We had a mark, just by Whitby Light, peeping, like. It used to break there, on the Outer Bar, it breaks across there. And we used to set off to row there, watching Skate Heads, watching t'Rock for a smooth. Why, we were done when we got to t'pier end.

---

* 'smooth' – the occasional wave that does not break; what in the earlier quotation was called 'a whole wave', 'an odde one'.

32 *The coble (the 'o' is pronounced short in Yorkshire and long in Northumberland) is the characteristic craft between Tweed and Humber. Some say it is a direct descendant of the Viking longship; but more probably it is unique to the east coast of England. The coble is a perfect example of a craft's having evolved to meet local conditions. Made to be launched off steeply-shelving, open beaches, it has a deep forefoot, yet a flat bottom. Instead of a keel, there is a long rudder which can be unshipped when launching or landing. The coble can be rowed, or sailed with the aid of a single dipping lug.*
    This fine model of a Whitby coble is on display at the Science Museum, London.

Popular opinion has it that the coble is of Viking ancestry. One source[2] states, 'The type of craft in use by the Yorkshire fishing villages was a direct descendant of the Viking ships … .' The late Edgar March, a leading authority on inshore fishing craft, was less categorical, maintaining only that: 'It is reasonable to suppose that the coble owes its design to Viking influence, the broad, flat keel aft being similar to that in the Nydam boat.'[3] G.S. Laird Clowes[4] arrived at the conclusion that the Viking influence reached the Yorkshire coast via Shetland, where the local boats were themselves only indirectly linked with the long-ships: 'On the east coasts … of both Scotland and England, all existing evidence tends to show that the origin of all our small boats was the Norwegian yawl or yole, a light double-ended boat such as has been found associated with the larger "long-ships" of Viking times … .' In other words, the suggestion appears to be that, rather than being traceable directly to Viking settlement and colonisation in the 10th century, the coble derives from the gradual extension south-wards down the east coast of a boat design hailing originally from Norway, but itself imitative of ship design in an earlier period of Norwegian history. A major difference, however, in comparison with both the Shetland yole and the original Viking longship, is the coble's square stern which evolved to facilitate launching and landing on open beaches. Also, one authority has cast doubt on the coble's supposed links with Scandinavia. While recognising that 'the shore boats of both [Scotland and the east coast of England] are believed to possess a common origin, namely the Norwegian beach whale-boats', the writer goes on to argue that:

> The coble ... is a type of craft quite different from every other English boat and, so far as can be ascertained, bears no relation to small craft of any other part of the globe, with the single exception of a class of fishing sampans in common use in most of the fishing villages in Japan. These sampans, like the east coast cobles, are beach boats and have to contend with a similar set of conditions. It is interesting to notice, therefore, how parallel circumstances existing on opposite sides of the world influence the introduction of craft with almost identical features.[5]

One of the small number of men who were still building cobles along traditional lines towards the end of the 20th century, Gordon Clarkson of

33 *Cobles at Staithes (the photograph is of the crab auction, c.1900). In 1817 it was estimated that there were somewhere between 250 and 300 cobles fishing off the Yorkshire coast between Redcar and Scarborough. Seventy belonged to Staithes alone, while Runswick and Robin Hood's Bay each had thirty-five. They were used for long-lining in the inshore fishery and for crabbing. In contrast to the sombre hues of the fishermen's dress, cobles were painted in vivid colours. Notice the length of the masts leaning against the staith: masts were made to equal the inside length of the boat, and oars were twice the coble's breadth at the widest point amidships.*

Whitby, had for a long time been sceptical about the 'Viking connection'. He was once in Oslo where he examined the Gokstad ships closely:

> *They have strong similarities* [to the Yorkshire coble]*, up to a point. Only up to a point. I'll tell you where the similarities are: they're clinker-built* [with planks overlapping] *and they have similar sawn frames. But there the resemblance ends ..... Of course, you get entirely different sea conditions. After all, you get fiords, deep fiords, where you don't need to land a boat. You can sort of go up to the edge of a steep side, and there you stay ..... They had far more dead rise,* had a Viking ship.*

Gordon Clarkson is probably unique in so much as he is not only a third generation Clarkson to build cobles, but also in that he has examined the Gokstad ships in Norway, has studied the Sutton Hoo ship in the British Museum, and has seen the Viking block ships raised from Roskilde Fiord in Denmark. 'If you have a look at the Sutton Hoo ship, *that* is nearer to a coble ... . the construction's rather similar in some respects; but the flatter bottom is as well. In other words, east coast style.' About the Danish ships he says: 'They have similarities as well, in construction. But nevertheless not quite the same as ours.'

What Gordon Clarkson appears to be stressing is that, whereas the method of construction is very similar for both the Viking ships and the Yorkshire coble, the actual design of the two types of craft is distinctly different. This is a plausible reconciliation of the conflicting views outlined earlier. That is to say, the Yorkshire coast was an area of Viking (chiefly Danish) settlement, which might explain the adoption of Scandinavian boatbuilding techniques, while allowing for the possibility that these were applied to an already existing, peculiarly local, type of craft.

An authority on the construction of British inshore fishing craft outlined the main principles of construction of a coble as follows:

> A coble has no keel; she is built upon a plank called a 'ram-plank'. This is carved from a solid balk of wood. Forward it is like a knife on edge, narrow and deep and shod with iron. It is dropped here 1½ ins. for weatherliness, and as it sweeps aft, it is flattened and broadened, so that the plank, instead of being on edge, lies flat. At its after end it is curved upwards, and made very strong, to withstand the shock of landing stern first on a wave-swept beach.[6]

Cobles are clinker-built; that is, the planks (or *strakes* or *strokes*) overlap each other, rather than being fitted edge to edge (*carvel* or *corker* built), producing a smooth surface. Another authority[7] describes how this was done:

---

* 'dead rise' – in this context, with a more pointed hull, not so flat-bottomed as a coble.

34 *John Chapman of Filey, boatbuilder, 1907. This may be the only photograph extant of an old-time Yorkshire coble builder at work, so it is worth examining it in detail. John Chapman has a pipe in his mouth; and the three men in guernseys are the crew of the newly completed, but as yet unpainted coble. On the right is Chapman's apprentice. He is holding in his left hand an implement called a 'dolly', which was used to clench the copper nails used in the boat's construction. His legs straddle the building ram which the boat has rested on. Hanging on the wall (directly in line with the head of the middle fisherman) is a selection of augers, long-shanked, hand-operated drills used in boatbuilding. Fastened to the long wall is a steam box. A strake was slid inside it at one end, the box was sealed, and then steam was piped in (it came from a boiler located outside the shed). Steaming made the plank more pliable. When it was removed from the box it was immediately cramped into place using wooden tongs. This is a fairly small coble, probably to be used for salmoning in Filey bay.*

In the early years of the 20th century, most fishing villages had their own boatbuilder. There was John Cole at Staithes, Jim Hutton at Runswick, Cowey at Whitby and Hopwood at Flamborough, to mention but a few. Often, these men were simply the local joiner, turning out anything from coffins or chicken coops to cobles. They worked without plans; and for a new coble charged about £1 per foot.

The hull was now built up on the ram plank, ... the first planks for'ard rise vertical; aft they lie horizontal until sufficient width of bottom is obtained. Then the strakes are given an upward tilt aft as well, the first strake to do this being called the 'rising stroke' or strake. The number of strakes varied considerably, even in boats of the same size, and much depended on the timber available; but they were always as wide as possible.

In fact, six or seven strakes were usual, and the topmost one inclined sharply inboard creating a 'tumble home', the purpose of which was to reduce the risk of shipping water as the coble heeled over when sailing at speed in a strong breeze. 'No matter how far she leaned over, she always had a plank square to the water', explained Bill Clarkson (coble-builder, Whitby).

35 *In 1976, David Wharton ordered a traditional sailing coble from J. and J. Harrison of Amble, Northumberland. The boat was built by the firm's foreman, Mr Hector Handyside, who had the foresight to photograph the different stages of her construction. Built of larch on oak, she is 26 feet 3 inches long overall.*

(a)   A coble has no keel. Instead, it is built up on a 'ram' or 'ram plank' which is scarfed (jointed) to the vertical stem. Thus, the stem is knife-like and forward-facing, whereas the ram is horizontal and flattens out until, at the stern, it has the appearance of a plank.

(b)   The ram is tilted upwards somewhat towards the stern. The baulk of timber on which the ram is laid is called a 'building ram'. Notice how the bow dips sharply downwards – this is the 'forefoot' – and the stern rises.

(c)   The planks are called 'strakes' or 'strokes'. The first one to be fitted – the 'sand stroke' (so named, presumably, because it rests on the sand) – is vertical where it joins the stem; but by the time the stern is reached it is practically horizontal. On the right of the picture the other sand stroke is visible; the first one, at the side nearest to the camera, being already in place.

(d)   With three strakes fitted, it is now possible to see the characteristic curve and sweep of the coble's shape developing.

(e)   Cobles are clinker-built. That is to say, the planks overlap each other and are clenched together using copper nails. This is in contrast to carvel-built craft whose planks lie edge to edge. Clinker construction is thought to ensure greater resilience and 'give' – essential qualities if a boat is to be landed through surf onto rocky shores. The cramps in the picture looking rather like large clothes pegs are being used to hold the strakes in place until they have been fastened together. They are called 'tongs'.

(f)   Traditionally, a coble has six or seven strakes (this one has seven). Notice how the top strake inclines inboard. This is called the 'tumble home'; and no matter how hard over the boat leans when under sail, there will always be a plank at 90 degrees to the water line.

(g)   This photograph illustrates perfectly the point that the timbers (ribs) and stern of a coble are fitted only when the hull is complete.

(h)   Stern and timbers are now in place.

(a)

(b)

(c)

(i)   The first thwart (seat), or 'thoft' as it is known in Yorkshire, is in place and resting on the inwire. Notice the slope of the stern.

(j)   The hull has been turned over to fit the 'drafts' (sometimes referred to as 'skorvels') – one is already in place. These are to protect the hull on landing and, like a sledge's runners, to facilitate the boat's being dragged over the beach.

(k)   The finished hull, painted up; and a very bonny boat.

(d)

(h)

(e)

(i)

(f)

(j)

(g)

(k)

Cobles were propelled by oar and sail (and often, in light breezes, by both simultaneously). Oars were made in two parts: a blade of ash lashed to a deal handle. An iron ring was attached to each oar and this fitted over a wooden thole pin. Leather tacked to the oar at its fulcrum and on the gunnel prevented chafing. The length of an oar was twice the coble's beam at the widest point. The sharply raked mast, which carried a single, dipping lug sail, was proportioned similarly: the same as the inside measurement lengthwise of the boat.[8]

Sailing a coble required great skill and judgement. With a reputation for being able to go very close to the wind, there was, however, great danger that the coble in a sea would gripe and broach to. In January 1871 three Staithes fishermen (Richard and Thomas Cole, and William Thompson) were drowned: 'The ballast had been shifted to the weather side in order to keep the coble stiff, and whilst under sail she had been kept too close to the wind, in consequence of which she broached to and instantly upset'.[9] Only a month later three more Staithes men perished when their coble *Sea Venture* capsized in a strong wind.[10] Such tragedies were sadly all too frequent, and one consequence was that, although fishing families usually worked together, some fathers would not have their sons in the same boat, in case of mishap. Maud Hind's brother, Bob, fished with his father, Robert Harland, while another son sailed in a different coble: 'in case something happened and they were all lost'.

Nevertheless, old fishermen recall sailing in cobles with obvious relish; and it was noticeable how they responded to enquiries about the sailing qualities of cobles in much the same phrase. 'They could go like yachts, some on 'em', was a typical and frequent response. This choice of words was almost certainly not accidental (although the incident in question was not within the memory of any of the men concerned). In July 1885, a sailing match took place between the coble *C.D.B.*, owned by a gentleman named Barstow, from York, and a yacht belonging to a Mr Thomas B. Doughty. The course was from Whitby West Pier to Kettleness and back again via the Rock Buoy, a distance of about nine miles. Mr Barstow layed £10 to £5 on his coble. 'Both craft made a good start, and each carrying as much sail as possible, sailed briskly away, the coble taking the lead, which it sustained all through the race, and finally won by about a mile'. Perhaps the respective qualities of the helmsmen had something to do with the outcome: 'Mr Henry Freeman [famous coxswain of the Whitby lifeboat] sailed the winning craft, and Mr Doughty navigated his own yacht'![11] In any event, this victory seems to have subconsciously entered the folklore of the coble at Whitby.

When sailing in a stiff breeze the three-man crew of a coble had plenty to do. The helmsman steered and held the sheet; another man was for'ard by

36 *Riding, as it were, 'upon a great furious horse'. J.R. Bagshawe was an artist who actually went to sea with the Staithes fishermen and drew them from life. In the above painting he captures exactly the strength and skill of the coble-men pulling for shore on an 'odd' wave or 'smooth'.*

37 *The coble was not an easy craft to sail. Lacking a keel, the deep forefoot and long rudder acted as a substitute; but there was always the risk of running away on a sea and broaching to. For that reason, the helmsman always held the sheet (the rope leading from the free edge of the sail) in his hand and never fastened it. That way, he could always let go and allow the sail to flap harmlessly, thus causing the boat to lose way. A second member of the crew worked the 'Andy Billy', two blocks so arranged as to enable the coble to be sailed very close to the wind. The third man was often at work bailing out (see page 66).*

38 *Were a coble to attempt a landing bow first through breakers onto a steep shore, the forefoot would bury itself in the sand and the boat would capsize. Consequently, cobles are beached stern first, as this remarkable early action photograph (taken at Staithes around 1905) demonstrates. It illustrates perfectly the relationship between the sea and shore conditions and the design of the craft.*

Obviously, in order to land stern first, the coble had to be turned round completely on the approach to shore. This was an operation requiring great skill and attended by not a little danger. The earliest known written description of the coble, dating from Elizabethan times, tells how it was done (see page 57). It is remarkable that when the late John William Storry described, several hundred years after this account, entering Whitby harbour in a coble he used almost identical language, save that for him the 'odd' wave becomes a 'smooth'.

the Handy Billy* working the tack; and the third man baled and shifted the ballast to the weather side as the boat went about. Tommy White recalled this with pleasure:

> *You never had your sheet tied. Oh, no. If you got a gust of wind you let the sheet go. A good sailsman never fastened it ... . O, I've seen us when we were hard over, with a bucket, bailing out, with the water coming at t'lee side. Bailing out. O, beautiful! Better than a yacht!*

Ballast usually took the form of bags of sand or gravel, but flint cobble stones were also used at Whitby. At Staithes, Runswick and Robin Hood's Bay stones gathered up from the beach often served (there was very little sand at these

---

* 'Handy Billy' – an arrangement of two blocks, fastened at one end to the 'inwire' (q.v.) and at the other to the foot of the sail, and which when tautened when tacking to windward held the sail off the mast and thus obviated the necessity to lower the yard.

places); and a big herring coble, a 'plosher', carried perhaps half a ton of ballast, which, with a full load of herring on board, had to be jettisoned at sea.

Most sailing cobles carried a spare, short mast (the storm mast) which could be stepped in bad weather and used with the sail reefed. A spare rudder was often carried, too, lashed to the inwire;* but if the rudder broke when fishing and there was no replacement at hand one of the two masts was put over the side and used as a substitute.

Writing in 1817,[12] the Rev. George Young estimated that on the stretch of coast from Scarborough to Redcar between 250 and 300 cobles were in use, with 70 fishing out of Staithes alone. Towards the end of the century, in 1896, there were 196 second-class boats (craft under 15 tons), chiefly cobles, bearing the Whitby registration, as against only 10 yawls, a bigger class of boat owned and crewed predominantly by Staithes men.[13] Thus, it is clear that, until comparatively recent times when the modern, powered keelboat was introduced, the coble was the principal craft in use on the northern stretch of the Yorkshire coast.

The coble is essentially an inshore fishing boat, normally returning to port each day. It is an open boat and one not designed to be lived in at sea. But at certain times of year some coblemen would go fishing deep-sea, and this, of course, required bigger boats of an altogether different design.

The origins of the deep-sea boats are just as obscure as those of the coble. The North Sea herring buss was probably a fore-runner. The English buss was of some forty tons burthen, three-masted and square-sailed, with blunt bows and the raised stern of the Elizabethan period. By the late 18th or early 19th century this had evolved into a craft, still three-masted and bluff-bowed, but now with a transom stern and a counter built over it. Lugs had replaced the earlier square rig. Yorkshire luggers are estimated to have been some 61ft overall (44ft on the keel), and of about 90 tons burthen. By 1820, this type of craft had also a jib and a running bowsprit. These were the five-men boats, or farmin or farm boats.[14]

Early in the 19th century there were:

> 28 five-men boats employed on this coast, viz. 14 belonging to Staithes; 6 to Runswick; 5 to Robin Hood's Bay; and 3 to Scarborough … . Each large boat is provided with two cobles ... [and] usually carries 7 people, viz. 5 men who have shares, one man who has half a share, and a boy who is allowed a small sum.[15]

Hence, the designation 'five-man boat' refers to the number of share-men, and not to the full complement. Also, 'farmin' and 'farm' have nothing to do

---

* 'inwire' – simply, a strip of wood fastened to the timbers along both sides of the cobles.

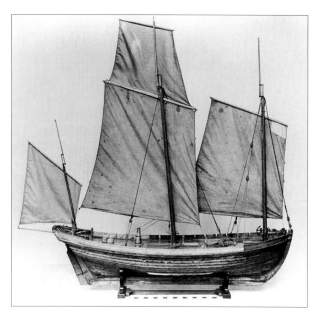

39 *Model of a Yorkshire lugger (Science Museum, London). The North Sea herring buss of Elizabethan times was probably the predecessor of the Yorkshire lugger. By the late 18th century lug rig had replaced the former square sails, but the vessel remained three-masted and bluff-bowed. By 1820, with the introduction of a running bowsprit and jib, the type had evolved into the 'five-man boat', itself in part the fore-runner of the yawl.*

with farming (as is sometimes supposed[16]), but are simply phonetic renderings of 'five-men' as pronounced in a strong Yorkshire-coast accent.* (In passing it might be mentioned that in the East Anglian herring fishery it was common-place for farmworkers after harvest was over to go to sea for the 'home season' in autumn.[17] Occasionally, such men came north on Yarmouth and Lowestoft boats to fish off the Yorkshire coast. James Cole recalled that they could be told apart from the true fishermen chiefly by their speech and lack of familiarity with the vocabulary of fishing. They were known locally as 'farmers' or 'Joskins'. It was not the custom of the Yorkshire boats to take on farmworkers.)

A five-man boat was launched at Scarborough as late as 1848, and in his evidence to a government inquiry John Edmond, foreman to Mr R. Skelton, builder of the vessel, gave a detailed description of it:[18]

> Her plank is one inch thick, and of wainscot; timbers [ribs] averaging six inches broad, five inches thick; wales, four inches thick and seven inches broad. She is copper fastened to the water-line, and her timbers are fastened with treenails [pegs, dowels] of fir, and one inch in diameter, through every plank …
>
> This is the only boat of this kind which Mr R. Skelton has built for the last 18 years; and there have been but three or four by the other builder … . There have been three built at Whitby the last few years for Filey … . There seems to be a reaction of feeling at Filey in favour of the five-man-boat, but

---

* 'faa-hve-m'n' – the two words have been run together, thus acquiring eventually the status of a single adjective.

the much greater expense is the chief barrier to its use. There is not one of these boats sailing out of Scarborough at present, nor has been for some years. Staith[e]s and Filey are the strongholds for them. The Staiths boats are usually built at Whitby; they are a little less than the Scarborough boats in their original cost, but are lighter in their construction, and wear out much sooner.

The five-men boats were used for the herring fishery, customarily from 15 July to 23 November, after which they were laid up for the winter. In February they were made ready again and long-lining commenced, lasting through to July. During the line fishing two cobles were carried on deck (sometimes known as 'caufs' [calfs]), but in the herring season only one. The five-man boat described by John Edmond had a length overall of 63ft 6ins (57ft 2ins on the keel); the extreme breadth was 17ft 3ins; and the depth of hold was 7ft 2ins. Twenty-three tons of ballast were carried. Exclusive of fishing gear, but including one small boat valued at £13, this boat cost £550.

According to Edmond, the craft which was to supersede the five-man boat, the yawl, was introduced by his employer, Mr Skelton, in 1833. The first, named *Integrity*, was built apparently 'on speculation'. Just over 34ft long overall, and 11ft broad, it cost only £60. Even allowing for any increase in price between 1833 and 1848, this was a much less expensive craft than the five-man boat, both to buy and to run (it could be worked with a smaller crew).

The Scarborough yawls derived from the Norfolk beach punts: undecked craft hailing chiefly from Cromer and Cley, which had taken to visiting the Yorkshire coast for the annual herring fishery. The Scarborough boats, however, were decked in, somewhat bigger, and, being intended for deep-water work, were given much greater depth. John Edmond reported:[19]

> They went on gradually increasing in size and strength until the year 1840, at which period they seem to have arrived at their most useful degree of capacity. During that year there were four built by Mr R. Skelton, of nearly equal size, shape and strength ... . Since that time a few have been built rather longer for Filey, and two by the above-named builder, with round counter-sterns. He has built 18 since their first introduction, and about the same number has been completed by Messrs Smiths, the other builder of this place [i.e. Scarborough]. There was also six built by another person, now retired. This is near the entire number in existence on this part of the coast. There were two or three built at Whitby in the early part of the above period [1833-40], but being small, built of larch, and iron-fastened, they have gone to decay.

The Scarborough yawls were built of American oak $^{15}/_{16}$in. thick, clinker-built, and fastened with copper to the waterline. Timbers were of English oak fastened with treenails of fir.

40 *Yawls in Scarborough harbour. The yawl was introduced and developed by a Scarborough boatbuilder in the 1830s. It derived from the Norfolk beach punts, undecked craft hailing chiefly from Cley and Cromer which had taken to visiting the Yorkshire port for the annual herring fishery. The Scarborough vessels, however, were decked-in and of greater depth, being intended for deep-water work ('fishing the off-ground'). They were constructed of American oak, clinker-built, and fastened with copper to the waterline. Their ancestry owed something, too, to the Yorkshire luggers and five-men boats of the 18th century (see plate 39 and page 67).*

In 1849, this type of yawl was to be found chiefly at Scarborough and Filey. One remained at Flamborough (three others having been sold away), one at Robin Hood's Bay, one at Staithes ('they want to sell'), and three or four smaller ones at Whitby. The Scarborough-based yawls were extremely versatile, some engaging in three distinctly different types of fishing in the course of the year:[20]

> These boats fit out in February each year for the long-line fishing, and as the spring advances, go off to the Dogger Bank; they then carry two cobles on deck, 22 or 23 feet in length and sixteen broad; they are thus occupied until May, when they commence trawling, that is the Scarborough boats, but those belonging to Filey do not trawl, but go on with their long lines until the commencement of the herring fishery, early in July. The herring fishing here and at Yarmouth employs them until the end of November, when, with the exception of half-a-dozen or so (varying with their success), they lay up for the winter. These go on trawling.

Thus, at Scarborough the yawl had ousted the five-man boat almost entirely

41 *Yawls leaving Scarborough harbour (note the cobles on deck, and the white-painted, lute sterns). The yawl was a versatile craft which engaged in several types of fishing, as the report of a government inquiry in 1840 mentions on page 70.*

by the mid-19th century; whereas at Filey and Staithes the older type of boat still found favour.

In 1869, as a consequence of the 1868 Sea Fisheries Act, systematic registration of fishing craft began. The records at Whitby[21] show that the Staithes fishermen's predilection for deep-sea boats had remained constant. However, whether or not these were the Whitby-built, smaller version of the old five-man boat to which John Edmond had referred so critically twenty years earlier is not entirely clear. Dora Walker, in her pamphlet *Whitby Fishing,*[22] takes the view that there was a type of Staithes boat, three-masted and with lug sails, which around 1850 was superseded by a boat designed by Marshall, a Whitby boatbuilder. Known locally as the 'Marshall lugger', it was a lighter craft, requiring fewer men to handle it, and with two masts instead of three. Later, probably in the 1880s, lug sails were abandoned and fore and aft sails took their place (the dandy or ketch rig). They were known as 'yawls'.

In 1869 there were 16 yawls (*Dependant, Ruby, True Love, Rose of England, Confidence, Good Intent, William Clowes, Princess Royal, Prosperity, Gem of the Ocean, Ann, Race Horse, Blue Jacket, Venus, Refuge* and *William Ash*) registered at Whitby and all but two were specified as fishing out of Staithes. One of the two,

William Ash, was skippered by a Staithes man, Richard Thompson, and it was certainly Staithes-owned subsequently (James Cole sailed in her in 1898); while the other, *True Love*, although St Ives-built and Whitby-owned, was Staithes crewed.

The mode of fishing engaged in by the Staithes yawls was the same as at Filey: long-lining and herringing. Tonnage varied, from just under thirty tons (*True Love*) to 39 tons (*Ruby* and *William Clowes*), with a mean of around thirty-five or thirty-six tons. Length of keel varied also, from *Rose of England*'s 50 feet to the 61 feet of *William Ash*, but in most cases keel length was 55 feet.

In all but two instances, there was a crew of either eight or nine, with some slight variation in the ratio of men to boys. Where there was a crew of eight it consisted always of six men and two boys; where it was nine there were usually seven men and two boys, but occasionally six and three. The exceptions in this particular were *Ann*, listed as carrying seven men and three boys; and *Ruby*, which, although at 39 tons one of the biggest boats, had a crew of only four men and two boys. The significance of these crew sizes is discussed in a subsequent chapter, but, briefly, it is that, given that each yawl carried one or two cobles on deck, when the big boats were laid up in winter there was a surplus of boys and men in relation to the number of cobles available, and this surplus had to seek alternative employment, usually outside the fishing, until the following spring.

Apart from the Staithes yawls, the boats registered at Whitby in 1869 were all either cobles or mules. The great majority of cobles measured nineteen or twenty feet along the keel,[*] were of two and a half or three tons burthen, lug-sailed, and carried a crew of three. Engaged mainly in line fishing, some also fished with nets in the herring season. However, a bigger type of coble was listed as being specifically for the herring fishing. These, too, were described as lug-sailed cobles, but their tonnage was in the range seven to ten, and they were thirty or thirty-two feet on the keel (suggesting an overall length of up to forty feet). Typical of this class of coble was Thomas Cole's *Good Intent*, 30 feet on the keel and carrying three men and a lad. Although not named as such in the Register, this, and cobles like her, was a herring plosher.

Cobles listed as belonging to Sandsend, Runswick, Staithes and Skinningrove were identical to those fishing out of Whitby; but those at Robin Hood's Bay tended to be smaller. Specified as being for crab and lobster potting, often without mast and sail, they were manned by only two men, had a keel length of 14 feet, and were of three-quarters of a ton burthen.

---

[*] 'along the keel' – as the coble does not have a keel, strictly speaking the term 'along the ram' ought to be used, but 'along the keel' seems to be more common.

42 *This rare photograph depicts an historic craft, the* William Ash *(WY 1). When in 1869, as a result of the Sea Fisheries Act, fishing boats were required to register, the first to be entered at Whitby was* William Ash. *Altogether 16 yawls were registered at the port at that time, although 14 in fact fished out of Staithes and the other two sailed from Whitby but were crewed by Staithes men. James Cole first went to sea in a yawl in 1895 at the age of twelve. In his first year he sailed as 'little lad' with his father and grandfather in the* Venus, *followed by three years in the* Dependent *and a year (as 'big lad') in the* William Ash. *Shortly before he died in 1975, James Cole recalled: 'I was t' lad. His job was to cook. Each man took his own food. I had to fry their beef and fish for them.'*

43 *Tees shipyards: on the left, at Stockton; and, right, Taylor's yard at Thornaby. Normally, a yawl had a crew of eight. Two three-man cobles were carried on deck for the off-shore fishing. When the season ended in November, six of the crew fished in the cobles throughout the winter until the following March or April. This left a surplus of two (usually the 'lads') without berths. As James Cole put it: 'You couldn't stand about' – so, groups of young fishermen went in the winter months to the Tees shipyards to work as riggers. In the early years of the 20th century, with Saturday overtime, they could earn about two pounds a week.*

44 *In the second half of the 19th century a new type of fishing boat was popular, especially at Whitby and Scarborough where there were deep-water harbours. This was the 'mule', which, as its name suggests, was a hybrid, having the bows of a coble and the stern of a yawl. Mules were used particularly for the herring fishery, which accounts for so many Scarborough mules in Whitby harbour in this picture.*

Apart from cobles and yawls, one other designation appears in the Register for 1869: the mule. The mule, as the name suggests, was a hybrid. It had the deep forefoot and bow of the coble; but, instead of a square stern, it had the pointed stern of the yawl. There were two distinct types. One, much favoured by Filey fishermen, was essentially a large coble with a pointed stern; while the other, the one to which the term 'mule' is commonly applied, was originally an open boat with a definite keel running the full length of the vessel, in contrast to the coble's flat bottom. These mules were built subsequently with a half deck for'ard, and, later still, became fully decked. Single-masted, they had one dipping lug sail.

However, the mules listed in the 1869 *Register* were almost certainly of the coble type. Contemporary photographs of mules[23] show them to be 'double bowed' and bigger, but otherwise cobles in every respect, save that some were fitted with a bowsprit and a small jib sail. Moreover, in the Whitby *Register*, larger herring boats (namely those with a keel length of from 29 to 33 feet and about five tons burthen) were described as having a crew of three men and a boy, carrying either a single lug or a jib and foresail, and were designated

45 *John Chapman of Filey with the newly built coble* Sunstar, *October 1911. This is a 'double ender' coble, sometimes referred to as a mule. Despite the Scarborough registration, this boat fished from Filey using lines and crab pots. Twenty-five feet overall, she weighed 3.27 tons, had a crew of three, and was skippered by William Cappleman. Wheeled under-carriages are still used at Filey, but nowadays tractors pull the boats, whereas in the old days it was horses.*

'coble' or 'mule' apparently indiscriminately. For example, when the *Register* opened in 1869 one of the first entries was of the *Beta*. Then owned by a John Miller Jr and skippered by Samuel Lacey, she was described as a lug-sailed coble fishing long lines with a four-man crew. Her keel length was 34 feet and she was six tons burthen. In May 1874 the *Beta* was re-registered. Thomas Storr was her owner by now, and John Storr her skipper. Tonnage and length of keel remained the same as in 1869 (suggesting that no structural alterations had been carried out in the meantime), but now the *Beta* was specified as being for herring fishing. Most significantly, she was designated mule, with lug sail *and jib*. In other words, it seems a reasonable inference that the *Beta* had the same hull both as coble and as mule, and that it was the variation in the mode of fishing and sail plan which justified the change of description.

This proposition is reinforced with the appearance the following year of what seems to be a new type of boat. A registration dated 5 October 1875 is of the *Scotia* of Whitby. Owned by James Webster and William H. Grier, and skippered by the former, she was 14 tons, 37 feet, crewed by five men and a boy, was specified as being for the herring fishing, and her type given as

'Keel – Lug sail'. In 1876 and 1877 similar boats were registered: *Garland* – 14 tons, 37 foot keel, 5-man crew; herring fishing, keel boat, lug sail; *Restitution* – 10 tons, 37 foot keel, 5-man crew, nets, decked keel boat, 2 masts and lug sails.

The *Scotia*, *Garland*, and *Restitution* (and others subsequently) are listed not as mules, but as keel boats. Yet their descriptions fit exactly what were known in Whitby as mules; whereas 'keel boat' has come to mean the larger class of modern, motor fishing vessel. Hence, it is important to distinguish mules as being either coble-type or keel-type. It was the latter that were most common at Whitby.

Whitby, unlike Scarborough, never became established as a successful trawling station. The harbour by the end of the 19th century was in a deplorable condition with the Bar silted up with sand and impassable to all but the smallest craft at half tide. Despite excellent access to railway sidings, facilities for landing and marketing catches were poor, and, to make matters worse, the Harbour Trustees had for years been in a state of bitter hostility amongst themselves. As the 20th century opened, stagnation appeared to have set in. Elsewhere, and notably in East Anglia, the herring fishery was thriving; and in the two or three years before the outbreak of the First World War attempts seem to have been made to modernise the herring fishery at Whitby. Several limited liability companies (such as Esk Fishing Co.; Rawcliffe Steam Drifter Co. [Staithes]; Staithes Fishing Co.; Streonshalh Fishing Co.; Saint Hilda Fishing Co.) were formed and a number of steam drifters purchased (mainly second-hand), from Yarmouth and Lowestoft, but also from Scotland. The war, however, extinguished these enterprises. Some drifters were called up by the government to serve as tenders and minesweepers in the Royal Navy; others were lost by enemy action, torpedoed or mined while fishing in the North Sea.

Peace in 1918 brought no improvement. The traditional markets for herring caught off the Yorkshire coast had undergone violent and profound change during the war. Germany was bankrupt, shorn of most of her former territory at the eastern end of the Baltic, and about to enter a period of frenzied inflation. Russia, with the two revolutions of 1917 behind her, was embarking upon a civil war which would last until 1921 and leave her spent and devastated. The bottom dropped out of the market for herrings: by the mid-1920s Whitby's steam drifters, and the odd steam trawler, had been sold off. The fishing outlook was bleak. Some fishermen returning from the war – and many had lost their lives in it – went into other occupations, which often meant leaving Whitby and its neighbouring coastal villages to seek employment, mainly in the Teesside area.

In the meantime, however, a revolution had occurred which, in the long term, was to affect the fishing community drastically (as in so many other walks of life): the spread of the internal combustion engine. The fore-runner of this revolution at Whitby was the *Star of Hope*, a vessel described as having lug and jib sails and a motor. Built at Hartlepool in 1909, she was registered at Whitby on 5 May 1911 under the ownership of Robert Wray Milburn with Thomas Verrill as skipper. Soon after came the *John the Baptist*, a motor keel boat, but still with lug sail and jib. Built at Filey in 1910 for a Hartlepool owner, she was brought to Whitby two years later by Skipper John Robert Storr. In 1915 the *Welcome Home*, a mule built at Whitby in 1897, was fitted out with a 15:20 horse power Kelvin engine; and later, in 1918 just after the war had ended, the *Faith* built at Flamborough in 1912 and fitted with a Kelvin 26 horse power motor was brought to Whitby where she fished under a succession of owners and skippers until 1935, when she broke her back going over the Bar.

These early motorised craft were, so to say, the first wave of the techno- logical revolution. Others emulated them in the 1920s and early 1930s, but as time went on the boats aged (some had never been built for motor propulsion in the first place, but had simply been adapted from traditional sailing craft). Advancing technology had made many of the engines obsolete; while else- where, and especially in Scotland, fishermen were modernising their craft. All these factors led to the second stage of the revolution: the advent of the modern motor keel boat.

As early as 1923, John Robert Storr had bought the 47-ft *Fair Maid of Perth*, built at Banff in 1915, renamed her *Pilot Me*, and brought her to Whitby.[24] Later, in 1932, two new, purpose-built boats came to the port. The *Venus* and *Galilee*, skippered by James Cole and Edward Verrill respectively (two Staithes men who had migrated to Whitby with its deep-water harbour as Staithes declined after the demise of the yawls), were built in Scotland at the Macduff yard of W.G. Stephen. *Venus* cost £780 (£360 for the boat itself, and £420 for the two Kelvin 26:30 engines).

More boats followed from Scottish yards: *Success*, the first canoe-sterned boat in the Whitby fleet, in 1933; *Endeavour*, still fishing in the 1970s and skippered by the original owner's younger son, in 1934; *Prosperity*, and *Easter Morn* (for Henry Duke, skipper of the unfortunate *Faith*), *Progress* and *Provider*, all built in Scotland in 1935.

Meanwhile, technological innovation had overtaken the coble, too. A few had had auxiliary motors installed in the 1920s, but these, although of great assistance to the fishermen, were often somewhat makeshift conversions. The breakthrough came in 1933, and the instigator was a woman, Miss Dora M. Walker:[25]

46 *The SS* Ethelwynne *of* Whitby *off* Venice *(from a painting). She was skippered by Capt. George Marsay and owned by the Harrowing Steamship Company (whose house sign, the Maltese cross, is painted on the funnel).*

Many fishermen on the northern stretch of the coast, if times were hard or in order to get through the bad-weather winter months, would sign on for a voyage or two with a local steamship company. A frequent trip was from a South Wales port with a cargo of coal to South America where, after discharging the coal, a fresh cargo of wheat was loaded at the River Plate. Coal out, grain home – that was the pattern, too, on the Black Sea route, often with a call at an Italian port. At Naples, Genoa and Venice there were dockside artists who, for comparatively little, would paint a portrait of the ship as a souvenir. These were done in simple colours and the style was rather simple; but the detail was extremely accurate. Most fishermen's homes had an Italian ship-portrait on the wall: it was clearly a most popular art form.

From childhood I had yearned to own a Whitby coble and fish it, and as it often happens that, when you intensely desire a thing, you get it – at a price! – I got my coble.

The price was a long spell of ill-health necessitating sea air. The outcome of doctor's orders was a house in Whitby and the opportunity to get a boat built, and to spend the interim of waiting in learning how to work gear, and boat. I was exceedingly lucky in having a friend willing to take the risk of a woman aboard his ship. He was at an age when a sailing coble, with the necessity of long spells at the oars, can be a heavy burden. My 'apprentice fee' … was a Kelvin engine.

Dora Walker's *Good Faith* was launched in February 1933. Built by Frank Clarkson at Whitby, she incorporated several new features:[26]

It was my plan to half-deck her, to protect the engine from the seas, and to have a long rudder affixed to a rod that could be raised or lowered in shallow or deep water. For the first year she had a petrol engine, but the prospect of having to renew the machinery frequently – which follows inevitably in boats ... caused me to change it the second year to an Ailsa-Craig diesel, made in a special light-weight alloy.

A year later, a rope fouled the *Good Faith*'s propeller when fishing, after which: 'I had a "hand hole" fixed over the propeller, with a brass valve that could be unscrewed at sea',[27] a feature which became standard in motor cobles built at Whitby.

Another important development in modern coble construction was the invention of the tunnel to accommodate the propeller shaft. Formerly, cobles were built according to classic design and methods and then the hull had a hole cut in it aft to take the shaft. Will Clarkson, by steaming the planks in a specially constructed steam box, was able to mould a propeller shaft, running approximately one-third of the length the boat, at the after end, without weakening the basic construction.

The coble came back into its own during the Second World War, as Dora Walker relates:[28]

> And then came the commandeering of the keel-boats. One after another they went. *Endeavour*, *Provider*, *Progress* and *Prosperity*. *Eastern Morn*, *Venus*, *Galilee*, *Success*. Last of all, the old *Pilot Me*. She steamed* out in the early morning – and the quay was empty indeed. Only the few cobles remained ... .
>
> The keel-boats were taken. But the veteran skippers were not retained despite their record and experience. They returned to begin again in open cobles ... .

In 1944 the bigger boats began to trickle back to their home port, where they resumed fishing according to the traditional seasonal pattern: potting, long-lining, *driving* (drift-netting) for herring. In 1945 an Inshore Fishing Industry Act was passed, to be followed in 1951 by the Sea Fish Industry Act, which established the White Fish Authority, and in 1953 by the White Fish and Herring Industries Act. One of the most important provisions of this body of legislation was to make available grants and low-interest loans to fishermen and owners for the acquisition of new wooden vessels and their gear.[29] A new wave of modernisation ensued, based on Scottish yards, but now at Whitby also.

Boats, both wooden and, later, iron, had been built on the site of the Whitehall Shipyard in Whitby's upper harbour since 1738. In 1871, as

---

* The entire Whitby fleet at this time was motor-propelled; yet the verb 'to steam' was, and is, invariably used to describe a boat under way.

mentioned in a previous chapter, the last wooden sailing vessel and the first iron screw steamer, the *Whitehall*, were launched; and from then until the early years of the 20th century Whitby enjoyed considerable prosperity in her shipbuilding trade. But the silting up of the harbour, the narrow span of Whitby bridge coupled with the rapidly increasing size of ships, and the advance of technology on Tyne, Wear and Tees saw the demise of shipbuilding at Whitby and an exodus of skilled men out of the town. The Whitehall yard re-opened again in the 1920s, but the national economic climate was unpropitious and it closed in 1933. Contracts to build lifeboats for the Ministry of Transport during the Second World War brought about a minor revival, and with it the formation of Whitby Boatbuilding and Repairing Company. Post-war legislation concerning the fishing industry provided yet more impetus, and in 1950 the 50-foot motor keel boat *Lead Us* was launched for Skipper W. Storr. Others followed: *Whitby Rose* (1957), *Accord* and *Statesby Rose* (1958), *Lead Us* (1959), and *Midas* (1960). Boats came to Whitby from Scottish yards, too: *Pilot Me II*, built by Walter Reekie at St Monance in 1948; a new *Provider* in 1958; *Golden Hope* the following year; *Wakeful* and *Achieve* in 1960; and a new *Venus* in 1961. *Ocean Venture*, built by J.N. Miller and Sons of St Monance in 1959, came to Whitby in 1962. In the meantime a new *Success* was launched at Anstruther. This was the third boat of that name to be owned by the Leadley family of Whitby, and, as Gloria Wilson points out:[30]

> All three have introduced something new to the town. The earliest, built by Walter Reekie in 1933, was the first canoe-sterned Scottish boat to fish from Whitby, and was also the first to have a short wave radio transmitter installed. *Success II* introduced seine netting to Whitby in the late 1950s. The latest *Success* [1960] … is the first Whitby boat to undertake full-time seine netting, instead of working pots, lines and drift nets.

The revolution which began, at Whitby, with the arrival of *Star of Hope* in 1911 had by 1960 moved through a number of stages, each one following the other at an ever quickening pace. Some twenty years after the advent of motorised fishing vessels at Whitby, at the beginning of the 1930s, came the first generation of purpose-built keel boats. In the late 1940s a second generation appeared equipped with various electronic aids which had been developed initially for military purposes during the war. And then, almost uninterruptedly, a series of boats had been built culminating, in 1960, with the Leadleys' *Success*, and with it what proved to be for most Whitby keel boats the abandonment of the traditional, seasonal pattern of fishing. One after another, the big boats moved over to seine netting and trawling as a year-round activity. In 1971 Skipper Jacob Cole took delivery of a new *Venus*. Built at Fraserburgh, she had a transom stern designed specifically for stern trawling. Other skippers adopted the same design (for example, *George Weatherill*, the first boat at Whitby to have a glass fibre hull in preference to the traditional wood, and *Eskglen*). In 1975 only *Endeavour* (Skipper Matthew Hutchinson) was still engaged in potting and long-lining.* In 1975, too, a new *Success*, the fourth of that name to be fished by the Leadleys, was launched at Whitby.† Her technical specifications, as reported by the *Whitby Gazette* (9 May 1975), were:

> Fifty-five feet long, with an oak frame, larch planking, and oak topside planking. Transom sterned, she has an 18 feet beam and 8 feet 4 inch draught.
>
> The *Success* is powered by an 8L3B Garner 230 h.p. (at 1150 r.p.m.) engine, and is fitted for trawling and seining. She is the first fishing boat in Whitby with a Kort nozzle – a fixed shield around the propeller which increases the vessel's towing power by 25 per cent. She is also the first Whitby vessel to be fitted with a 2 rope bin on the starboard side, which facilitates automatic storage of ropes below deck when seine netting.
>
> The vessel also has a complete 110v and 24v electrical system, with a back-up system which can be run from a Lister generator independent of the main engine; a 450 Decca auto pilot, and Mark 21 Decca Navigator; a Mastra combined seine and trawl winch with Beccles Coiler; a Cattermarine (type 300) power block; Saxon King SSB ship-to-shore radio; Redifon VHF radio telephone; Feruno radar and echo sounder; and Scandinavian Tenfjord steering.
>
> All the latest safety equipment has been fitted … . There are watertight bulkheads for'ard and aft of the fish room, and both the bulkheads and the fish room are insulated with Quelflam and aluminium. There is a complete CO_2 smothering gas system in the engine room.
>
> The *Success* has a fuel capacity of 1300 gallons, and carries 200 gallons of fresh water.

Success cost £100,000. The days when a new coble cost £1 a foot to build lay then still within living memory. Some, like Tommy White, recalled the exhilaration of sailing with the sea coming in at the lee side. He remembered, too, having to row a herring plosher in a dead calm from Skinningrove to Whitby, about ten miles; and James Noble and two others once took an hour and a half to make Whitby harbour from Saltwick Nab, about half a mile, in a sudden northerly gale: when he stepped from the coble onto the quay, his 'arms felt longer than his legs'. No one, other than for nostalgic reasons, could possibly bemoan the passing of that kind of hard, physical toil; and,

---

* *Endeavour* landed drift-net-caught herring in 1974, the only boat to do so at Whitby. She also fished off-shore for salmon in summer, an innovation so far as Whitby keel boats were concerned.
† Whitby Shipbuilding and Engineering Co. went into liquidation in 1965. Re-opened subsequently as part of Intrepid Marine International, it built *Success*, the first Whitby-built keel boat for over ten years.

despite the modern aids, as exemplified by *Success*, fishing remains one of the most hazardous industrial occupations. Not all innovations have been wholly beneficial, especially with regard to the conservation of fish stocks. Moreover, as in society at large, there have occurred among fisherfolk marked changes in life-style, outlook, beliefs, family life and income.

George Ewart Evans, writing about rural communities in East Anglia, observed: 'the majority of country people up to the end of the last century [i.e. 19th century] cultivated their land and got their living in essentially the same way as they had done since the time before the Romans came to these islands.' By that he meant that 'they relied on their own muscle power assisted by animals'.[31] 'Sails' instead of 'animals' would render this statement true for Yorkshire inshore fishermen. Yet it is doubtful whether a single working fisherman could now sail a coble; and, as such skills have become redundant, so it is no longer necessary to transmit them to succeeding generations. For the first time, vast areas of knowledge have fallen, irretrievably, into disuse. It is to the recording of some small part of that knowledge that this study is dedicated.

Five

LONG-LINING

47 In the Dawn *by J.R. Bagshawe (c.1906).*

FISHERMEN who leave the sea to take up shore-based occupations almost always find themselves doing unskilled, manual work. In terms of the onshore economy, they are deemed to be devoid of useful skills and their only major resource in the labour market is their physical strength. But the fisherman *qua* fisherman presents a very different image. Afloat he amasses a quite considerable body of knowledge and lore relating to winds and tides, the behaviour of the sea, habits of fish, the contours of the seabed, and the landmarks which enable him to navigate to and from the fishing grounds. He learns, too, the characteristics of the raw materials from which he makes his equipment (or, as he would call it, his 'gear'); and acquires a variety of craft skills which enable him, for example, to convert rope, twine, hazel sticks and iron into crab pots. Many of the simple (but effective) implements used in the making of the gear he creates himself, and even when his materials are factory-made he quickly learns their peculiarities and capabilities. The inshore fisherman is a great improviser, and, especially in past time, would utilise whatever lay at hand in the construction of his gear.

Nowhere are this knowledge and resourcefulness more evident than in the process of fishing itself. Evident, yet, in a sense, not evident; for the fisherman's main activity takes place at sea where direct observation by the outsider is rare. It is this circumstance which makes detailed description of fishermen at work so difficult. Even going to sea with them only solves the problem in part, since so much of what goes on is done at speed, and to ask questions would be to risk being a nuisance, and to place oneself too close to the activity might constitute a danger. Moreover, certain methods of fishing have gone out of use entirely and still others have been modified by the advent of new, synthetic materials and technological innovation (such as plastics and radar), so that to observe them now would in any case be impossible.

A further difficulty facing the social historian is that, like most occupational groups, fishermen have their own specialised language and vocabulary which are virtually incomprehensible to the outsider (and even to other members of the community who are not themselves fisherfolk). A parallel case might be the farm horseman who, until comparatively recently, used a vocabulary which was highly specialised and which also varied considerably between different regions of the country. The naming of the parts of the harness and the words of command given to the horses often changed completely over quite short distances. Now, when tractors are mass-produced, standardised and universal, a carburettor is called a carburettor, be it in Cornwall, Cumberland, or wherever.

The point of these remarks is two-fold. First, it is important to stress that a concern with language when writing history is much more than just a formal philological exercise. Words express ideas, emotions, attitudes, beliefs and aspirations; as well as describing material objects. If a material object falls into disuse, so in time does the word which describes it, so that eventually both are lost. A spoken word, therefore, may itself be an historical fact, just as valid a fragment of evidence as, say a shard from a Roman pot or a word in a printed document.

To offer an example. Until recently every coble and keelboat fishing out of Whitby carried a 'gog', or 'gog-stick'. A gog was a piece of hazel about 18 ins long and some 1½ ins in diameter. At one end a V-shaped nick was cut in it, perhaps 1½ ins deep, so that it looked like a very crude, wooden, two-pronged fork. It was in fact a disgorger: as the lines were hauled on board, the grooved end of the stick was fitted over the cord to which the hook was attached, slid down, and pushed into the fish's gullet, thus disgorging the hook. The purpose was to prevent the line snapping, which might have happened had the hook been simply wrenched out by force. So, why have gogs ceased to be used? On those keelboats which abandoned line fishing in favour of year-round trawling or seine-netting such an implement became redundant. Yet one keelboat and many of the cobles continued to go long-lining. However, cotton cord eventually became virtually unobtainable, having been superseded by nylon. This new material, extremely strong and resilient, made it possible for the men to simply shake or pull fish off the hooks without fear of the line's breaking, thus saving time at a point in the fishing process when time is of prime importance.

Eventually, not only will even fishermen not know what a gog was, but the word itself will probably cease to exist. It might be objected, however, that to know what a gog was and how it was used scarcely constitute a profoundly important historical fact. But, in reply, it could be argued that, should a multiplicity of such objects and processes, and the terms which describe them, disappear from use and, ultimately, from the language, then our knowledge and understanding of a particular occupation, its evolution and response to external change, will be seriously incomplete. Fortunately, many of the terms long in use by Yorkshire fisherfolk still belong to their active vocabulary; and, where this is not so, there were men and women alive in the late 1970s who could describe them in terms of their own direct experience.

The second problem confronting the social historian is how best to present a substantial body of quite complex, technical knowledge (much of it existing only within an oral, as opposed to written, culture) in such a way that it can be readily understood by anyone unfamiliar with the work of inshore fishermen. In the present chapter (and in those on potting and netting) the materials, the making up of the gear, and the actual fishing itself are described to a large degree through the medium of the fisherman's speech. In this way it is hoped that there will emerge, not only a reasonably clear understanding of the work process, but also a sense of the knowledge and skills deployed by inshore fishermen.

* * *

Like the farmer, the fisherman had his seasons, with every season requiring its own special gear. The habits of the fish were the principal determinants of each type of fishing: the appearance of shoals of herring, the migration of salmon, lobsters and crabs, the spawning of flatfish, and so on. Since these habits were immutable, so to a great extent were the traditional fishing seasons. Nature's rhythm was reflected in man's work. In contrast, the bulk of Whitby's present fleet of keelboats engages in a single type of fishing all the year round.

In the past, a typical year for a sailing coble or mule began about the second week in October with the winter line fishing. This method alone was used up to the end of February, when it was carried on simultaneously with potting for crabs and lobsters. In May spring fishing commenced. Boats took on board herring nets and long lines, stouter than the ordinary winter lines, and engaged in netting and overing. This involved catching the small spring herrings in the nets to use as bait on the big over hooks. Springing lasted a month or six weeks and then the cobles started driving (drift-netting) for herrings. After the First World War, when the bottom fell out of the market for herring and as motors were introduced, the pattern changed somewhat. John William Storry recalled how, after the spring fishing, he and his partner John Richardson would go in their motor-mule, the *Fortuna*, down the coast to Grimsby for the dogfishing: 'We've been up towards Blakeney, Cromer way. We used to go right up to them, across t'Wash – it's eight hours from Grimsby, South. Dogfishing; baiting with salted herring. June, July, August – then we'd come back home and go trawling.' In August, however, most Whitby boats began the main herring fishery which lasted through to the back end of September or into October, when the winter line fishing came round again.

This main seasonal pattern – winter lining, spring fishing, herringing – seems to have been general on the north-east coast of Yorkshire since time immemorial, and vestiges of it remain today. A few motor cobles at Whitby and Staithes, Filey and Flamborough still combine line fishing and potting;

48 *Usually, a coble had a crew of three men who worked together on a share basis. The week's earnings were divided by four: one share each for the crew and one for the boat. If the skipper was also the owner he received two shares, but was responsible for the boat's upkeep. Each man provided his own gear. However, the catch was sold as one lot and the shares were equal. Thus, labour was co-operative and the system of payment egalitarian. This is the three-man crew of a Staithes coble. The man holding the 'tommy tin' in the middle is Richard 'West' Verrill.*

Sometimes a crew was made up of two men and a boy (the 'tratter' or 'trat lad'). In that case, there were only three shares (one for each of the 'share men' and one for the boat). The lad, who had only a short line in comparison with the men's two long lines each, fished his own gear and kept the proceeds – good or bad – for himself. When it came to shooting the lines at sea, Robert Storm of Whitby recalled, 'the trat lad was often given t' best spot'.

and, even though the herring fishery on the Yorkshire coast had almost disappeared, one Whitby keelboat, until 1978, adhered fairly closely to the old cycle.

Skipper Matthew Hutchinson reckons his boat's year from 1 September. In 1969 *Endeavour* (WY1) drift-netted for herring until about the third week in September. Then, after a short interval to paint up and overhaul the boat, potting started and carried on until the middle of November when the pots were put ashore and the long-lining season started. This went on until March, when *Endeavour*'s crew began to work three fleets of pots and four lines simultaneously. Line fishing ended at Easter, and an extra fleet of pots was put in until the back end of June when herringing came round again.

The year 1974-5 was very similar for *Endeavour*, except that there was no herring fishery. Instead, salmon nets were taken aboard towards the end of

49 *Landing a coble at Robin Hood's Bay was particularly hazardous. The boat had to be steered along a submerged channel with rocks on each side. Posts were used as marks (one is visible in the centre of the photograph). However, because of the headland in the background, Bay Ness or North Cheek, it was sometimes possible to land at Bay when Whitby was stormbound. There was no harbour at Robin Hood's Bay, and, except in very fine weather, boats had to be dragged up the slipway onto dry land, a laborious task which required a great deal of co-operation amongst the fisherfolk.*

May, so that potting and salmoning were carried on side by side until the first week in July, after which it was salmon fishing full-time up to the last day of August.

In the 1970s, overing ceased completely. The change-over to round-the-year trawling and seine-netting is the chief reason, but the serious depletion of herring stocks in the North Sea as a consequence of intensive exploitation also contributed to its demise. However, until then, the seasons remained fairly constant, and, although several of the details relating to dimensions and gear have changed, this description of line fishing off Whitby, dating from 1838, would be instantly recognisable to the crew of the *Endeavour*:

> The lines are shot across the tide, left on the bottom for several hours, usually during the time of a tide's ebbing or flowing, say six hours. While the lines are shot one man keeps a lookout, the other two wrap themselves in the sail and go to sleep in the bottom of the coble. Each man has three lines, each line 200 to 240 fathoms, 240 to 300 hooks to each line are tied or

whipped to a length of twisted horse hair called 'snoods', each about 2½ ft long, fastened to the line 5 ft apart.

When the lines are baited they are regularly coiled up on an oval piece of wickerwork like the bottom of a clothes basket, called by Yorkshire fishermen a 'skep', at Hartlepool in Durham a 'rip'. The lines are baited by wives and children before the coble proceeds to sea, all are fastened together and when each is 240 fathoms the length of the whole is nearly 2½ miles. An anchor and buoy are at the first end of the line and the same at the end of each man's set of lines, or four anchors and four buoys to each coble's entire line. The buoys at the extremities are tarred dogskin, inflated like bladders with pole and flat, intermediate buoys are usually cork. The anchors are large stones, as an iron anchor is liable to get fast among rocks.[1]

A description of line fishing off Scarborough dated 1769[2] presents an almost identical picture: again, there was a three-man crew to each coble, and each man fished three lines (whereas by the next century it was usual to have only two lines per man).

Fishermen made much of their own gear, and, as the references to horsehair snoods and dogskin buoys imply, they used whatever natural materials there were at hand. In other words, they improvised as much as possible in order to minimise costs. However, in the case of long lines, the main length of the line itself (the baulk) was manufactured (although James Cole could just remember a Whitby man named Hustler or Oastler who spun lines for local fishermen). Horsehair snoods seem to have given way to cotton by the end of the 19th century. An example of a hook attached to a horsehair snood may be seen in Whitby Museum: twelve to fifteen strands from a horse's tail were used. Exhibited, too, are whorls for spinning lines, hardwood in the case of those from Whitby, but those from Filey are made from brass and steel.

Lines were – and are still – measured in 'haaf pieces'. The pronunciation of this term is 'half piece', but the origin lies unmistakably in the Swedish *haaf* (the main sea), and, in any case, more than two pieces constitute a line. Pieces on the Yorkshire coast measured 30 fathoms (180 ft), but sometimes they were 45 fathoms, the length preferred at Hartlepool where Staithes and Whitby men occasionally bought their gear. The overall length of a line varied slightly. Tommy White worked lines made up of ten 30-fathom haaf pieces (the usual length today); whereas Will Richardson had twelve 30-fathom pieces to a line, or eight 45-fathom pieces. Lines at Staithes tended to be longer than those at Whitby, up to fourteen haaf pieces.

Lines were bought from manufacturers' agents in an untreated condition, and the first task before they could be made up was to bark and tar the white, cotton baulk. Like many other activities connected with the fishing, this job was done in the home. Tommy White recalled: 'We'd have a stick and a bucket

of tar in the house. T'old man would pull the line through the tar. Then he would take it and hang it up in the gas house [the gas works]. Dry it in the gas house, up by the railway.' But, before tarring, the lines were first barked. Bark was known locally as 'cutch'. Originally, it had been made from the bark of oak trees, but this was largely superseded by 'catechu', a substance deriving from the tree *Acacia Catechu* which grows in Malaya and has a very high tannin content. The word 'cutch', then, derived from the Malay *kachu*.

Fishermen bought cutch from dealers ('It looked like jet'), broke it up into nut-sized pieces, and boiled it in a bucket until it dissolved. The method of treating the lines was explained by John William Storry:

We used to bark 'em first in cutch, boiling hot. Then we dried them, till they were like wool, and the bark that was in them held the tar. You had boiling tar and pulled them through with a tar-stick – that was a piece of hazel and a little ring (out of an old sail, a little brass 'cringle', we used to cut them out of old sails) – so's t'line would go through. You pulled the lines through [the ring at the end of the stick which was immersed in boiling tar]. I've been all morning pulling through, five or six lines. Red hot! You had to hold a cloth over the tar bucket while the man behind you was pulling them through. You used to hold the tar stick in one hand a lump of rag in the other so you didn't lose any tar: the tar used to run back into the bucket again out of the cloth. But it used to burn your hands, though. You got many a splash in t'face, when the stick used to slip, the tar used to 'blash up' and burn you.

There were considerable variations in the number of hooks attached to a long line. In recent times, there were usually 280, but at the time of sailing cobles there would be between 300 and 400 hooks, while the Staithes lines had 25 to 27 score (the usual unit of calculation), i.e. 500 to 540. The spacing, or setting, of hooks depended chiefly upon the type of fishing the line was to be used for. There were, for instance, 90 big hooks on an overline, set about three fathoms apart. But the usual settings were known as 'feeak and 'eeak' (or 'hook and a miss'), 'two feeaks and an 'eeak', and ''eeak and 'eeak'.

A 'feeak' represents one coil of the line as the fisherman hauls it in and arranges it on the skep. The word 'fake' ('feeak' is obviously a local dialect variant) has been found in a printed source dated 1627, and its oral usage no doubt pre-dates that. Its meaning in the 17th century, in a nautical context,

FACING PAGE:

50 A Filey fisherman. Before the advent of cheap rubberised wellingtons, fishermen, if they could afford them, wore leather thigh boots. They cost two guineas a pair in the early years of the 20th century, the equivalent to a shareman's earnings in a good week. Consequently, great care was taken of them, even though it cost six shillings to have them re-soled and heeled. When at last they could be worn no more, the boots were cut up and pieces were tacked onto the oars at the point where they pivoted on the coble's gunwale. This man is also typically wearing off-white, moleskin trousers (note the absence of flies: instead there is a button-up flap, hence 'whole-fall' trousers).

51 Fishermen at Staithes, c.1905. Fisherfolk's homes were often clustered apart from those of other inhabitants in a community; and the fact that their work was carried on at sea out of sight of the rest of the population gave fishing as an occupation an air of mystery. The separateness was emphasised, too, by the fisherfolk's speech, rich in dialect and specialist terminology and varying even between adjacent villages. There was much intermarriage, and custom and superstition were strong. Also distinctive was the way fisherfolk dressed. The men in this group at Staithes have two sartorial features in common: each man has headgear of one kind or another (note the sealskin cap worn by the man second from the left – these were at one time greatly favoured, dating possibly from the time when boats from the Yorkshire coast fished off Iceland), and they are all wearing guernseys.

was 'one of the circles or windings of a cable or hawser as it lied in a coil'.[3] ''Eeak' is simply the dialect pronunciation of 'hook'.

Lines set feeak and 'eeak and two feeaks and an 'eeak were both winter lines. A feeak and 'eeak line was one where on the first coil there was a snood and hook attached, the second coil was devoid of hook, and the third coil, again, had a hook attached to it (hence the alternative description, 'hook and a miss'). A line set two feeaks and an 'eeak carried fewer hooks, spaced wider apart, with two hookless coils of the baulk occurring between each snood. When fish were plentiful the feeak-and-'eeak line was more advantageous, but if they were scarce the two-feeaks-and-an-'eeak line was preferred since it involved less labour to bait and was less expensive, as less bait was required. The 'eeak-and-'eeak setting was used only on dog-lines (lines used to catch dogfish). This was because dogfish tend to congregate in dense packs, so that as many hooks as possible were baited and every feeak of the line carried a snood.

John William Storry, when fishing in mules in the 1920s, worked lines which had a mix of small and big hooks: 'Every twelve feeaks we put an over hook, for a bit of herring or squid bait', so that there were 390 haddock hooks and 49 over hooks on the same line.

Once the set of the line had been decided, the length of each snood (pronounced 'sneead') could be determined. The essential point here is that when two snoods are laid alongside the baulk they do not meet (if they did, a tangle might ensue as the line was fishing). Therefore, the length of a snood corresponds to the length of one feeak, which itself depends upon the type of material from which the line is made, for, as Matthew Hutchinson explained: 'Cotton stretches; nylon stretches; new hemp runs up [shrinks]; and old hemp stays as it is'. Consequently, the length of feeaks on lines used on board *Endeavour* ranged from 3ft 3ins to 3ft 8ins, depending upon the material, and the length of snoods roughly corresponded. Thus, a modern nylon line, or one made from cotton, is set at 3ft 3ins or 3ft 4ins; a new, unshrunk hemp line at 3ft 8ins, while 3ft 5ins is sufficient for a year-old hemp line which is being refitted with hooks and snoods. However pedantic the enumeration of these measurements may seem, it reveals nonetheless the fisherman's knowledge of his raw materials, and, in a small way, may be likened to the carpenter who knows the grain of different kinds of wood. So the fisherman, from experience of his craft, learns the characteristics of rope and twine, and their behaviour under stress of the sea.

Snood cord was bought from the manufacturers' agents in hanks or ready-wound into balls. Most fishermen had a snood board, an implement they made themselves. It was a piece of flat board about 4 ins wide and in length exactly half that of the snood. That is to say, if the desired length of each snood was 3 ft, then the snood board would be 18 ins long. Cord was wound tautly and neatly round and round the board lengthwise until the surface was covered. Then, with a sharp knife, a cut was made across the board, with the result that the formerly continuous length of cord fell into equal, 36-inch pieces.

When cotton snood cord became difficult to obtain and was replaced by nylon cord, fishermen found that, as it was cut, the nylon snoods splayed and unravelled at the ends. At first, a man would take a cigarette from his mouth, apply it to the end of the cord, the nylon would melt, and thus 'seal' the strands together. But this was a time-consuming business, until one day Matthew Harland, a retired bridge-attendant at Whitby, hit upon a simple and efficient solution. While the cord was being wound round the snood board, the blade of a knife was left to heat in the fire. Then, when it was red-hot, the cut was made, and the cord was not only severed but also sealed simultaneously. Here is another small example of the workman's ingenuity.

The next step was to whip hooks onto the snoods. John Verrill of Staithes remembers that his father would sit down, gather up the loose snoods from the snood board, and tie the bundle lightly at one end. Taking some whipping thread which had been pulled through Stockholm tar, he would begin to whip on the hooks. The bundle of snoods hung over one side of his knee, and, as each hook was whipped on, the completed snood would be passed over to the other side of his knee, so that there was no chance of getting into a tangle. To tar whipping thread, the bobbin was dropped into the bucket of hot tar, but keeping hold of one end of the thread, which was then wound anew round an empty cotton reel.

Even an implement as simple as a hook had its own terminology in fishermen's speech. The barbed point was called the wither, the curved part the crown, the straight part the shank, and the flattened end was called the flat. As in most jobs, economy of effort compatible with efficiency and good workmanship was the rule. John William Storry reckoned to whip on 300 hooks in a day: the first hundred in an hour, the second hundred in one hour ten minutes, and the third hundred in about an hour and a half – 'After that you got tired.' He would make six turns of the whipping thread round shank and snood to fasten them together, followed by two clove hitches and 'back it with three on the flat'. Some fishermen, he said, overdid it, and then there was so much whipping 'it looks like a horse's leg'.

With hooks whipped on, the snoods could now be fastened to the baulk. Two half-hitches were made round the baulk with the free end of the snood, leaving some 1½ ins to 2 ins of cord hanging spare. This spare end was then twisted round the main, or standing part of the snood and fastened to it by a knot, so that for the last inch or so nearest the baulk the snood was double thickness. This was called the kelkin, and it had a purpose: as the lines were hauled on board the fish were taken off and each hook was tucked into a kelkin so that it did not blow about in the wind and become entangled, or catch in the fisherman's flesh or clothing. At Staithes, a line with hooks secured in the kelkins was said to be kidged.

When making up an over line the spacing between hooks was measured by taking the baulk, opening the arms wide apart, and thus extending the line across the chest. Three such movements measured three fathoms. But for the ordinary winter lines most fishermen used a line-set, a length of flat wood, rather like a long ruler, which had various measures marked on it. Others cut notches in the kitchen table and measured off the feeaks that way.

52 *Long-lining constituted the backbone of the fisherman's year. Beginning in October, it went on until as late as May or June, when preparations for the herring fishery began. A single line might have as few as 300 hooks or as many as 500; so, with each man having two lines, a three-man coble could fish up to 3,000 hooks in a single night. It is obvious, therefore, that prodigious quantities of bait were required along the coast when long-lining was at its height during the winter months. And this is when womenfolk became absolutely indispensable; for it was they who, while their menfolk were at sea, gathered bait, prepared it, and got the lines ready.*

This superb photograph by Frank Sutcliffe, taken at Whitby about 1898, epitomises the interdependence of women, men, boat and gear in the Yorkshire inshore fishing industry.

Once the hooks had been whipped on and the snoods attached to the baulk a line was complete; but, before it could be used for fishing, additional equipment was necessary. First, anchors were required to hold the line to the seabed. These had to be buoyed (to show where the line was, and also, of course, to make retrieval possible). Anchor and buoy were joined together by a tow line. Anchors could be bought factory-made, but were just as likely to have come from the local blacksmith (who made many of the fishermen's small pieces of equipment, and fittings for boats, in addition to his more usual employments). Nowadays, buoys are made from cork and, increasingly, from plastic; but in past time they were either cork or of animal origin. The only recollection of this was by James Cole who said that in the late 19th century Irish boats occasionally fished for herring off the Yorkshire coast, and dog-skin buoys were used on their nets. If one broke away in rough weather the local men would take it up and use it as a buoy for their own lines. More usual were pigs' bladders and sheep's stomachs (both called bladders indiscriminately). Fishermen would cadge them off butchers, wash them, and hang them out in the wind and sun to cure. Then warm Stockholm tar was poured inside and the bladder inflated. A cotton poll (bobbin) had first been inserted into the neck and bound round with snood cord. When the bladder was fully blown up a stopper, called a bladder pin, was plugged into the poll to prevent air escaping, and the outside of the bladder was either tarred or painted. Often, the boat's registration number would be painted on, too.

At Whitby line buoys were known as enders (even if they came in the middle of a line, as was sometimes the case), or as bowls. At Staithes it was more usual to call them bunches, or cork bunches, if that was the material used. Buoys marking the extremities of a line were named starts, bowl-starts, or bunch-starts. The word 'start' in this context means something which stands, or starts up, and has nothing to do with 'beginning'. The start itself was a pole which fitted through the buoy, with a small flag made out of rag or canvas at the top and weighted at the bottom by a piece of iron which kept the start upright in the water. Attached to the iron fitting was a ring on a swivel (made by the blacksmith and costing, round about 1910, 'a tanner [six old pence] apiece'). The line tow was fastened to the ring.

John William Storry told how fishermen used to keep an eye open for canvas floats which had broken away from the herring nets. He called these floats hummocks (another local name is pellets), whereas Manx fishermen called them mollags, and Scotsmen knew them as mullocks. A mullock was a canvas bag, about 18ins to 2ft across at its widest point, and in shape reminiscent of an inflated hot-air balloon. According to that analogy, the lower, flat end of the mullock consisted of a wooden disc. Will Storry used to cut away the lashings binding the disc to remove it, and make five or six short incisions in the top of the bag 'as if you were cutting into an orange to peel it'. The pole, or start, was pushed through, and the canvas gathered into pleats at top and bottom which were bound to the start. When the line was shot at sea each end of it was marked by one of these bowl-starts.

One last piece of gear was needed before the line could be used to fish, and this was a bowl-start joined by a tow to an anchor, but quite independent of the line itself. It was called a kessen-bowl, or kess. Sometimes a line would break as it was being hauled in. When this happened an anchor with a kess attached would be put overboard immediately. The coble then sailed to the opposite end of the line (which was also marked by a buoy) and started to haul in the line back over. But sometimes the line would snap a second time or become fouled on the seabed: then a second kess would go overboard and the fishermen would be forced to grade for the lost line. The coble would be positioned up-tide of the line mid-way between the two kess-bowls. It would then be allowed to drift between the two bowls dragging behind a grade (pronounced 'grathe'). A grade was a kind of grappling iron, but one which had the hooks fairly close to the stock. If they were lucky, the grade caught the line and the fishermen were able to retrieve it: 'You can tell when the line's hooked. It gets heavier and the grade lifts off the bottom.'

Several fishermen explained the origin of the term 'kess-bowl' as meaning guess-bowl, since it enabled them to 'guess' the whereabouts of a broken line. This is a perfectly rational explanation which fits the actual purpose of the kess. However, John Hunter's reasoning that it was so called because it was a buoy that was cast away with the lines was probably more correct in a strictly philological sense, since much of the Yorkshire fishing dialect derives from the Viking settlement and *kesta* in Old Norse meant 'to cast' giving *casten* in Middle English, with the variant *kest*.

Evidence placed before the Commissioners in 1878 when they visited Newbiggin in Northumberland provides a detailed breakdown of the costs and materials for a fleet of six lines (the usual complement by then for a three-man coble) and, incidentally, summarises the foregoing description (see Table III).

Table III   Cost of a fleet of six long lines in 1878

	£	s.	d.
One Line	0	13	0
Cotton Snoods	0	7	0
Hooks	0	3	6
Cutch	0	5	0
Half bobbin of [whipping] thread	0	0	4
Making a total of	1	8	10

This multiplied by 6 gives as the cost of a fleet of 6 lines 8 13 0

There are besides:		s.	d.		£	s.	d.
6 anchors @		2	0	=	0	12	0
4 tow lines @		3	0	=	0	12	0
4 buoys	Sheepskins	4	6				
@ 7s. 6d.	Iron	1	6	=	1	10	0
viz.:	Shank	1	0				
	Tar	0	6				
					11	7	0
Add bait					0	4	6
Total cost of fleet lines					11	11	6

Source: *Sea Fisheries Report*, 1879, p. 74.

With a total value of £11 11s. 6d. a set of lines represented an appreciable investment at a time when one pound would be regarded as a good week's income by a fisherman. Also, that sum makes no allowance for time and labour expended in making up the lines, which, as we have seen, were quite considerable.

Long lines (but not overs) were baited on shore, mainly by wives and children. This was a lengthy, repetitive and dirty job, but quite fundamental to the fishing enterprise. The preferred bait was mussel, although if these were unobtainable limpets served as an alternative (see Chapter Nine). Generally speaking, baits were classified into hard and soft, depending partly upon the actual texture of a bait, but also upon its ability to stay on the hook when subjected to the pull of a strong tide. Thus, whelk (pronounced locally 'willock') was a hard bait both in texture and in that it would stay on the hook virtually indefinitely until taken by a fish. In the same category were paps, a colloquialism meaning 'breasts' or 'teats'. It is a term highly descriptive of the appearance of a variety of large sea anemone which lives in crevices under rocks near low-water mark. The men would gather paps at spring tides,* cut them into strips, and use each strip as a bait. So good were they that they could often be retrieved intact from a landed fish's gullet and used again the next day.

Another hard bait, but relatively soft in texture, was the razor-shell. James Noble recalled that these were much favoured by Flamborough fishermen, and that the Dukes, who moved from Flamborough to Robin Hood's Bay and then to Whitby, used them whenever they were available. They were pulled out of the sand as the tide receded. The fishermen called them 'hoss arses' (horse arses), a vulgar but accurate description of their appearance. Other soft-textured hard baits were sand worms (lug worms) and nereid worms which are known in the local dialect as 'thosks'. Sand eels, a hard bait, were used occasionally, and squid (invariably pronounced 'squib') and scallops ('queens' or 'queenies') were favoured if they could be got off the trawlers, which brought them up in their nets; otherwise they had to be bought and transported by rail from Hull, Grimsby or Hartlepool. Herring and mackerel, the usual baits for the over lines, were hard baits, too.

Apart from mussels, the only other soft bait was telpies (hermit crabs). These were often brought up in the crab pots and were kept as line bait. Nowadays, mussel is used almost exclusively, and, from lack of either time or

---

* Spring tides have nothing to do with spring *per se*. They are tides which have a big rise and fall (i.e. they go out a long way and come in a long way). Conversely, neap tides have only a comparatively small rise and fall. Governed by the moon's phases, each type of tide (springs and neaps) occurs twice in every lunar month.

53 *At Flamborough, depending upon weather conditions, the fishermen could land their boats at either North Landing or South Landing. Consequently, the village itself was built not by the waterside, but on the headland roughly equidistant from the two landings. This meant that the fishermen had a long, steep climb before them after they had drawn up their cobles out of the water. In autumn and winter, when the line fishing was at its height, all their gear had to be carried up to be baited ready for the morrow. Donkeys which in summer had carried children on the sands of Filey and Bridlington now bore different burdens; but their owners were glad enough to lend them to the fisherfolk in exchange for their keep.*

inclination (or simply because they are no longer so readily available), fishermen seem reluctant to utilise alternatives.

A highly specialised bait was once used in the turbot fishery at Scarborough (for which that port was famous). An account published in 1837 mentions that fresh herring or haddock was the usual bait, but adds, 'Many years ago … the Dutch purchased of the Thames fishermen the lesser lamprey for turbot bait to the value of £700 per year. The Scarborough fishermen were accustomed to obtain a supply [of lamprey] by land carriage from the River Wharfe, a distance of about sixty miles.'[4] To go to so much trouble and expense in the pre-railway era when overland communication was extremely difficult speaks highly of the effectiveness of lampreys as a bait.

Another use of the terms hard and soft is to describe the nature of the seabed. Hard ground is rocky, while soft ground (or mild ground) consists of mud, clay, sand or gravel. With the advent of trawling and the attendant risk to the line-fishermen's gear, the coblemen worked mainly the hard ground where the trawlers could not go. Off the Yorkshire coast there are areas of both hard and soft ground.

54 *Coiling 'basket lines' at Staithes in the 1890s. Although the pattern of fishing along the Yorkshire coast was basically the same everywhere, there were occasional variations, depending partly upon the fisherman's own preference and partly upon the size of the line. For example, although the flat skep was most usual, some fishermen had wooden 'trays', while often the great lines used in the spring fishing were coiled in baskets.*

It is remarkable how well the general contours of the seabed and the type of bottom were known by fishermen long before sophisticated navigational aids and submarine surveys came into operation, as this description, written in 1769, demonstrates:

> Scarborough is situated at the bottom of a bay, formed by Whitby rock on the North, and Flamborough Head on the south. The town is seated directly opposite to the centre of the west end of the Dogger Bank ... . Though the Dogger Bank be, therefore, but twelve leagues[*] from Flamborough Head, yet it is sixteen and a half from Scarborough, twenty-three from Whitby, and thirty-six from Tinmouth Castle ...
>
> It is to be remarked, that the fishermen seldom find any cod, ling, or other mud fish[†] upon the Dogger Bank itself, but on the sloping edges and hollows contiguous to it, the top of the bank being covered with a barren, shifting sand, which affords them no subsistence; and the water on it, from its shallowness, being continually so agitated and broken, as to allow them no time to rest. The flat fish do not suffer the same inconvenience there; for

---

[*] A league is three nautical miles, or 3,041 fathoms.
[†] Bottom-dwelling fish, especially flat fish.

when disturbed by the motion of the sea, they shelter themselves in the sand, and find variety of suitable food. It is true the Dutch fish upon the Dogger-Bank; but it is also true they take little, except soles, skates, thornbacks, plaise, &c. It is in the hollows between the Dogger and Well-Bank, that the cod are taken which supply the London market.

The shore (except at the entrance of Scarborough Pier and some few other places) is composed of covered rocks, which abound with lobsters and crabs, and many other kinds of shell-fish: Beyond these rocks, there is a space covered with clean sand, extending, in different places, from one to three or four miles. The bottom, from hence, all the way to the edge of the Dogger-Bank is a scarr, in some places very rugged and cavernous; in others smooth, and overgrown with variety of marine plants, corallines, &c. some parts again spread with sand and shells, others, for many leagues in length, with soft mud and ooze, furnished by the discharge of the Tees and Humber.[5]

That admirable description was written, of course, long before trawling had been introduced into the North Sea, but we can see the effects this had upon line-fishermen from the following extract which is taken from the minutes of evidence submitted to the Sea Fisheries Commission when it met at Staithes in 1863. Professor Huxley, one of the commissioners, is questioning Richard Verrill, a fisherman for 48 years:

Where do you shoot your long-lines during these months [November to March] – We shoot them about six miles off, from that to ten; then we change the ground. There is hard rocky ground for seven, eight or ten miles, and then we come into soft ground again. That is the place that they can trawl over with their smacks.

Do you prefer setting your lines on the hard or soft ground? Which yields the most fish? – The hard ground; the bait will lie longer there.

The smacks cannot come there, can they? – No …

Do they ever go over the soft ground? – Yes; it is there where the damage is done.

Have they ever carried away your lines? – No.

Are there in a season's fishing many complaints of lines having been carried away by trawlers? – There is a soft ground here that runs about a quarter of a mile in breadth to four miles in length, and they put their trawls in that and drag them along; if we have our lines there they take them away altogether. In point of fact we dare not put them down there now owing to the trawling.[6]

The same pattern, more or less, of soft and hard ground alternating prevails off Whitby. With lines baited, the coblemen would sail out to the Rock Buoy, three quarters of a mile north-north-east of the piers, and then set a course north-east by east for six or seven miles. They were heading for the Doaks, a popular ground for the Whitby men.

The Doaks are 'like three little hills' situated at distances of between two and nine miles offshore and about six miles in extent. It is hard, rocky ground with, lying beyond, the Mussel Ground, a soft area consisting of sand, gravel, red clay and, as the name suggests, beds of tiny seed mussels, a favourite food for plaice and other species of flatfish. But it was the Doaks where the coblemen usually shot their long-lines.

The best time to shoot, explained John William Storry, is at half-tide, irrespective of whether it is flooding or ebbing; and, as described in the 1838 Report, the lines are shot across the tide (for reasons which will emerge shortly). First to go overboard is the bowlstart, attached to a tow and an anchor. The depth of water over the Doaks varies from 26 to 32 fathoms and, as Matthew Hutchinson emphasised, the length of tow must be 'at least twice the water' (his tows were 70 fathoms when fishing on the Doaks). The tow is bent on (tied, fastened) to the stock of the anchor, while the line itself is bent on to the lower part of the stock near the flues (flukes).

As the anchor, with tow and line attached, sinks to the bottom the coble is pulled ahead and the coils of the line are paid out from off the skep by a man standing towards the stern of the boat. He never touches the baited hooks or snoods (unlike in over fishing, which will be described later), but instead picks up two or three feeaks of the line at a time and flings them overboard. In the meantime, the forward motion of the coble and the force of the tide tighten the line and cause it to billow slightly under water, or, as Will Storry described it, 'to sweep':

> There wants to be plenty of tide going, so that the line sweeps. If you shut a line at a slack,* it just lies where you put it. You won't get much fish: it doesn't travel along t'ground. It has to sweep like a trawl-net. As you're shutting, that line's going along the ground … . But the line's catching fish as it's going down, as it's travelling. But if it's dead tide and you shut the lines, they don't budge.

Another disadvantage of shooting lines at slack water is that the bait lies motionless on the bottom and becomes prey to such 'varmints' as starfish and small crabs.

If a line is shot at half-tide, it leaves three hours of a tide to run. It takes about one hour to shoot the lines, then there is an hour's wait while the line is fishing. At the end of that hour the fishermen start to hale the line. The maxim was to hale 'North side of the ebb; South side of the flood'. Given the set of tides and the configuration of the land in relation to the position

---

* i.e. shoot a line at slack, or dead, water (when the tide is neither coming in nor going out).

55 *Elliot Duke ('Old Elliot') with tray lines at Robin Hood's Bay in the early 1930s (photograph by Leo Walmsley).*

of the fishing ground, lines are shot with one end (the off-end) further from the shore than the other (the in-end). The off-end is usually shot first, and, when the entire line has been shot, the coble heaves to. The line is coming on board over the north, or port, side of the boat. However, if this were continued once the tide has started to flow the line would become fouled under the boat's bottom due to the force of the tide, so the line is switched to the south, or starboard, side of the boat and haling continues until completed.

Fishing is an occupation which places great emphasis upon co-ordinated team-work. As the lines are being haled, each of the three men on board has a specific job to do, and the success of one man's work depends very much upon the efficiency and co-operation of the other two. One man rows the coble, keeping as steady a course and speed as possible; another man hales the lines; while the third man kleps (gaffs) the fish as they break surface and takes them off the hooks, using a gog if necessary. The six lines were usually shot in two fleets, or strings, of three, with each man having one of his two lines in each fleet. Once all six lines were back on board, the coble headed home as fast as possible to catch the market (the earlier a boat's fish was sold the better the chance of a good price).

The method of fishing just described was the regular winter lining engaged in by cobles and mules and, later, by keelboats. It is still carried on at Whitby by a few motor cobles. However, two types of line fishing came to an end at the port during the 1960s: overing, and dogging – fishing for dogfish.

Dogging is still carried on at Grimsby, the main market for this fish; but it is a type of fishing which, in historical terms, is of fairly recent introduction. In the 18th century dogfish were regarded as merely predatory pests, and their appearance in great numbers was frequently noted with anxiety. In 1766 vast quantities of haddocks appeared off the Yorkshire coast, but when the Scarborough coblemen went off, 'At the distance of three miles from the shore, they met with nothing but Dog-fish, in immense quantities, which had followed the shoal of haddocks.'[7] At about the same time, Charlton was attributing a decline in the amount of fish landed at Whitby to the prevalence of dogfish and proposing a radical solution:

> The fish we have on our coast are, salmon and trout in the river Eske, … and, in the open sea, cod, ling, butt [halibut], bratt [turbot], plaise, scate, coal-fish, herrings, mackerels, haddocks, whitings, gurnets, dabs, sand-fish, lobsters and crabs. We have also dog-fish, porpoises, and several other species of fish which are not eatable, as they live by preying upon such as are sold in our markets, of which they have greatly diminished the breed of late years … [and] at present we seldom or never send any fish to foreign markets: Nor (as it is believed by many) shall we ever more have it in our power to send any considerable quantity abroad, unless ways and means can be found for destroying the dog-fish, which are grown so numerous on our coast. But this is not to be done without the assistance of the legislature, by which, if a small premium were offered for every score the fishermen brought in, their whole breed might in a little time be extirpated, (as was the case formerly with the wolves here in England) to the no small emolument of the fishermen who live upon our coast.[8]

Charlton was wrong, however, to dismiss the dogfish as 'not eatable', although it is not surprising, at a time when prime fish were prolific and communications bad, that they should have been regarded with contempt. Yet, strangely, the dogfish, despite its unattractive name, unpleasing appearance and indifferent flavour, has been successfully smuggled into the channels of mass consumption. As one commentator has pointed out:

> The British housewife's taste in fish is notoriously finicky. She has a few archetypal images of the edible fish, based on the cod, the herring, the plaice, and one or two others. Apart from 'rock salmon' – the splendidly

56 *In 1909 J.R. Bagshawe spent a week in the Staithes yawl* True Love, *long-lining on the Dogger Bank some forty miles east-south-east of Hartlepool. The yawl carried nets which were shot first to catch small, spring herrings for bait. Then the great lines ('overs') were baited, and shot and hauled from the cobles which had been launched from the deck of the yawl through a gap in the bulwarks. The catch was mainly cod, ling and skate; but some surplus herring was landed, too.*

In this sketch, drawn from life, Bagshawe shows a cod being taken off the long-line. The coble's parent yawl is in the background.

ambitious euphemism under which, until recently, it was possible to slip dogfish into the fish and chip shop fryer – she is extremely reluctant to extend this list.[9]

Thus, it was the spread of fish and chip shops, beginning in the later decades of the 19th century, which turned dogging into a worthwhile enterprise for fishermen. Also, modern technology has made it possible to utilise the skins of dogfish (which are very leathery and have the texture of emery paper) in the shoe industry.

Once Whitby fishermen acquired powered keelboats, they began to venture down the North Sea to Grimsby. From there they fished in the Wash off the north Norfolk coast with their 'eeak and 'eeak dog-lines. Herring or mackerel was the usual bait, and the method of fishing was similar to the winter long-lining, except that the 10-piece lines carried more hooks, because of the closer spacing. It was important, too, said Jeff Waters, to establish that dogfish were present before shooting the full fleet of lines. Therefore, a couple of short lines (about eight pieces each) were shot first, called by the Yorkshiremen 'tittlers' or 'feelers'. If the tittlers came up with a good haul of dogfish, the rest of the lines were shot. If not, the boat moved to a different part of the sea. But when a boat found itself among a big shoal of dogfish (and especially one which contained a high proportion of the heavier bitches, or she-dogs), catches could be prodigious: as much as 1,000 stones from 10 lines.

Spring fishing was mainly for skate, cod and conger-eel. The lines were stouter than those used in the winter fishing, but the same length (10 haaf pieces). Big over hooks were fitted, set three fathoms apart, and each one was baited with half a spring herring. The boats caught their own bait: 'We used to take maybe a dozen nets. Sometimes you never got no bait, and you couldn't go that night, so you came back in.'

Overs were always baited at sea, and this affected the method of shooting the lines. Unlike the ordinary winter lines which were coiled on wickerwork skeps, over lines were arranged either on wooden trays or in baskets. If a tray is used, the line is laid out in two piles of coils placed side by side. To begin, the coil to which the first hook is attached is set down on the left-hand side of the tray, so that when the line is shot it is the last hook to go overboard. So, one hook and four feeaks are placed on the left-hand side of the tray, then the second hook and four feeaks are placed on the right-hand side. As this is done each hook is hooked over the four coils to keep them together. Then the third hook goes to the left on top of the first hook, the fourth to the right on top of the second hook, and so on, until the entire line is coiled in two piles.

When shooting overs, the tray is placed amidships on, let us say, the starboard side of the boat. A man stands on either side of the tray, while behind is a tub of bait. The after-side man (that is, the man nearest the stern of the boat) picks up four feeaks of the line, to which the first hook is attached, 'dags' a chunk of herring onto the hook and flings hook and feeaks overboard. While he is doing this, the fore-side man (who preferably should be left-handed) is dagging bait onto the first of his hooks. He throws his hook overboard; and so it goes on, each man rhythmically alternating with the other until the line is shot.

The method is the same for basket-lines, except that these are coiled slightly differently. The baskets used are similar to ordinary tub-type fish baskets, but are without handles. They have cork fitted round the upper rim, into which the hooks are pressed to keep them in place. The end of the baulk is left hanging outside the basket and the feeaks are coiled inside. When the first hook is reached as the line is being coiled, it is stuck into the cork rim. When the second hook is reached, that is stuck into the rim on the left-hand side of the first hook. The third hook is placed to the right of the first hook, and so on. It is a kind of 'odds and evens' system, with 'odd' hooks going always to the right of the first hook, and 'evens' to the left, round the rim of the basket until all 90 hooks are in position.

The reason for these two systems (which are essentially the same in principle) is, of course, to facilitate a two-man baiting and shooting operation. It is vitally important that (a) the line is coiled in the correct sequence, and (b) that the two men maintain a regular rhythm. Failure to do either results in a messy and dangerous tangle.

Just as dogging occasionally produced thousand-stone catches, so from time to time did overing have spectacular hauls. Will Storry remembers one vividly. It happened when he was fishing in *Endeavour*.

> *We once went off Staithes, fourteen mile, about Nor'Nor'East … . And it was a dark night. T'wind was southerly, and rain, very dark (it wants to be dark for skate). And we shut fifteen overs – it took two of us to hale them. We got 280 stone, of skate! Great, big skate! Well then, the next night we went (we shut the same gear), and we got 180 stone. A **hundred** and eighty. Scarcening. And we went the following night for 40 stone … . All down in a hole, down off Staithes. Two hundred and eighty stone. I'll allus remember.*

Overing ceased sometime in the 1960s and now the future of any kind of long-lining hangs in the balance. In comparison with the general rise in the cost of gear, the price of bait has increased disproportionately. More crucially, however, few womenfolk are prepared now to put up with the daily drudgery of shelling mussels and the dirt, smell and domestic inconvenience which accompany it. Sometimes a retired fisherman can be persuaded to do it, but most fishermen now have to bait their lines themselves when they come ashore from the fishing. Moreover, whereas not too long ago line-caught fish fetched a somewhat higher price on the market because of its superior quality and freshness, now it brings no more than trawled fish. One reason, apparently, is that when a line fish is gaffed the klep leaves a small red mark in the flesh ('about the size of a tuppenny piece') which the consumer, not knowing its origin, dislikes.

On the other hand, the keelboats engaged permanently in trawling tend to be bigger, newer, and more expensive (both to buy and to operate). With fuel costs escalating rapidly, ever bigger catches must be made to compensate. Moreover, trawling (even by inshore keelboats) is a mode of fishing which keeps men at sea for five days out of every seven; whereas the line-fishermen spend some part of every day at home with their families. In terms of job-satisfaction, too, line fishermen claim that the seasonal pattern of lining, potting and salmoning offers a more varied and interesting life, than does year-round trawling and seine-netting. Unquestionably, some line fishermen (and especially those fishing from cobles) see themselves as being freer and more independent than their trawling colleagues. But the decisive factor in the end will probably be the economic one. To some extent this will be determined by international trends, although British and European Union policy may well in the long term be crucial.

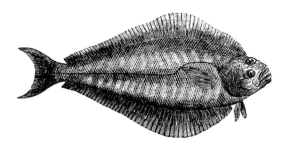

HALIBUT

Six

TRUNKING AND POTTING

57 *Packing crabs for market, Flamborough, c.1903.*

'THE TAKING of crabs and lobsters', wrote Young in 1817, 'is carried on both in summer and winter, chiefly by the elder fishermen.'[1] Later, in 1876, Isaac Storm of Robin Hood's Bay, looking back to the time when he first started fishing, recalled that 'Thirty-eight years ago only a few old men and young lads were fishing for crabs'.[2] Two other pieces of evidence reinforce the implication that the crab fishery was of secondary importance in the fore part of the 19th century: out of 84 fishing craft belonging to Staithes in 1817 only eight were engaged in catching crabs and lobsters. Also, the prices paid for these delicacies compared unfavourably with those of white fish. Whereas the wholesale price for haddocks was often as high as 8s. a score, and with cod and ling fetching, on average, 18s. a score, crabs were sold at prices ranging from 1s. 6d. a score to a maximum of 4s. Then, as now, lobsters were valued more highly, bringing three times the price of crabs.

The reason for the relative unimportance of the crab fishery lay almost certainly in the problem of poor communications. Shellfish is highly perishable, and should be cooked when the creatures are still alive. Alive or boiled, crabs and lobsters are heavy in proportion to their bulk, and in the pre-railway era the high cost of transportation to inland markets must have rendered them inaccessible to all but the more well-to-do classes, a circumstance necessarily limiting the scope of the market. Even in those days, however, substantial profits could be made. The guard on the Whitby to York stagecoach had a regular round of customers in the county town to whom he sold lobsters carried illicitly on the coach. So successful was he in this enterprise that he subsequently retired to live in a handsome house built out of the proceeds which, until demolished recently, was known to Whitby inhabitants as 'Lobster Hall'. But fishermen had none of the advantages of the resourceful guard's free transportation and, until the advent of railways, had to depend on a chiefly local market.

Such a market, of course, was limited, and could easily be satisfied, especially as, according to contemporary accounts, shell-fish were abundant. As it happened, the then prevailing method of catching crabs and lobsters was one which sacrificed quantity to quality; and it may be argued that the demise of the traditional method and its replacement by new equipment and techniques in the 1850s was a direct response to the economic opportunities offered by the rapidly widening network of railways and the new and populous markets which this opened up.

Before about 1850 the method used for catching crabs and lobsters was called trunking, a form of fishing which had virtually died out by the 1860s, except at Cromer and Sheringham, in Norfolk, and at Flamborough, in Yorkshire. The following account of trunking is based mainly on the evidence of a Flamborough fisherman, Moses Smith, to the Sea Fisheries Commission in 1863.[3]

A trunk (called also bag-net or hoop-net) consisted of an iron hoop to which was attached a net bag. A 5-ft bar of round iron was formed by the village blacksmith into a circular hoop with a diameter of some 21 ins. A basket-like bag of netting with a mesh of about three inches hung below the hoop to a depth of three feet. Stretched tightly across the widest part of the hoop were two cords, closely parallel to each other, called the bait band. As the name suggests, the bait was placed between the two bands and held secure by a sliding knot (such a device is known today as a snotter). Three straps of rope, 'bridles', spaced equidistant around the circumference, led from the hoop to the main warp which was itself topped by a cork buoy. The trunk was a simple implement, but its very simplicity demanded time and skill to operate it.

A two-man coble normally had a fleet of 24 trunks. These were baited with freshly-caught dabs and small plaice: 'The bait cannot be too fresh for crabs,' remarked John Warcop, a Bridlington fisherman, in 1876,[4] whereas a lobster will take rotting bait. The trunks were piled flat in the coble and taken to the fishing ground. This was rarely more than a mile offshore and almost invariably on a rocky bottom. The depth of water ranged from a few feet up to ten fathoms, the maximum at which trunks could be operated effectively, but usually they were shot at a depth of three fathoms. Trunks were shot mainly at night, but fishing was carried on by day if there was a swell which stirred up the bottom and made the water cloudy, such conditions being known as a crab swell. Clear water by night, cloudy water by day – this was the maxim when trunking.

Each trunk was shot separately and was marked by its own buoy, the two outer pots in the line carrying larger buoys to indicate the extremities of the fleet. Each pot was about eight fathoms from the next. Fishing was continuous: as soon as all 24 had been shot, the coble returned to the first trunk and began haling. In this way, the entire fleet would be haled and shot up to fifteen times in a single night's fishing.

Great care and skill had to be exercised when haling. A trunk lay flat on the seabed, with its net bag collapsed under it. Attracted by the bait, crabs and lobsters crawled into the centre of the hoop. The fishermen came alongside the buoy, took hold of it gently, and carefully, drew in the slack rope. Then

they hauled in the tow with a steady overhand motion. There were two crucial moments in the process: the first was when the trunk was lifted off the bottom, and the other as the hoop broke the surface of the water. Crabs are relatively slow creatures which in any case easily became entangled in the netting. But lobsters are very agile and good swimmers, and if they detected a strong tremor as the rope was seized by the fisherman above they would quickly swim out of the hoop. Similarly, in the turbulence created by the hoop's breaking surface a lobster, with a strong flick of its powerful, fan-like tail, would try to catapult itself over the rim of the hoop back into the sea. Trunking, therefore, was an active method of fishing, whereas the creel-type pots which succeeded trunks might be termed passive, a point which is implicitly made in this exchange between the commissioner and Jordan Woodhouse, a Flamborough fisherman, in 1863:

> You think the trunk a better way of fishing than the pot? – It is a deal harder way of catching them.
>
> What is the advantage of using the trunk? – Why any tailor could catch them with a pot, but it takes an expert man to catch lobsters in a trunk.[5]

The invention of the creel-type pot (as is so often the case with advances in fishing technology) is surrounded by uncertainty. The willow pots, shaped like a bee-hive and characteristic of the south coast and west country, are thought to have derived from Dutch eel pots. Paradoxically, given the tenacity with which some of them clung to trunks, the crab fishermen of Norfolk are often credited with the invention of creels, and it was stated definitely in 1876 that such pots had been introduced to Whitby by two old fishermen from Sheringham.[6] In any case, if, as is believed, creels first came into existence on the Norfolk coast, Yorkshire fishermen had ample opportunity to copy the new invention: local boats followed the herring as far south as Yarmouth every autumn, passing among the Cromer crab grounds on the way; while Norfolk fishermen at that time often came crabbing off the Yorkshire coast from the last week in March until June or July (indeed, it was a source of complaint that small-sized crabs were taken live from the Yorkshire grounds to be returned

FACING PAGE:

58 *Flamborough fisherman making a crab pot. The Yorkshire coast is one of the best crabbing grounds in Britain, and Flamborough always had an especially high reputation for its crabs. Pots are shot in fleets attached to a warp, rather like charms fastened to a chain bracelet. An east-coast pot consists of bows of hazel fastened into a flat, wooden base. This framework is covered with netting which the fisherman 'knits'. Usually, a pot has two entrances ('smouts'), consisting of net funnels along which the crab clambers attracted by the bait, only to fall, trapped, onto the bottom. There is also a net 'door' through which the crabs can be retrieved (notice the pot by the stone 'copper': the smout is visible on the left and the door, open, is on the right).*

to the sea off Cromer to replenish local stocks – it was evidently possible to distinguish a 'Yorkshireman' by its distinctive light-brown colouring).[7]

But no matter who invented pots, any impetus to find a less time-consuming, more efficient method of catching shellfish must surely have come from the new economic conditions created by the advent and spread of railways. As early as 1838 a perceptive observer forecast that, as a consequence of railway development, 'In districts where a hamper of fish is now only brought by coach to patrician mansions, it will be generally within reach; while the population of large towns will obtain an addition to their permanent food;'[8] and Thomas Smales, a Whitby fish merchant, stated that from 1847, 'The price of all fish went up after the railway was made.'[9]

The structure of the creel-type pot varied in its details from place to place, but essentially it consisted of a slatted wooden base ballasted at each end with pieces of iron or heavy stones. Into the base were fitted three or four arches of bent hazel rods and the whole covered with twine netting. One or more apertures were made in the netting to allow the crabs access to the bait, which was secured in a bait band.

The introduction of pots round about 1850 and the expanding market created by railways had profound economic consequences. There was a crisis of over-fishing and, in turn, a serious depletion of crab and lobster stocks. By 1876 the situation had become so acute that the Government, despite its strong *laissez-faire* predilections, felt obliged to set up a Royal Commission with a view to imposing certain restrictions on the taking of shellfish. The evidence submitted to the commission allows us to trace the changes which had occurred in the previous fifty years (some of which have already been described above) and also to summarise the crab and lobster fishery in the last quarter of the 19th century, thus permitting comparison with subsequent developments.

The commissioners visited Whitby, Robin Hood's Bay, Scarborough, Flamborough and Bridlington. Everywhere the story was the same: more men in more boats fishing with a greater number of the new pots and catching, per man, fewer and smaller crabs and lobsters. So serious was the situation on the Norfolk grounds that local fishermen had themselves initiated legislation to restrict the size of crabs and lobsters landed for sale. At Anstruther in Scotland similar limitations had been agreed on a voluntary basis as early as 1866: 'The fishermen there,' reported Thomas Thompson of Scarborough,[10] 'made the rule to return small crabs, and did so, and the markets made the rule not to buy any crabs under five inches. This practice was carried out for 10 years. It proved very beneficial, and there are more large crabs caught there than anywhere.'

Such self-imposed restrictions were extremely uncommon amongst fishermen. They all recognised the risks attached to over-fishing, yet they were
forced by economic necessity to maximise their catches. It was a vicious
circle, and one which increasingly they felt impotent to break themselves, yet
all the time hoping that some outside agency would do it for them. William
Purcell of Scarborough was voicing the wishes of many crab fishermen when
he asked the commissioners for 'protection'. By this he meant, he said, 'a law
to prevent the sale of unsizeable crabs and lobsters'. However, in the absence
of a legal limit, shellfish were sized according to their market value.

At Whitby, and the system there was typical for the whole Yorkshire coast,
a crab of full market size was 5 inches or more across the broadest part of
the shell and was known variously as a size crab, or a tale or tally crab. In 1876
such a crab was worth 6d. retail. Four-inch crabs were sold two for one in
relation to tale crabs, while a 3½-inch crab sold for one penny. Below 3ins
crabs were sold at Whitby to children at a half-penny each; but at Staithes
such crabs were given away to children. At Flamborough, up to the 1840s,
such small crabs were regarded as children's perquisites:

> The small crabs were given to the boys for pocket money, and they could get
> 2d. to 3d. of a morning. Now [1876] the boats get nearly 8s. for small crabs,
> 3½ to 4 inches long, in a morning … . The small crabs are bought by the
> poor people. The population of Flamborough are two-thirds fishing and
> one-third agricultural. The crabs are hawked about among the agricultural
> class.

At the other end of the scale, a 6-7 inch crab was regarded as 'extra size'.

A sizeable lobster was 4½ inches in the barrel (the barrel being the main
trunk of the body); below that lobsters sold two for one. A 4-inch lobster was
known as 'half-size': anything less went under a variety of names, the dialect
changing over quite short distances. At Whitby an undersized lobster was, and
is, known as a ninty or poke, while at Runswick and Staithes it was a nanycock,
and at Hartlepool a nancy. Another dialect term in use at Whitby describes
a crab which has somehow lost its big claws: it is known as a miffy.

A full-size lobster in 1876 was worth 9d., and small ones fetched 3d. or
4d. But the most prized catch was a spawning, or berried lobster, which went
for 1s. 6d.: 'There is a premium for these, as they are much sought after, the
berries being used for a sauce for turbot'.

The crab and lobster fishing began usually at the end of March, when the
weather became more settled, and went on into July (at Whitby the customary
date for the end of the season was the 6th). After that crabs begin to moult
their shells and go soft, or light. A few old men fished for lobsters in October,

and the odd boat would try for a lobster at Christmas when prices reached at least twice the summer level. But essentially it was a fishing season lasting three to four months and, as many fishermen argued, there was therefore no necessity to impose a close season. The real damage, they said, had come about as a result of the increased number of boats engaged in the crab and lobster fishery and the superior efficiency, in terms of quantity, of the new pots. Whereas in 1817 there had been no boats at all crabbing full time, now, in 1876, there were twenty. At Staithes the number had risen from eight to 35, and at Robin Hood's Bay it had nearly trebled. In the previous fifty years the increase at Flamborough had been from 30 to 70 boats. Moreover, each boat now fished more pots than had been the case with trunks, a point which was made forcefully by James Dalton: 'Fifty years ago there were not half a dozen boats crabbing from Scarborough. There are 50 boats now. Fifty years ago [they] used to take 30 trunks per boat. Now [they] take birdcages or creels and [the fisherman] carries 35 to 40 in his boat. Some boats, however, take 100 creels.'[11]

On this occasion, the 1876 commission was sufficiently impressed by the fishermen's pleas to recommend legislative action (perhaps this was because only inshore fishing interests were at stake); and the Bill which came into effect the following year imposed a number of important restrictions. Crabs must not be bought or offered for sale which were less than 4¼ inches across the broadest part of the back, nor should they be carrying spawn, or be soft. The sale of berried lobsters was also prohibited and a lobster had to be, before it could be sold, 7 inches from the tip of its beak to the end of its tail 'when spread as far as possible flat'. These regulations, with only slight modifications, have remained in force ever since.

There has been little change, too, in the method of fishing for crabs and lobsters in the past hundred years, and such as have occurred are the result of technological innovation on the broader plane, rather than from within fishing itself. By far the biggest impact was caused by the motorisation of fishing vessels which extended the scale of crabbing operations considerably: boats could carry more pots at greater speed and over longer distances.

Although the change-over from trunks to pots had obviated the necessity of constant attendance by the fishermen when crabbing, the new creels still need to be visited daily to rebait and remove the catch. Pots are heavier than trunks and are shot joined together in fleets: hauling them was a laborious business. To make the job slightly easier fishermen utilised the natural swell of the sea – as the coble slid into a trough the man haling reached overboard as low down the tow as he could and pulled in as the coble lifted onto the crest of the wave. On the southern stretch of the Yorkshire coast a method

59 & 60 *Shooting a fleet of pots off Robin Hood's Bay. In the warmer months, crabs and lobsters move in close to the rocky shore. If the weather was calm, as in the picture above, the pots were shot in shallow water. If a storm blew up, however, and the fishermen did not have time either to bring their pots ashore or move them into deeper water for safety, the sea could quickly pound an entire fleet into a broken, tangled mass (top).*

Around the turn of the century, faced by intense competition from steam trawlers, many families moved from the villages to the deep-water ports. Among them were the Dukes, who left Flamborough first for Robin Hood's Bay and later for Whitby. It is Dukes who are depicted here, hence the coble's Hull registration (Flamborough was in the Hull district).

of shooting and haling pots was used designed still further to minimise the labour involved. There, pots were spaced along the tow according to the depth of water to be fished in. Thus, if the water was 10 fathoms, then the pots were set 10 fathoms apart on the tow, 'the object aimed at being that, when hauling, one pot will be in the boat before the next one leaves the bottom, so that only the weight of one pot is felt at the same time'. Another device was haling and shooting 'under run':

> When hauling crab pots the men usually work with the tide, and if changing ground all the pots are hauled, and the crabs and lobsters taken out, and the pots rebaited and shot again in the new position. When the ground is not to be changed, and the tide permits, the fleet of pots is under run – that is, when the first pot is hauled it is cleared, re-baited, and put overboard the other side of the boat, and so on until the fleet is finished.[12]

Haling pots in an open sailing coble was a backbreaking task demanding great physical strength, and, not surprisingly, attempts were made to find mechanical aids to ease the labour. The real breakthrough came with the invention of engine-driven pot-haulers. Several fishermen had them installed in existing craft, but the first Whitby coble to have a pot-hauler incorporated in its design was Dora Walker's *Good Faith*, launched in 1933. Also, as powered boats got bigger, so did the number of pots each one could carry. Consequently, in the event of bad weather a motor coble could often put to sea, retrieve its pots and return to harbour; whereas a sailing coble would be stormbound.

Apart from the recent substitution of synthetic twine for the hempen variety used formerly, the design and construction of the crab pot itself has changed very little. Moreover, although, as noted earlier, working the new, creel-type pots required fewer active skills than did trunking, the actual making of a pot is, if anything, more complex and demands greater craft.

Acquisition of the wherewithal to make pots again highlights the inshore fisherman's ingenuity and resourcefulness. Of the three basic materials used in the construction of a pot – wood, iron or stone, and twine – only twine had to be bought.

During spells of bad weather when putting to sea was impossible, fishermen would spend much of their time combing the shore in search of anything of value that had been washed up. Lengths of timber, especially if it was hardwood, were good finds which were sawn into boards for making pot bottoms. Many fishermen constructed these themselves, but others bought them ready-made from local joiners. Prices varied from the 4½d. per bottom charged at Loftus sawmill around 1900 to as much as 2s. 3d. in later years. The cost in 1978 was 50 new pence.

Once the pot bottom had been made, the next step was to fit a number of arches (bows) into it. These were made from hazel sticks, and the gathering of this raw material constituted an important part of the fishermen's seasonal activity. North Yorkshire is an area of big landowners and extensive estates, some of it woodland grown for timber, but also to serve as coverts for game. Here hazel grew in abundance. Some landowners were generous in allowing fishermen access to their land; others not. Whitby men often ventured up the Esk valley as far as Grosmont in search of hazels (invariably pronounced "ezzells'), but usually they went up the coast to Sandsend to the Marquis of Normanby's woods, as Will Richardson recalled:

> We went mostly to the Marquis's, to Mulgrave Woods. You got a permit through the Mission to Seamen. Mr Heslop, the Missioner, used to get you one. Just tell him when you wanted to go and he'd get you a permit from the gamekeeper. And you'd go in groups, so many at a time, maybe ten of you. We used to walk to Sandsend, get your hazels, and if you didn't want to carry them back, you had them brought by the Lythe carrier – there used to be a van, a horse and cart.

A similar system prevailed at Staithes in James Cole's day:

> There was a house down Ridge Lane called 'Nine Chimneys' where the gamekeeper lived. One side of the lane belonged to Sir Charles Mark Palmer and the other to Turton (we weren't allowed in there, he didn't give a free day). But old Sir Charles Mark Palmer, he gave a free day for the fishermen to go and get hazels: a special day in spring, perhaps the beginning of March. You went yourselves and got them. And if you couldn't go that particular day – if it was a fine-weather day, then you used to go to the gamekeeper and just explain to him that you were at sea that day and he gave you a chit, so that if anyone came to you, you were all right.

Despite such arrangements, hazelling was a task which occasionally brought fishermen into conflict with authority. Edward Verrill was once told this story by a Whitby fisherman who, in his youth, had been cutting hazels without permission in Mulgrave Woods when he was surprised by the Marquis's son.

> An old chap once told me a tale, and it was a true tale. He once went for 'ezzells. So, he was just nicely getting cutting these 'ezzells and a young feller went tiv 'im. He says (effecting a posh voice):
> 'Hey! What are you doing here?'
> 'Why,' this chap says, 'I's cutting a few 'ezzells.'
> He says, 'You can't have them, they belong to my father.'
> 'Oh,' he says, 'where did your father get them?'
> The young man says, 'He got them from my grandfather.'
> 'And where did he get them?'
> 'Well,' he says, 'he fought for them.'
> 'Right,' says the fisherman, 'I'll fight **you** for them, an' all!'

Such anecdotes are probably apocryphal, but they illustrate nonetheless the acute awareness of social differentiation.

Once hazels had been gathered, they had to be sawn into the appropriate lengths and bent into bows. Holes were drilled in the pot-bottom to receive the bows, but, hazels not being of uniform thickness, the holes had often to be enlarged. Also, in order to ensure a uniform curve to the bows, a simple implement, made by the fishermen themselves, was used, called a bow-bender. And, just as much of the work attached to making up lines was carried on in the home itself (setting hooks, tarring, and so on), so it was with pot-making, as Edward Verrill explained:

> *In them days there was nae brace and bits — they had an auger. Maybe shove a poker in t'fire, and sometimes shoved t'hazels up t'chimney to get them to bend. Aye, I've seen them do that: shove 'em up t'chimney, then they bend easily, with the heat. Or maybe shoving a poker in t'fire, then running outside to make the hole a bit bigger.*

The next step, once the basic framework of the pot had been constructed, was to lash ballast at each end. Within living memory, ballast took the form of flat stones gathered from the shore: 'If they could get a bit of iron they used it, but nearly always it was flat stones. And at Staithes they were always a smaller pot, for cobles, and the stones nearly filled t'pots up!' Nowadays, ballast is invariably metal, a favourite being old cast-iron window sash-weights, or broken fire grates, which are dense and heavy in proportion to their bulk.

It remained now only to cover the pot with netting, which was done with tarred hemp twine. To make a pot from start to finish took about half a day, a considerable investment of a man's time in addition to the cost of materials. Pot-making was carried on when men were unable to put to sea because of bad weather or once they had come ashore after a night's fishing. It was a time when men often got together and yarned as they worked, and sometimes it afforded an opportunity for a man to demonstrate his speed and skill in a competitive way: 'I've covered a pot in an hour. "Dead Eye" and "Banger" were watching and I telt 'em I could dae it in an hour and they said I couldn't. But I did it – just on the hour,' reminisced James Cole proudly.

Covering a pot with netting (it is called braiding or knitting) is a complex process, since the net must conform to the curvature of the bows, and there are circular, tapering funnels into the pot to be made, too. These funnels, through which the crabs enter the pot to reach the bait, go under various names according to locality. On the southern stretch of the Yorkshire coast they used to be known as pipes, while elsewhere they are called spouts. But at Whitby the term is smout, a word of Nordic origin meaning 'hole' or 'opening'.

Although the basic design of the pot has remained essentially unchanged since its inception, much minor modification and experimentation has been carried on in the hope of improving its catching qualities, especially with respect to the more valuable lobster. Thus, preferences vary as regards the arrangement of smouts and doors (the tie-up section of netting through which the pot is baited and cleared of its catch). James Cole, for instance, always put two doors in his pots, so that, no matter which side of the boat the pots were being haled, there was always a door facing him and he could thus economise on time and labour when clearing or rebaiting:

In Staithes we used all four-bowed pots with one smout in, right through from side to side ... . When we came to Whitby they were all three bows. They were about twenty-four inch, and they had two smouts ... one at each end. I always put two doors, one at each side; some just puts one door. But that way you had to turn the pot round.

Laurence Murfield was another Whitby fisherman who experimented with the design of pots and who was largely responsible for introducing parlour pots to the Yorkshire coast. Parlour pots have four bows and a netting compartment, the parlour, at one end with a smout leading into it from the main pot.

You see when you bait a three-bowed pot with two roads in, one on the opposite side to the other, a lobster can go out just like that after he's had a feed. But why they don't go out in a parlour pot we just don't know. Instead of going out they go straight into the parlour, and they stop there, they don't go out ... . I once read a book – it was during the war – and it was about Canadian lobster-catching. And there was a diagram in it, and I kept it ... . Eventually I made some parlour pots, and put one at each end of the fleet of pots. And every time you pulled 'em up, in the clear water, there was always either one or two lobsters inside. But parlour pots are big and awkward to handle: they take twice the amount of room up ... . Now, when I was at school there were no three-bowed pots ... but when I was eighteen my father made what was called 'flapper-smout pots' ... and I did very, very well with them. Instead of the top of the smout being tight, it was slack and used to hang over, and that made it more difficult for a lobster to come out. Before that, we put cane smouts in, a ring [a circle of cane was put into the inner end of the smout to hold it open]; *but a lobster would just swim out. So my father says 'We'll alter that', and he made more or less what the smouts are today. Now then, there was one year he made a fleet of 'one-eyes'. Instead of the two smouts in a three-bowed pot, he only had one. So, he had a fleet of those for a while. But the four-bowed pots in them days when I left school, they were neither shape nor make!*

Potting is still an important activity for Yorkshire coblemen and the crews of some of the smaller keel-boats. Whitby alone accounts for about thirteen per cent of the national catch of crabs and lobsters. The basic implement, too

– the pot – stays essentially unchanged, although, as James Cole's and Laurence Murfield's remarks suggest, fishermen are constantly experimenting and adapting their gear in an effort to outwit their quarry, or in order to lighten their own labour.

Attempts to mass produce pots commercially have had little success. Nowadays, however, bottoms are usually bought ready-made; while imported cane or plastic tubing have largely supplanted hazels (even though these remain abundant locally). Hemp twine is virtually unobtainable, having been replaced by synthetic substitutes. Thus, in potting as in other types of fishing, the trend has been away from self-sufficiency and towards money transactions. Despite these pressures, however, the making of the pot itself remains a craft carried on by the fishermen themselves.

Seven

FIXED ENGINES, JAZZING, BLASHING AND DRIVING

61 *A Filey fisherwoman,* c.*1907.*

It is said that in some parts of Scotland agricultural workers would, at the annual hirings, stipulate that salmon should not be served to them more than so many times a week, so abundant, and therefore cheap, was that fish in the rivers and off the coasts.[1] In general, however, the salmon has been regarded as an aristocrat in contrast, say, to the herring, whose appeal has always been more democratic. Perhaps the present scarcity of herring, and consequent sharp rise in price, will bring a more discerning appreciation of its qualities. Yet, traditionally, the salmon was priced dear and the herring cheap. Both occupied an important place in the Yorkshire fishermen's calendar, and, given reasonable luck, made a substantial contribution to their yearly income.

Salmon and sea trout were so prolific in the River Esk in the 1770s that part of the catch was exported by ship to London to be sold on the metropolitan market;[2] but by 1817 they were 'now very scarce, the quantity being much diminished since the establishment of the inland alum-works',[3] an early example of the effects of industrial pollution. It was industry, too, which in the course of the 19th century turned the Tees and, to a somewhat lesser extent, the Humber into dirty rivers, and caused the disappearance of salmon from those waters. The demise of the alum industry, however, allowed the Esk to purify itself and it has remained ever since one of the most important salmon rivers in England; and, although the river itself has long been closed to all but licensed anglers, the great quantity of fish which annually congregate off the harbour mouth waiting to go upriver to spawn has created an important sea fishery. Not that salmon are confined to the estuary of the Esk alone: Tees Bay, Scarborough and, particularly, Filey and Bridlington bays all are, or have been, excellent salmon grounds.

In 1817 cod and ling were fetching 18s. per score wholesale at Whitby, whereas salmon and sea trout were going for 6d. to 1s. a pound.[4] A little more than a century later, in 1923, the price had risen to between 2s. and 4s. a pound.[5] By 1978 salmon were fetching £1.82 a pound on the quay at Whitby (cod was selling at £4.80 a stone).[6]

As these figures suggest, a good salmon season could set up a fisherman for the rest of the year, and many were glad to abandon pots and lines to go salmoning before the herring season began in earnest in late August. Here is a succinct description of how it was done:

The method of shooting the net is to leave one end at the water's edge and then pull straight out, paying out the line at the same time. Just before the end is reached the boat circles round so that when the net is shot it forms a shape of a hook [called, on the northern part of the coast, the 'yuck'], the curved part being to turn the fish into the net. The boat then lays off, and when a fish strikes (this being known by the corks disappearing under water), the men pull to the place, and haul that part of the net up, take the fish out, and drop the net again.[7]

Strictly speaking, the end of the net left at the water's edge should be unattached, so that it can drift freely with the tide. All fishermen, however, fasten pieces of metal or stone to the net, ostensibly, as Robert Allen put it, to 'slow down the drag'. Over the years, increasingly heavy objects (even anchors) have been used, so that, technically, the nets have ceased to be free-floating and have become, to use the authorities' phrase, 'fixed engines'. The fishermen call it sand-fishing or, more commonly, fishing 'in t'sand', and it is a method which is still in use. Two other methods of catching salmon and trout – jazzing and blashing – have virtually gone out of existence, but driving for salmon is enjoying a resurgence of popularity.

Jazzing was a way of fishing for salmon peculiar to Whitby. The east and west piers incline towards each other leaving only a relatively narrow harbour entrance (since 1913 breakwaters have extended the harbour mouth even further seawards). East of the piers lie the scaurs forming Whitby Rock, while to the west extends the Long Sand. After a storm, as the sea is subsiding, and while the Esk is still swollen and brown following rain over the inland moors, is the time to go jazzing, for it is then that the salmon make a rush to swim upriver to spawn.

There were usually two men and a lad to a coble when jazzing, and the work was hard and quick. Fishing within a certain distance of the pier-end was prohibited, but, at the risk of prosecution, the law was often ignored, thus adding a certain spice to the enterprise. Albert Hunter often went jazzing as the lad and, 60 years later, his description still had a ring of excitement about it:

We'll say there was a nice bit of sea and you couldn't get outside, fairly rough and on the ebb tide. Just after half ebb, half ebb to low water: you came away at low water, because then it was no good at all. You see, what happened was that during the flood tide the fish came up into the river. Then, as soon as the tide started to ebb, they wanted to be back out … . There's been fifty or sixty got at a time at that job. But, by! it was hard work, there's no doubt about it.

Let's be honest, you could only jazz between the pier ends. You used to start from one side [of the harbour mouth] and go up the river in a straight line. And as the tide took hold of the net it made it into a half-circle, like a bag. The fish would come and lie against the net. Now, the man who was hauling the bottom rope – that's the *one with the leads on, the lint – started to get his lint in first, to form the bag (a great big bag it was, as well). 'Course, the boy always had the cork rope; that was supposed to be the boy's job. And you had to pull! You weren't just pulling the corks, you were pulling the coble as well (because the man at the oars couldn't back-in quick enough).** *Well, what happened was: the fish used to run down the net, hoping to get out. But you had to go faster than the fish! And that was the fish that you caught!*

You never took your end up; you left it going, and away you went back. You would maybe get one that time. If you were lucky you would maybe get two or three, it all depends on how they laid. If they were lying up *the net they came more or less straight into the coble, but the ones that were running down the net, they were difficult.*

Since jazzing took place in fairly rough seas, capsize was always a possibility, and the present writer can remember many occasions when watching from the pier a coble rose poised on the breaking crest of a wave and seemed destined to founder, only to slide back into the trough at the very last moment due to the skill and timing of the oarsman. To the spectator, jazzing seemed to be an exhilarating, as well as an arduous, experience.

Blashing, on the other hand, needed calm conditions – the smoother the better – and was carried on at night. Not salmon, but sea trout were the main quarry; and these on a still night would swim in with the tide to lie in pools close to the shore beneath the rugged cliffs. The fishermen, knowing the trout's habits, would approach silently in their cobles. George Frampton recounted what happened next:

We used to work six nets. There's all different 'shots', as we call them – High Scaurs, Jetticks, Killin Bight. Say you went to High Scaurs, you would 'take the fall'. You would wait until just turned high water, and you had proper marks. At High Scaurs you couldn't see the shafts [long fingers of rock jutting out from the shore], *they were covered, but we knew exactly where the end of the shaft was. So, you put your weight down just at the end of the shaft, and then you had a proper mark, a named stone, where you shot in with four nets. You covered all that in, but as the tide ebbed the shaft was baring, till, at the finish, when the tide had ebbed out as far as you wanted it, it was all bare. But there was still so much water near the shore for you to get in with the coble. Then you blashed.*

In other words, having formed an arc with the nets from the seaward end of the shaft to the shore, the fishermen quietly positioned the coble, and then, making as much noise as possible, blashing, they drove the startled trout seawards and into the nets.

Sometimes, the four nets would be left and the men would make a number of blashes by shooting two nets in a half-circle from the shore, before returning

---

* Cobles were backed, stern first, when jazzing; and some say that the demise of jazzing is due to the disappearance of the square-sterned rowing coble.

62 *This Filey fisherman, with a magnificent salmon in one hand and a sea trout in the other, has good reason to look pleased. Then, as now, salmon was a luxury fish; and a good summer salmoning could set up a family for the winter ahead. In 1817, when haddocks could be had for as little as 1s. 6d. a score, and turbot and halibut for 2d. a pound, salmon were bringing from 6d. to one shilling per pound. Prices today, of course, are much higher; but the differential is about the same.*

at dawn to blash the big shot. On good nights scores of sea trout could be taken in this way.

The implement used for blashing was quite simple: a long hazel stick or bamboo, sometimes with a flat piece of wood nailed to one end. The water would be beaten with this, in the same way that a beaver slaps its tail to sound the alarm. George Frampton, remembering when he and Laurence Murfield went trouting together, said: 'I was at the oars and he was at t'stern. He was blashing with his stick and I had a biscuit tin with a screw through into one of the timbers. I was kicking the tin, and we were shouting at the top of our voices! By God, we'd have frightened anything!'

Salmon nets used for fishing 'in the sand' were 60 meshes deep, each mesh being 6½ inches from knot to knot, but trout nets had a smaller mesh. Originally, both kinds of net were made from hemp; then flax was introduced, at first half and half, and then all flax. Both materials, being natural fibres, required constant attention.

Most fishermen had two sets of nets with one set in use at any given time and the other ashore being 'sweetened'. As a net was fishing, seaweed, mackerel, plankton, jellyfish ('blebs') and other 'rubbish' became entangled in the meshes. Despite ceaseless cleaning out, fragments remained and this caused the nets to be luminous in the water. Also, the fishermen believed that the salmon and trout could smell the nets when they became dirty. So, every few days, the nets were taken ashore for cleansing. First, all the bits and pieces were shaken out or picked out by hand; then the nets were steeped in tanks containing a solution of alum (hence the expression 'aluming the nets'), and afterwards hung over old masts on the quayside to dry and bleach in the sun and wind. Within living memory, the alum tanks at Whitby were owned by Paul Stamp, the landlord of *The Fleece*, a harbourside public house. He also had barking coppers, tanks of boiling cutch, in which the lines and herring nets were barked to preserve them. Salmon nets and new trout nets were always white, but trout nets were often barked at the end of the first season to prolong their life.

Apart from the routine cleaning and aluming, nets had to be taken out of the cobles daily to be spread and dried off. A heap of wet nets in the bottom of a coble would quickly rot, and there was always a risk of them igniting by spontaneous combustion. Today, salmon nets are made of monofilament: they last several seasons, require no cleaning beyond a shaking as they come aboard out of the water, in periods of bad weather lie in a heap indefinitely, stay in the boat from the beginning of the season in May to its end on the last day of August, and never need barking or aluming.

Sand-fishing for salmon can take place in any weather other than in rough seas; jazzing went on as the sea subsided after a storm and when there was a 'fresh' down the river, and trouting required still, calm nights. The ideal conditions for the most common method of salmoning, driving or drift-netting, were when there was 'a bit of jowl on'. A jowly sea is one where the surface is whipped by a fresh breeze into choppy waves. Sometimes the breeze blows across the tide and then the surface is even more turbulent. But a jowly sea is not a rough sea. There is no rolling swell or big breakers, and, possibly because the motion of the water agitates the organisms on which the fish feed, jowly weather is regarded as best when driving for salmon. The technique is quite simple: nets are put overboard to hang suspended from the surface by corks like a curtain in the water. They are joined to the boat by a warp or swim, and boat and nets drift freely with wind and tide. A catch is made when a fish swims into the net and is enmeshed by its gills. The old salmon fishermen at Whitby rarely ventured much beyond the Rock Buoy, about a mile offshore, but today's fishermen in their motor cobles and even in keel boats will fish four to six miles out using the new monofilament nets.

Of all the fishermen's seasonal activities, salmon fishing is perhaps the most unpredictable. For example, 1977 was a bumper year; catches were heavy and prices high. In 1978, despite continuing high prices, very few fish were caught (some said it was because the wet summer had enabled the fish to enter the swollen river more easily than usual), and it was one of the worst

63 *Mending salmon nets, Old Dock End, Whitby. Salmon nets needed a great deal of attention. They were expensive to replace, and unless they were kept clean could easily rot. After about a week's fishing, the nets were taken ashore to be mended and cleared of sea-weed and other rubbish. They needed cleansing, too, of the minute fluorescent organisms which stuck to the meshes, thus making them visible to the fish. Therefore, every so often the nets were brought ashore and steeped in a solution of alum to sweeten, cleanse and preserve them. Then they were dried and repaired before being taken to sea again in the cobles.*

seasons in memory. But there is nothing so uncertain as fishing, as George Frampton's story illustrates:

> We went for a fortnight and never got a fish. There wasn't a lot getting landed, cobles were getting ones and twos and threes; but it didn't matter where we went, we got nothing. So, my father says, 'These nets is going to be no good. I think we'll take them out at t'weekend and dry them off.' Anyway, it got to the Thursday, me and my brother went (he [father] couldn't go). We went in the afternoon and there wasn't a coble in t'sand. 'Cos it was a flowing tide* and there's only odd fish then. We went off t'Steeple, a mark, and we shut the nets with two yucks. My brother was at the oars and I was shutting, we only had about three yards to go, when he says, 'Mak' sharp!' And when we looked, coming past Upgang were all these threshers. Thresher sharks, with big long tails, threshing, come hell for leather! Coming like a speedboat! Then we saw the nets . . . . The in-yuck went down. Then the off-yuck started to go down. Then the threshers seemed to vanish.

---

* Sand-fishing for salmon was usually on an ebb tide.

With the prospect of a good catch, and being a hand short, George was put ashore to run to fetch his father. He dashed along the beach to Whitby. On the west pier he met a fisherman who ferried him across the harbour to the east side in his coble. 'The old man was in "T'Duke"', George explained, but he called him out and, together, they rushed back to the Long Sand.

> *We started to hale from the in-end and we got eighteen. Altogether we finished up with thirty-three or thirty-four. We shut again, but by that time there was cobles all over! We went off that night, driving, and we shut off the Buoy and got fifteen or sixteen, all summercocks.* And we never looked back after that.*

Thus the unpredictability of fishing.

SALMON

Eight

HERRING:
'THE FISHERMAN'S HARVEST'

64 *Herring mules setting sail at Whitby, c.1910.*

ENGLAND's chief rival for maritime supremacy in the 17th century was Holland. Of all the reasons advanced at the time to explain this state of affairs one was cited more than any other: 'the Dutch usurpation of our fishery'.[1] So great was the sum of money derived from the sale of fish – and especially herrings – caught in British waters that:

> they [the Dutch] have not only maintained their wars many years against the Spaniard, both by land and sea, … and, at length, they have not only wearied him in the wars, and brought him to good terms and reasonable composition; but also it is most apparent, notwithstanding the huge charge of their wars so long continued, which would have made any other nation poor and beggarly, they, on contrary, are grown exceeding rich and strong in fortified towns and beautiful buildings, in plenty of money and gold, in trade and traffick with all other nations; and have so increased and multiplied their shipping and mariners, that all other nations and countries in the world do admire them.

The basis of Dutch affluence, it was alleged in 1614, was the herring caught off Shetland and the east coasts of Scotland and northern England which was salted and barrelled on board ship and then carried by fast sailing vessels, called herring-yagers,* to the Baltic countries to be sold. With the proceeds other commodities were bought, mainly for use in shipbuilding, so that when the yagers returned to Holland they were laden 'with hemp, flax, cordage, cables, and iron, corn, soap-ashes, wax, wainscot (oak boarding planks), clapholt (split oak for barrel staves), pitch, tar, masts, and spruce-deals, and hoops, and barrell-boards, and plenty of silver and gold, only for their produce of herrings'. Herrings caught off East Anglia towards the end of the season were converted by the Dutch into brand-herrings and sold in France 'for Lenten-store … and they do return from these places with wines, salt, feathers, rosin [resin], wood, Normandy-canvas, and dowlas-cloth [coarse linen cloth from Dowlas, Brittany], and money, and French crowns'.

Preparations for this great herring fishery, upon which so much wealth was founded, began in the middle of May when

> the industrious Hollanders begin to make ready their busses and fisher-fleets; and, by the first of their June, are they yearly ready, and seen to sail

---

* The word 'yacht' derives from *yager* or *jager*, the 'g' in the Dutch being pronounced like the 'ch' in the Scottish word *loch*.

out of the Maeze, the Texel, and the Uly, a thousand sail together, for to
catch herrings in the North-seas. Six-hundred of these fisher ships, and
more, are great busses; some six-score tons, most of them a hundred tons,
and the rest three-score and fifty tons; some eighteen and sixteen men a-
piece; so that there cannot be, in this fleet, of people, no less than twenty-
thousand sailors ... . And thus north-west and by north hence along they
steer, then being the very heart of summer, and the very yolk of all the year,
sailing until they do come unto the isle of Shetland ... . From this place,
being nigh two-hundred leagues from Yarmouth, do they now first begin to
fish; and they do never lose the shoals of herrings, but come along amongst
them, following the herrings as they do come, five-hundred miles in length
... [And] it is Bartholomew-tide, yearly, before that they be come from
Shetland, with the herrings, so high as Yarmouth.

The autumn fishery off Yarmouth, which lasted until St Andrew's day
(30 November), was the culmination of this great annual migration of ships
and men, and there the Dutch were joined by Frenchmen from Picardy and
Normandy. There, too, were 'all the herring-fishermen of England', including
those of 'the North-countries beyond Scarborough' who came in 'poor little
boats, called Five-men cobbles'.

Tobias Gentleman's account has been quoted at length because it describes
a pattern of fishing which persisted until very recent times. In the 19th
century Staithes yawls ventured as far north as Aberdeen to catch herring,
drifting southwards with the shoals; and vessels from Staithes, Scarborough
and Filey continued the fishing down to Yarmouth, before returning to their
home ports to lay up for the winter. Off the Yorkshire coast the main herring
season was in August and September, harvest months in the agricultural
calendar. And, indeed, in a very real sense it was the fisherman's harvest, too.
'The herring fishery is of principal importance to Filey', wrote a local Methodist
preacher in 1870. 'This may be considered the harvest of fishing. What is
caught with the lines does little more than secure for the fisherman and his
family present sustenance, and sometimes not even that; the herring fishery
is looked to for the means to obtain their varied and expensive gear, and to
meet every special want.'[2]

By the 1870s Yorkshire harbours were packed in the late summer months
with vessels come to share in the herring harvest. Zulus and fifies from the
Moray Firth lay alongside stately East Angliamen, together with boats from
Cornwall's Mount's Bay and from the Isle of Man. There was the local fleet,
too: yawls, each carrying up to ten men and boys; ploshers (or, as the Filey
men called them, splashers); mules and cobles. Filey alone in 1870 sent 34
yawls to the fishery.

65 *For these youngsters at Scarborough in August 1903 the herring fleet is but a scarcely noticed backcloth to their holiday games. The herring fishery to the fishermen, however, was the culmination of their year. On the Yorkshire coast it lasted from July to September.*

The catching of herring, no doubt because of its great importance both to fisherfolk and the nation, has received more attention than any other type of fishing carried on in the British Isles.[3] For this reason the present account will offer only a fairly general survey of the Yorkshire herring fishery in the era of sail, albeit in the words of first-hand observers; but, in order to emphasise the long continuity of the fishery until its recent demise, there follows a description of herringing in the early 1970s by a Whitby keel-boat skipper. However, to begin, here is a report dated 1870 of how Filey yawls were equipped to catch herring.

[Each boat had] about sixty nets of long length, that is 50 yards. There are four lashings or strings at equal distances on each net; these are about 18 feet in length, and are tied or lashed to a strong rope or ropes which will extend 200 yards in length. This rope is called the 'warp'; the warp is kept afloat by barrels placed about 25 yards apart; these barrels have small ropes attached to them 18 feet long, with which they are fastened to the warp, so that the warp sinks about 18 feet from the surface of the sea, and the top of the net will be about 18 feet below the warp, and the depth of the net is about 18 feet, so that the lowest part of the net in fishing is usually about 54 feet from the sea's surface. Sometimes, however, the lashings are shortened; this is done in very fine weather, as then the herrings swim much nearer to the surface. A herring coble carries four men and about half the number of nets that is carried by a yawl; it does not use a 'warp'. The nets are simply hung by ropes and cork, and swung with the barrels.[4]

Filey's Methodist ministers were indefatigable observers of the local community and it is fortunate that the Rev. George Shaw has left a description of a voyage he made on board a Filey yawl. It complements admirably the account of the gear cited above.

At two o'clock one Monday afternoon in about 1867 the Rev. Shaw sailed in a yawl for four or five hours directly off-shore to join the fleet of English, Dutch and French vessels already congregated on the fishing ground. As darkness fell the sails were lowered, with the exception of the mizzen, and the boat was put with her head to the wind. 'And now let me attempt to describe the scene' writes the Minister:

> The hatches were taken up, and the warp – a rope 1,000 fathoms (2,000 yards) long, and about four and a half inches thick – was paid out over the

66 *A good catch of herring at Whitby, c.1909. The fishermen on board a mule are counting out a good catch of herring. Alongside is a Whitby-registered yawl. Yawls were used for long-lining and for the herring fishery. In winter they were laid up on the mud of the upper harbour and the crews went lining in the cobles.*

vessel's side, the men at the capstan allowing it to go out at the required rate. Barrels to float the warp were tied by one man, while the nets were tied to it by another, the barrels being thrown overboard as they were tied, and the nets carried over by the warp itself. As the nets sink and the barrels swim, you will perceive that the warp is kept under the water by the former and prevented from sinking by the latter. The process of paying out occupied rather more than an hour, and when this was finished there were 100 barrels and 120 nets in the water.

Once the nets had been shot the crew had dinner, then went below for a chat before turning in for an hour or two. One man remained on watch, and about midnight the rest of the crew were roused to 'look on'. The Rev. Shaw came up on deck to find a coble being lowered into the water. With the skipper's permission, he joined the two men in her and they set off to look on:

> The men pulled along for some time, and not a word was spoken … . After rowing about a quarter of a mile we pulled to the fleet [of nets], and took in a barrel, by which we hauled up the warp, which one of the men thrust over the bow of the coble … . The net was then reached and lifted partly out of the water. In the small portion I saw there were scores of herrings entangled in the meshes … . Putting the warp overboard we went about another quarter of a mile, and examined another net with the same result, and after repeating the process two or three times, finding herrings in every instance, rowed for the vessel … . The master said as we stepped on deck, I am glad to see you back, I have never had my eye off you since you left. I learnt then that it was only in very fine weather they go out in a coble to look on, and that generally they haul in the warp and look at the nets nearest the vessel. The report that herrings were in the nets gave great satisfaction, and very soon preparations were made for taking in the nets. The men went to the capstan and commenced turning it round. By this means the warp was drawn in; as it came on board one man loosed the barrels, another 'paid' it into the hold, and two others shook the herrings out of the nets on to the deck, part of which fell through an opening into the well beneath … . This process lasted about three hours. At length the whole fleet was in and we had captured about 30,000 herrings. The sails were immediately hoisted and we were on our way with all speed for the market. As the vessel sped through the water, the decks were cleared and washed; the barrels &c., placed in the same order as before, all ready for the next night's work … . About ten o'clock the same morning we reached Scarborough, and a sample of herrings … was sent on shore by a man in the coble, whom I accompanied. We landed at the pier and proceeded to the place of business. The herrings were thrown on the ground, a bell was rung, a crowd of buyers and others collected, and the lot knocked down at 6s. 9d. per hundred, a capital price, and we moved off gratified that our night's fishing had netted something like £90.[5]

67 *Small cobles, as well as the bigger plosher, were used in the herring fishery. The photograph shows a crowd of cobles taking a tow from a paddle-steamer (possibly the* Camperdown *of* Middlesbrough) *to the pier ends. Normally, if a coble was being towed any distance on the open sea, it was towed stern-first. On the right a heavily laden collier is being brought to her moorings.*

It was not until the 1870s that Scottish boats began to take part in the herring fishery off the north-east coast of England on any substantial scale. In 1871 a hundred vessels were fishing from the Tyne, including some from the Moray Firth 'who have never been to the Tyne before, [and] who have brought quite a superior class of boats and nets with them'.[6]

The superior nets were machine-knitted on a loom invented by a Scot, James Patterson, and improved subsequently by Walter Richie of Leith. Made of cotton, they were finer, lighter, and much easier to handle than the old-style nets made of flax or hemp. The Scotsmen were innovators in other ways, too; as March has described:

> When the Scots fishermen came South with their fine cotton nets and light 3½ inch warps, they introduced a new method of fishing and computation. They never scudded [cleared of fish] their nets at sea, everything was bundled into the hold together – warp, buoys, nets, herrings and all, then sail was made immediately and the luggers were racing for market long before the rest of the fleet had hauled their heavy twine nets and hemp warps. The

68 *A Scottish 'zulu' off Scarborough. It was in the 1870s that the Scotsmen began to appear in the English east-coast ports for the annual herring fishery. They came in their lug-rigged fifies and zulus. Note the crutch, just aft of the mizzen mast. When the boat was fishing – riding to her nets – the huge main mast was lowered into the crutch. The same practice was adopted on the Yorkshire mules.*

Scotsmen cleaned their nets in the calm waters of the harbour, and the fish was shovelled into two-handled round baskets, holding a quarter of a cran … . The catch was sold by the cran, nominally a thousand herring, but naturally varying with their size and packing.[7]

The practice of counting herring individually (as opposed to measuring them in bulk, in crans) persisted longer at Whitby than at Yarmouth. John William Storry remembered widows and old women being paid 1s. 6d. a day for doing this tedious job; and Thomas ('Pipey') Peart told of the comic-sad occasion when Mary P— had stuffed so many herrings down her drawers while counting (she was going to take them home to eat) that, falling overboard accidentally, she nearly drowned!

The arithmetic used to count herrings was disadvantageous to the fisher-men. Four herrings made one warp, 33 warps (132 fish) were a buyer's hundred, and 10 buyer's hundreds made a thousand. Ten thousands constituted one 'last' (that is to say, notionally 10,000 fish, but in fact 13,200). At Whitby a similar calculation was used, but only 31 warps made up a hundred, as this eye-witness account, relating to the 1880s, of the landing, sale and despatch or herring shows:

Next morning [on returning from the fishing ground] the boats with good catches entered the harbour to discharge their fish, or had to wait until the tide permitted. On occasion, at low tide, the fish was landed on the sands. Those with smaller catches filled their 'punts', as their small dinghies were called. Every vessel had its small boat. For the purpose of marketing, a big

69 *The Scotsmen brought with them machine-made, fine cotton nets buoyed by big inflatable dans. Edgar March comments: 'They never scudded their nets at sea, everything was bundled into the hold together – warp, buoys, nets, herrings and all, then sail was made immediately and the luggers were racing for market long before the rest of the fleet had hauled their heavy twine nets and hemp warps.'*

basket was filled with herring and turned out into the market, to be bid for by the army of buyers. Some of the cargoes of fish were landed on the pier, and had to be carted in barrels through Haggersgate [a very narrow street in those days] for transference to the fish train. The herrings were sold in hundreds, with ten thousand to the 'last'. The hundred was, in reality, more

70 *Scotsmen at Whitby emptying a quarter-cran basket of herring. Salt is being scattered on top of the barrels of fish. The Scottish fishermen brought with them also a new, more equitable method of counting herring, based on the 'cran'. A cran was nominally one thousand fish, and consisted of four basketsful. Thus, if the herring were big, there were fewer than a thousand; if small, then there were more.*

71 *Scots fisherlassies at Scarborough. Scots lassies followed the fleet down the coast all the way from Lerwick to Great Yarmouth. Independent, fun-loving and very hard-working, they were always a welcome sight to the holiday crowds, who watched the girls deftly gutting the herring and packing them into barrels ready for export. The white building in the background, left, is the Bethel Chapel where many of the Scarborough fisherfolk worshipped.*

than a hundred. The counting into a basket was done by taking a couple of herring in each hand, and as each four fish, called a 'warp', was deposited, 'one, two, three, etc' was shouted until the 'thirty' was reached; another 'warp' was added, when the teller shouted 'tally'. Thus there were 124 fish to the 'hundred' ... . In counting the herrings a record or tally was kept by means of a piece of chalk and a board. A stroke was made for each hundred, and when four strokes had been recorded a diagonal line was drawn across from the top of the first to the bottom of the fourth. This scored 500 or five 'hundreds', or actually 620.

Most cargoes were discharged at the Old Quay, then called the New Quay, above the bridge. From Collier's Ghaut to the far end of the wooden quay was covered with barrels packed on end to a great height. These were divided into sections, a space being allotted to each firm of buyers. The packing of the fish was carried out by men who received the herring in baskets from the boats. As the baskets were emptied into the barrels, the fish were sprinkled with rough salt or ice. When the barrel was filled, paper, straw and sackcloth provided a covering which was fastened by a hoop. The barrels were then placed in carts and hurried to the train.[8]

By 1880 more than two hundred boats were fishing for herring off Whitby; and in 1885 it was reported that over eighty boats came from Cornwall alone,[9] their home ports being mainly Penzance, Mousehole, Fowey, St Ives and Newlyn. As a general rule, boats from Mount's Bay, Penzance and St Ives had pointed sterns, while the others were transom-sterned. They carried two masts and were lug-rigged. Unlike the east coast boats, which were clinker-built, the Cornish craft were of carvel construction. A crew of six or seven men was usual for the herring fishery, but sometimes Whitby men were taken on for the season (Tommy White twice sailed on a Penzanceman).

These Cornish luggers were excellent sailing craft: three boats in company once made the voyage from Mount's Bay to Scarborough in 70 hours, despite being becalmed for a spell, and, later, having to lower sail in a heavy squall.[10] A few fished the off-ground with the bigger Staithes yawls, venturing as far as 60 miles from land, and putting down their fish in salt while remaining at sea for several days. Usually, however, the fishing ground was three to seven miles off Whitby.

The Cornishmen are remembered in Whitby for their religious faith, good seamanship, and their fondness for cabbages! 'They were awful chaps for cabbages', commented Will Richardson; and James Cole told how a Penzance fisherman who married a local lass was known ever after by the nickname 'Cabbage'.

Behind this image as cabbage-eaters lies a fairly involved explanation. Except when they came into harbour to discharge their catch, or to seek refuge from bad weather, the herring fleet anchored offshore by day in Whitby Roads. But on Saturdays all the boats came into port. Then, 'the nets of many of the boats were transferred to carts, piled up like a load of hay, and taken to some field and spread to dry. Others suspended their nets on a pole hung high above the deck, and extending across between the two masts.' As well as this task, provisions had to be brought to last the men until the following Saturday. Consequently, fishermen out shopping were a common weekend sight:

72 *Cornish herring boats in Whitby upper harbour, c.1900. For a few weeks of each year, Whitby and Scarborough were hosts to a multitude of strange craft and their crews. Pictured above are Cornish boats ('Penzancemen') from Mount's Bay, Penzance and St Ives. They were excellent sailing craft: three boats once made the voyage from Mount's Bay to Scarborough in 70 hours (despite being becalmed for a spell!). Two-masted, they were lug-rigged and of carvel construction. Each one normally carried a crew of six or seven.*

73 *Far from home, visiting fishermen lived on board their boats and did their own cooking and 'housekeeping'. The Cornishmen are remembered in Whitby as being great ones for cabbage soup. On Saturdays they bought sacks of fresh vegetables in the market, and were affectionately nicknamed 'Cabbage Jacks'.*

This was usually done by using one of their herring baskets as a carrier, a two-handed job. This they filled with bread loaves, potatoes and other vegetables, especially cabbage … . One of their favourite foods was cabbage soup. A large piece of meat was placed in a big metal pan, sliced cabbage was added, and sometimes a raisin and suet pudding known as 'plum duff'. The soup* … was very palatable.[11]

Whitby fisherfolk looked forward to herring time. For all the labour involved, the weather was usually fine and work not so arduous as during the winter fishing with its storms and bitter weather. The harbour at weekends was packed with visiting craft. Friendships could be renewed. It was a time for exchanging gossip and news. It was a time for gaiety. Apart from the fishermen, Scots lasses followed the herring down the coast and were renowned for their good humour and chatter. They came to gut (gip) the fish which were then salted and packed into barrels. Standing at long, raised wooden troughs on the quayside, gipping knives at work almost faster than the eye could follow, their

* This recipe is almost identical to that used by Russian peasants to make cabbage soup (*shchi*).

74 *Counting herring on board a Penzanceman at Whitby, c.1900. Herring were sold by the 'last', nominally, 10,000 fish. Four herrings made a 'warp', and 33 warps made a 'hundred'. Since 100 'hundreds' made a last, it meant that the fisherman was paid for 10,000 fish, whereas the buyer in fact received 13,200. When the herring were actually being counted, one of the crew would keep a record by making a stroke with a piece of chalk on the board for every hundred. After four upright strokes, the fifth was diagonal, crossing them out, and the shout 'Tally!' was raised, meaning that 500 fish (620 in practice) had been counted out.*

In the picture above, herring are being counted according to this method into baskets. The boy in the centre holding board and chalk is keeping tally.

bright dress and strange, cheerful accents brought colour into what was too often a rather sombre existence. Maud Hind, remarking on how few treats children had when she was a little girl, recalled with evident pleasure the singing and dancing round the bandstand on Whitby pier 'when t'lasses came'.

Herring time held out the promise, too, of extra money; money which would buy a new dress, settle a debt, go towards new gear, or be set aside to pay for a new boat. But the herring is an erratic visitor, and some seasons brought only disappointment and the prospect of a hard winter ahead. In 1870, for instance, the *Whitby Gazette* reported at the beginning of September: 'The herring fishery ... has, this season, been an entire failure. This, of course, could not be otherwise than a great calamity to the Cornish and other fishermen who are away from their homes, as well as to our own men.' But on 1 October the same newspaper announced that the herring fishery 'has lately been very successful', with nearly 450 truckloads of fish, above a thousand tons, despatched inland by rail in six days.

Not that an abundance of fish necessarily meant an abundance of money for the fisherman. He would have preferred a season of steady catches and steady prices; for a glut of fish meant much work for small return. The season of 1884 was described as disastrous not because of too few fish, but because there were too many:

> Off Scarborough and Whitby countless thousands of herrings were caught and sold at prices varying from 3d. to 8s. or 9s. per hundred. In the height of the season many of the Scotchmen, on ascertaining the state of the markets, threw their catches overboard, rather than be at the trouble and cost of landing the fish even to sell it as manure.[12]

With chance so much involved, there is little wonder that fishermen, like gamblers, are always hoping that their number will come up. They wish no harm to their fellow fishermen, but it is always in the back of their minds that they will strike lucky, 'get among the fish', and take the top of the market. Such occasions stand out, become talking points, and are savoured over and over again many years afterwards, as James Cole's recollection shows:

> *I mind one year in a plosher, the* Venus, *we landed 110 cran in five nights' fishing. Three men: me and my father and my Uncle Tom. We always did very well – I was fortunate, I dropped in with two lucky fellas. But it was a hard go for three men, five nights. We landed 110 cran; and when we reckoned o' t'Saturday night (we allus reckoned on t'Saturday, you know) we had £50, and then there was the expenses to come off after that. It would be about 1907 ... . And we got £13 apiece, which was talked about. It was a lot of money ... . When me and Billy Butler – he was a Filey man really – sat on t'pier just afore he died, he says, 'Dis tha remember that Friday morning, Jim? – we were both towed by t'same tug?' (The boats used to knock off*

75 & 76 *The herring lassies were the photographers' and postcard sellers' favourites. Only rarely was a faithful impression of their toil recorded by the camera. The scene is Scarborough at about the turn of the century.*

trawling to tow you in summer time if it was a fine morning, and the arrangement was a shilling a cran for towing: if you had twenty cran you paid twenty shilling). So he says, 'Do you mind that Friday morning when you towed alongside of us?' – he was in a herring coble. He says, 'We had sixty cran and you had twenty or thirty.' I says, 'Aye, I mind t'morning.' And he says, 'You got eight shilling a cran on t'Friday morning and seven shilling on t'Saturday.' That's how it didn't mount up! That's how we had to have this 110 cran for £50. But it was in the paper about a coble getting all that money in one week.

The First World War, bringing in its wake the loss of traditional markets in central and eastern Europe, brought, too, the collapse of the herring fishery. Yet Whitby's decline seems to have set in before then. According to F.W. Horne:[13]

From 1897 to 1900 the number of Cornish vessels visiting Whitby decreased to some dozen or twenty; and by 1905 the Cornish craft had ceased to come, and the Scotch boats only ran in to shelter from rough weather on their way to and from the Yarmouth fishery. After the extensions to the Piers were completed [in 1913], and the wooden quay built along the pier side, there was a little flutter for a couple of years in the herring fishing industry, but it died away. After the last war [1914-1918], a Captain Barton tried to attract herring drifters to the port, but after a couple of years they gave up and returned to Yarmouth.

77 *Mending herring nets, Scarborough, 1876. For the Yorkshire women, the herring fishery meant blessed relief from the hard, monotonous grind of flither-picking, skaning, and baiting the long lines. But there were still nets to mend …*

78 *Mending herring nets, Whitby, c.1900. The* Mary Ann *was a herring mule. Note the crutch in which the mast rested when the boat was at sea and riding to her nets. The woman has attached a butcher's hook to the upright of the crutch to hold the net taut while she repairs the torn part.*

Horne attributes the early demise of the herring fishery at Whitby to a series of poor seasons. A more likely reason, however, was the state of the harbour. As early as 1885 the *Whitby Gazette*[14] noted that:

> While one or two places on the coast have improved their facilities for landing fish, Whitby has done nothing, and this year we have had more

complaints than usual about the unsatisfactory state of the harbour ... . The chief source of complaint is the insufficiency of water in the harbour at ordinary times for the proper accommodation of such class of boats as hail from Yarmouth, Lowestoft and Penzance. The fact is, there is now a lesser draft of water in the inner harbour than there ever was, and this having been communicated to the owners of the larger class of craft hitherto accustomed to trade at this port during the herring season, they have given imperative instructions to their skippers not to enter Whitby harbour with their cargoes of fish, but to take them to either Hartlepool or Scarborough.

That August 1885, 91 fewer fishing boats used the port than in the same month the previous year.[15]

Scarborough maintained its primacy as the chief Yorkshire herring port up to the outbreak of war in 1914. At Staithes landings were made only if the catch was light; otherwise the boats made for a bigger port. Nonetheless, Edward Verrill recalled the busy scene in the fore part of the last century:

There must have been thirty or forty ploshers going then, bigger boats. They used to lay up the winter cobles; they had them up t'beck at Staithes. Old Johnny Cole – he was boatbuilder, undertaker, everything – he had two or three men, and they painted them up, the winter cobles. So, when they'd finished the winter fishing they'd take all the small ones up and then they would bring all t'big herring boats down. Sometimes 'osses used to pull them up, if the tides didn't answer: take them so far up, then use 'osses. And if the tide would be down of a night they'd take the ploshers out of a morning and anchor them in Staithes Wyke, when t'weather was fine in summer. Then, all go away at eve, get ferried off. Jibs and sails if it was a fine night. And if they only got a few herrings, two or three thousand, or owt like that, they'd whip into Staithes. Decent catches – go to Hartlepool. Maybe get a tow with some o' t'steam drifters. Or perhaps they would go to Scarborough, pulling until they got there, or sailing with a favourable wind. They used to sell t'herrings at Staithes about eight o'clock of a morning. There used to be all flat carts there, all waiting to buy their herring. They used to count 'em out in warps – 33 to a hundred. Women used to count them; then they used to lay t'rowlers* on their heads and carry them up to t'buyers ... . all the carts lined up. They'd take some to t'markets [on Teesside] when they went on a Saturday. But a lot was hawked all round Cleveland, in the mining villages, farms, all over. Flat cars and gallowas.

Between the wars, herring fishing on any substantial scale virtually disappeared at Whitby, and was at a low ebb all along the Yorkshire coast. But in 1945 the Scotsmen came south again, repeating the centuries-old migration. They came in smart, varnished keelboats, often ring-netting in pairs. In 1945, 30 Scottish boats made Whitby their base. The next year 60 boats arrived; and

* 'rowler' – a doughnut-shaped, circular pad (roller); at Runswick known as a 'ree'ath' (wreath), at Whitby a 'bun', and at South Shields in Durham a 'weeze'.

79 *The Flamborough long-sword dancers, c.1910. The famous Flamborough sword dance may be connected with the making and repair of nets. Brought to this country by the Vikings, sword dancing is thought to represent ritual killing and resurrection. In contrast to other Yorkshire long-sword dances, where they are made of steel, the Flamborough dance is performed with wooden swords which, some folklorists believe, denote the tools ('needles') used to make and mend fishing nets.*

in 1948, 120 boats crowded into the harbour. The sea, following years of neglect caused by depression and war, was teeming with herring. In 1938 only 6,000 cwts were landed at Scarborough, and none worth mentioning at Whitby. Ten years later 18,000 cwts of herring were sold at Scarborough and 106,000 cwts at Whitby.[16] But by the early 1960s catches had again dwindled, herring stocks were seriously depleted, and only the odd Scottish boat ventured south as far as the Yorkshire ports.

The only Whitby boat to have fished in later years was *Endeavour* (WYI). Her skipper, Matthew Hutchinson, preferred the traditional drift-net method, which is essentially the same as that used by the Dutch 350 years ago. Such few changes as have occurred may be deduced from his description of the herring fishery:

You set off just as the sun's going down if the ground is within say, an hour's steam of the harbour. The echo-sounder's going. You get into the position where you think the herring should be, and you steam about a bit in that area. You either find them, or you don't find them. If you find them you hang on till nearly darkening and when you see them [on the echo sounder] *rising off the bottom you run over the top of the shoal, into the wind, five or six nets out of them, on top of them. You shoot your nets – you shoot about seven nets before you come to your mark* [of the fish on the echo-sounder's screen] *– and shoot the rest of your nets through them. So, you shoot before the wind so that the boat pulls the rest of the nets through the mark of herrings. Then it's up to God and Providence.*

There could be up to thirty nets with the smaller type of vessel, but with the Scotchmen (if they're still going) there could be up to sixty or seventy. They go probably 20 nets out of the mark. Endeavour *would have twenty or thirty nets in all, depending on the time of year. Now, springtime, we'd use thirty, because there's only a thin swim* [of herring]. *But when you get your thick marks later on in the year you put on about twenty nets because you get a heavier swim, and also if you don't get anything the first shot, with the darker nights you can always get another shot in.*

Each net is about 45 yards by 15 yards. You can regulate the depth. You have your corks on the nets and that keeps them straight, but the bottom rope is heavy enough to sink the corks; so you have a strop: it's from each individual net – it could be up to 10 fathom long – reaching up to a mullock. By tying the rope up you can vary the depth of the top of the net from a fathom to ten fathom below the surface.

The bigger boats work a warp. It's a heavy rope that goes underneath all the lot: it's a big help in hauling and has a lot of advantages with a bigger boat, but with a

---

80 *'Lowstermen' off Scarborough. The aristocrats of the herring fleet were undoubtedly the elegant, stately Lowestoftmen, pictured here at Scarborough. Notice the forward rake of the masts; and the Yarmouth steam drifter on the left. The Suffolk port relied on sail long after the Norfolk men had gone over to steam.*

small boat like ours we don't work a warp. Others work a very light warp. But we only work herring when it's fine weather, and in fine weather a warp can be a nuisance: it can pull through your net because you haven't a gale of wind keeping your nets tight.

This time of year – spring fishing – you'd have your nets down three or four hours; whereas when the herrings are thick you leave them no more than an hour, because by the time you come to the end of them there can be as much as you can pull in.

We have a crew of four normally, but you want no less than six at herringing, and with a warp you want seven. There's one man haling the bottom-rope. Three men are in the hold: one towards the cork-rope; one towards the bottom-rope; and one at the middle lint. Any herrings they shake out; and they stack the nets.

In a boat like ours, after we've haled five nets (say we've been getting a cran a net, a good hale) we'll knock off, box the herrings – which is the modern-day method – have a fag, and, it's funny, if you're having a decent hale of herrings, you're always thirsty. I don't know what it is … but you're always thirsty.

Herringing? It's a job you either love, or you hate: there's no in between. There's just something about it. I suppose drift-net herringing, it's one of those things, Man against Nature – more or less equally. We have echo-sounders now, of course; but for some unknown reason the herrings can swim the opposite way to our shot, and you get nothing.

Before the introduction of echo-sounders after the Second World War, and, more recently, of sonar, fishermen used simpler methods to detect the shoals of herring. On moonless nights one of the crew would lie in the bows looking down into the water searching for the tell-tale phosphorescence – fire – which gave away the herring. From time to time he would strike a knotted rope's end against the planking: if fish were there, they scudded away with a flash of silver bellies. Another device was to lower a weighted, very fine, piano wire into the sea: fish would hit against it and the tremors could be felt by the man on deck holding the line. Whales were regarded by Yorkshire fishermen as being a very good omen, and if a grampus, or herring whale, came up to blow, it meant that herrings were about. Some men, it was said, could smell the herring, although Matthew Hutchinson thinks it more likely that what they could smell was the foul air given off when a herring whale surfaced, unseen on a dark night, to blow.

Herring is no longer abundant in the North Sea. The massive catches of the 1940s and 1950s took their toll, and the presence of big fleets of foreign vessels – Danes, Dutchmen, Poles, Germans, Russians – just out of sight of land beyond territorial limits, scooping up fish, big and small indiscriminately, has depleted herring stocks to a dangerously low level. One consequence is that the government has imposed restrictions on British fishermen in the hope that the inshore spawning grounds will recover.

A direct effect of the scarcity of fish and the limited season is that herring fetch high prices (especially when compared with the £50 for 110 cran caught

81 *Clearing the pier ends, a variety of sail heading for the fishing ground – Penzancemen, cobles and mules.*

in five nights' fishing earlier this century): 'We last went herringing in 1974,' explained Matthew Hutchinson.

We were salmoning at the time and we'd been doing all right; then it just slackened off. All the lads aboard the Endeavour *were keen on herringing, so we said, Right, we'll have a go. And we put the nets aboard. There were only four or five days left before the ban, and I had herrings every night that year. The first night we had ten cran, landed in Whitby for £15 a cran. That was on the Thursday morning. On the Friday morning we had about ten cran and we got £7 a cran. I was very disappointed. We didn't go off on the Saturday night because it was Bank Holiday, or something. And on the Sunday night we went off and got fifteen or sixteen cran. I says, 'We're not going to Whitby to give 'em away'; so we went to Scarborough. And we averaged £20 to £25 a cran. We had three landings that week in Scarborough, and we finished with £790 for the first three days of the week, and then the ban came on and we had to stop. There used to be a custom that if you earned £1,000 in a week you were given a bottle of whisky by the fish selling company. The buyer at Scarborough came to me, and he says, 'Well, you've tried, lad. You've made a good start and you've over £700 for three days. Whether you get another herring or not, the bottle's yours for trying.' Yes; he sent me a bottle through to Whitby.*

An industry which is as old as recorded history is on the verge of extinction. Countless millions of nutritious herring have in the past been spread on the land as manure; dumped back, dead, into the sea; or, latterly, have been consigned to pet-food factories. Man has almost succeeded in eliminating a seemingly inexhaustible resource. If, as a result of bans on fishing, the North Sea herring ever does recover there will have to be strict international legislation to prevent their being decimated yet again. It might help, too, if it were made obligatory to use the traditional drift-nets. In contrast to ring-netting and modern 'hoovering' methods – trawling up the shoals resting on the sea bed during daylight – the old ways at least had the merit of lengthening the odds. Belatedly, there are signs that government is prepared to intervene to help to restore herring stocks. It is to be hoped that it is not too late.

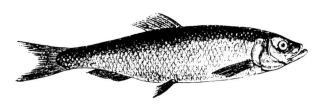

HERRING

Nine

WOMEN'S WORK[1]

82 *Hawking fish, Whitby, c.1908.*

WIVES and daughters of fishermen brought up children, cooked, cleaned, washed and, more often than not, bore the chief burden of responsibility for seeing that the money spun out until another share-out day came along. Except, perhaps, with respect to the last particular, their lot was much the same as that of any other working-man's wife or daughter in late Victorian and Edwardian England. But, over and above their many other duties, fisherwomen played a vitally important rôle in the production process – that is to say, they were, literally, a major and indispensable part of the fishing. Moreover, for both good and ill, their work was carried on to a large extent inside the home itself. It was a good thing in that the family was kept as a tightly-knit unit and mothers and children were not constantly separated, and also in that wives and husbands were engaged upon a joint domestic economy. Yet the tremendous burden of responsibility which women had to bear, as well as the debilitating effect of the hard, physical work itself, wreaked havoc upon their health.

Jane Harland died 10 months after the birth of her 10th child, at the age of forty-six. The next youngest was only three, while Maud, the eldest daughter was twenty-one. Maud's parents had never wanted her to be a fisherman's wife, and Maud herself had since childhood vowed that she would never marry one: it was too hard a life. However, with the death of her mother, and with father and two brothers at sea, Maud found herself, as eldest daughter, fulfilling precisely the rôle of fisherman's wife. Until she married (her husband, Hind, was a bricklayer) five years later when 'another sister was old enough to carry on', Maud's days began in this fashion:

> I've seen my father go out (get up, you know) about two o'clock of a morning. We had no gas fires nor nothing of that. He used to light the fire on. And he had an awful habit of doing the fireplace as well before the fire was put on: he believed in it. And then he used to go down the pier [to find out the state of the sea], and then he used to come back, and I used to many a time, oh! I used to think, I wish t'cobles wouldn't get off today ... . And he used to shout upstairs: 'Come on! Come on down, t'tea's ready, we're going off'. We had to come down. Get mi tea, and then, as soon as they went off, we used to bring the mussels in and we used to start – my auntie used to help me a lot. And sometimes the mussels were all froze, you know. You got bad fingers with them.

The key to comprehending the wearying, unremitting repetitiveness of women's work in the fishing community lies in Mrs Hind's reference to mussels. If the man's main task was to go to sea to fish, then the woman's chief responsibility was to prepare (and, very often, to gather, too) the bait. The scale of this work was enormous.

Up to about 1914 it was usual for each long-line to have 26 to 28 score hooks (that is, between 520 and 560 hooks). Each sailing coble, such as the one Robert Harland, Maud's father, fished in, carried a crew of three, frequently two men and a lad (the 'tratter'); and each man fished two lines, while the lad fished one line. Thus, as a crude guide, for a single night's fishing the number of hooks to be baited for the crew of a three-man coble ranged from a minimum of 2,600 (two men and a lad fishing five lines, each with 26 score hooks) to a maximum of 3,360 (three men, six lines, each with 28 score hooks). The yawls and mules, both bigger classes of boat, used an even greater amount of bait; and, given that long-lining was the dominant mode of fishing from the Humber to the Forth, it is obvious that prodigious quantities of bait were used every year.

By far the most popular and effective bait were mussels; but these became increasingly difficult to obtain. When the Commissioners investigating the state of the sea fisheries took evidence at the *Angel Hotel*, Whitby, in October 1878, a Staithes fisherman, Joseph Verrill, began by complaining of the depredations of trawlers, which had resulted, he alleged, in the destruction of spawn and small fry, and the carrying away of the line-fisherman's gear. What he might have mentioned, too, was that the increased landings of fish by the trawlers had had the effect very often of depressing the price on the market with the consequence that line-fishermen were having to double the quantity of their gear in an attempt to achieve the same financial return as formerly:

> The gear of the hook and line fishermen now is twice the length, and has twice as many hooks as formerly. The lines used to be 60 fathoms per 'piece', and four pieces made a 'line'. They have now eight pieces of 60 fathoms each. They used to be 16 score hooks, now they have 28 score hooks. They do not catch so many fish as they used.[2]

Arising out of this increase in the number of hooks used in an effort to compete with the trawlers, there was, of course, a very considerable upsurge in demand for bait.

> 'It is a puzzle now,' Joseph Verrill told the Commissioners, 'to get the bait … . The men cannot get the mussels now for love or money … . The bait at Staithes is so expensive that it does not pay to go out fishing. They are now buying mussels from Hamburg, which cost here 4s. 4d. a bag. A bag will bait four lines. The Tees mussels costing 5s. a bag will only bait two lines. The Boston mussels they cannot get at all.' Does not doubt that the fisherman will have to pay £200 for bait at Staithes this winter. The mussels are of no

83 *Runswick, c.1905. Women bore the biggest burden of responsibility for the children's upbringing, in addition to their many other duties. Pregnancies were frequent (as were miscarriages), and families tended to be large.*

use as bait unless they are fresh. They are now using limpets wherever they can pick them for bait … . They could catch many more fish now if they had plenty of mussels. The more bait the more fish. The man that 'pinches' his lines for the bait, the fish 'pinch' him.

So, it was partly to try to cut down on overhead expenses, but also to meet real shortages of mussels, that there was a growing reliance on limpets (called in the local dialect 'flithers'); and up to the early years of the 20th century, and sporadically since then, flither-picking was a permanent feature in the lives of fisherwomen and girls along the Yorkshire coast. Indeed, for most of the year, the long-lines dominated the daily routine.

Once the men had gone off, wives, sisters and daughters went down onto the bleak, exposed scaurs. They set out dressed only in their ordinary, everyday clothing. The long-lining season coincided with the most bitter months of the year. Many a day there was an icy easterly or northerly wind blowing off the sea, but, providing the boats could get off, the bait had to be gathered. So, be it rain, hail, snow or shine, the women took their wicker baskets (called

84 *Gathering driftwood at Whitby, a photograph taken c.1900 by Frank Meadow Sutcliffe. Keeping a good fire was essential: it was needed for warmth, cooking, bathing and washing clothes. To save money, women and girls would go onto the scaurs to gather bits of sea coal and driftwood. A typical entry in the log book of Staithes school, dated 3 February 1886, reads: 'Most wretched attendance this morning, probably owing to a ship having been wrecked under the cliff near Staithes, laden with coals, children being occupied by their parents in gathering them up.'*

swills) and ventured onto the scaurs. A pair of men's leather sea boots cost a guinea (a good week's income for a fisherman at that time, and there was many a week if a gale was blowing that his income was 'nowt'), rubberised wellingtons had not been invented yet, and all the women had to wear were flimsy shoes or, if they were lucky, lace-up boots or wooden-soled clogs. Ankle-length dresses over a quilted petticoat offered a little warmth and protection from the chapping wind; but when they got wet from the rain or tide, as they almost invariably did, the sodden, heavy material flapping against their legs must have caused intense discomfort. Some wore tight-fitting outer bodices in the style of the period over their dresses, and an apron or pinny; while others donned cast-off men's waistcoats for warmth. Over their head and shoulders they wore black, woollen shawls which were crossed over their chests and the ends tied behind the back. Hand-knitted, woollen half-mittens completed their dress.

This description is based chiefly on the outstandingly detailed photographs taken by Sutcliffe in the 1880s and 1890s. Sutcliffe was a pioneer of the 'naturalistic' school of photographers; yet some of his pictures seem in retrospect somewhat posed and composed. No criticism is intended in this observation, since he was constrained by technical factors, and, unlike many of the amateurs who flocked to Whitby in the wake of his success and who saw only the picturesque, he knew better than most the harshness of fisher-women's work:

> The amount of hard work these fishermen's wives and daughters undertake is marvellous. Let the photographer follow them when out flither picking on the rocks, he will soon be wet through up to the waist, and then when they have got their baskets full, let him climb with his apparatus, but a featherweight compared to the weight of their loads of flither, with them, up a cliff side some 500 ft. high, he will then think that the woman's work by daylight is even harder than the fisherman's toil and danger at sea by night.[3]

To an observer on the cliffs above, the flither pickers must have looked at a distance rather like rooks pecking in the fields. Moving over the rocks they were continually bent, seeking to spot the limpets, and, finding them, stooping or crouching to slide the blade of a knife between shell and rock. A sharp, prising action and the creature's hold was broken and it was transferred into the swill. Only when the swills were full could the women cover over the flithers with dillis (a seaweed, *Dilsea Cornosa*), and set off along the scaur back home.

Pictures by another Yorkshire photographer, Fisher of Filey, show that the fisherwomen there wore what might be termed 'a traditional dress'. That is to say, their costume was common to all fisherwomen in the town, and yet peculiar to them as a group. That the dress depicted in Fisher's photographs (they date from about the 1880s) was at one time more universally worn by fisherwomen on the Yorkshire coast is suggested by entries in Munby's diary for 1865.[4] Once, in January, he was on Scarborough sands when he met some bait-gatherers, all women, who wore white jerseys with long sleeves, short skirts, tarpaulin coats and strong boots. A few days later he met a lass he knew, Sarah Ann, who, he wrote,

> looked fresh and strong and clean and bonny as ever – she is 20. Had on a handkerchief tied over her bonnet [and] round her face – old shawl tied close round body – white jersey sleeves, a striped linsey kirtle to the calf, blue wool stockings, and stout highlows. She carried both a sack and a basket, with a tarpaulin next her back.

Early March 1865 found Munby in Whitby where he noticed 'a good few young women and girls with kerchiefed heads and rough clothing'; but the women who overtook him on the road near Staithes the next day, 'coming

85 & **86** *These studies of fisherwomen are studio portraits by W. Fisher, a Filey photographer who, like Sutcliffe at Whitby, has left a detailed pictorial impression of the local community. Fisherwomen wore a distinctive costume or 'traditional dress'; but it was based upon practical considerations. In bitter weather the women and girls had to go onto the rocky scaurs to gather limpets ('flithers') to bait the lines. Consequently, they wore strong, warm clothes, as is evidenced by this lass's short, stout cloak; the shawl wrapped across her chest to keep out the damp, cold wind; the wrist-length, long-sleeved, white woollen jersey worn under the bodice; and the thick, hand-knitted, woollen stocks.*

Notice the doughnut-like object on the girl's wrist (there is another at her feet). This was placed on the head to act as a cushion when heavy loads of bait or lines were being carried. Names for it varied from village to village, but amongst them were 'bun', 'wreath', 'roller' and 'weeze'. Also at the girl's feet are two small baskets (the woman in the other plate is holding one in her left hand). On the northern part of the coast these were known as 'swills', but at Filey the fisherfolk called them 'mawns'. They were used to put flithers in which had been gathered from the rocks. The baskets were tied to the women's backs, and so the bait was carried up the cliffs (which is why the women's skirts are fastened with laces just below the knee: so that they could clamber unhindered). It was James Cole's opinion that a woman at Staithes or Filey worked harder than a man who went off to sea.

two miles from woods with loads of faggots, kindling, on their heads', were 'all in bonnets, bare arms [it was a fine, sunny day], cotton frocks kilted, short blue or grey skirts, brown or black stockings, and strong shoes'.

So great was the demand for flithers at Staithes at that time that the scaurs there were completely bare of them, and the women, as many as 130 altogether, Munby notes, were forced to venture far afield. Some went north to Saltburn,

87 *A Staithes lass. Although fisherlasses had a deserved reputation for being bonny, a good few died, worn out, in middle age.*

while others had gone to neighbouring Runswick Bay where, understandably, the intrusion had been resented bitterly. Eventually, tempers had become so heated that the women of the two villages had fought each other, 'scratted', on the scaurs; whereupon the Justices had intervened and allocated certain days of the week to the Staithes women, much to the chagrin, no doubt, of the fisherwomen of Runswick.

In the end, the Runswick Bay flithers were exhausted, too, and the Staithes women were forced to go ever further afield. As the flithers on the scaurs at Whitby were needed by that port's fishermen, it was not uncommon for Staithes women to go to Robin Hood's Bay to gather bait. James Cole recalled how they would walk to Whitby and spend the night with friends in the fishing community, early the next day walk to Bay, pick their flithers, carry them on their heads back to Whitby, put the flithers on the carrier's cart for Staithes, and then walk home. It was a journey of about thirty-five miles.

Even more remarkable were the Filey women, who, before the linking of Filey and Scarborough by rail in the late 1850s, would sometimes set off just after midnight, walk to Robin Hood's Bay, pick their flithers, and return the same day – 44 miles! By 1865, however, the women's lot had improved somewhat, although it was still extremely hard by present-day standards. They would travel to Scarborough on a Monday or Tuesday by a train which left Filey at 9 a.m. They went third class on tickets marked 'FISHWOMAN' costing 3d. each way. This was a special concessionary rate, says Munby, that had been agreed by the railway company as a result of pressure put upon it by some 'ladies'.

88 *Even routine jobs, such as doing the weekly wash, were time-consuming and laborious in the early 1900s. This photograph of the fisherwoman at work with her poss-stick and peggy-tub was taken at Staithes.*

89 *Filey flither-pickers, 1865. At the time when this photograph was taken, 1865, many Filey women went each week to Cloughton, north of Scarborough, to gather bait. At Cloughton they lodged for the week in widow's cottages, paying 3d. a night each to sleep three in a bed, and taking their own food with them. Some days, they would walk further north still, to Robin Hood's Bay, gather bait, and walk back to Cloughton with their loads. This was in the coldest months of the year, when the long lines were down. Notice the mawn on the girl's back and the way her skirt is tied so that it looks like a pair of breeches. This was to leave the girl's hands and legs unencumbered when she climbed the cliff with her load of bait. Notice, too, the women's sturdy boots; very necessary for clambering over the wet, slippery, weed-covered rocks in search of flithers.*

At Scarborough the women took their baskets from the goods van and set off to carry them to the village of Cloughton some five miles distant. There, there were a number of old, stone-built, thatched cottages with walls a foot or more thick which were occupied by 'widow women'. It was in these that the Filey women took lodgings until the Friday, paying 3d. a night, sleeping three to a bed, and bringing their own food with them from home: 'a bit o' bacon and a cake, a bit o' pie or owt o' that'.

Every day, as the tide went out, the women went onto the scaurs to gather flithers (indeed, a bag of flithers was known as a 'tide', the amount which could be gathered in that time).

By Friday each woman had gathered seven or eight baskets of flither, far too many to carry themselves, so carts were hired in the village to transport the baskets to Scarborough station. The charge was a penny a basket; the women walked. Finally, the baskets were transferred from the carts into a special van attached to the train which arrived back in Filey at 5 p.m.

Once the bait had been gathered and the women had returned home, the flithers or mussels had to be skaned. Skaning is the process of removing the soft part, the actual bait, from the shell. Limpets are univalves and thus the soft body could be removed from the shell virtually in one movement. Most used knives, but for skaning flithers Mrs Marion Cole (*née* Allan), Whitby, preferred a spoon specially sharpened round the lip. Thus, with one twisting movement the bait could be scooped out of the shell in much the same way as one scoops clean the cap of a boiled egg.

Mussels are bivalves and skaning them required speed, dexterity and considerable strength in the wrists. A right-handed person would hold the mussel in the palm of the left hand, while the skaning knife (often a bone-handled, steel dinner knife with a short, pointed ground-down blade) is held in the right hand. The first movement is to cut away any beard with bits of stone or broken shell attached (the beard is the tough, hair-like growth with which the mussel anchors itself to a rock or to other shells). Then the tip of the knife is forced between the two halves of the shell, near to the muscle which hinges them together, with a twisting movement of the wrist, the knife blade is forced round with the tip cutting simultaneously between the inside of the shell and the soft body, severing as it does so the meat from the shell. The left hand tilts slightly, the two halves of the shell are prised apart, and the final movement is the tip of the knife repeating the action of cutting out the soft part from the other half of the mussel.

The entire operation takes only a few seconds, and, after practice, skaning becomes a very mechanical and repetitive activity. But a woman might have to skane several thousand mussels daily. Sometimes the mussels are themselves covered with barnacles which can cut the hands. As the shells are forced open a saline liquid flows out and this and the dirt sticking to the outer shell coarsen the skin, split fingernails, and penetrate cuts or grazes. The skaned mussels were next dropped into a jar, and a woman knew from experience

90 *Caving a long-line. Lines were coiled on flat, oval-shaped, wickerwork skeps. Sometimes, before baiting, the lines were so tangled and full of rubbish – seaweed and bits of old bait – that they had to be tipped off the skeps, picked clean and recoiled. This is called 'caving' a line. If a hook was missing, some women knew how to whip on a new one; but usually that was part of the man's work.*

91 *Baiting lines, Whitby, c.1905. It was probably the needs of the photographer which caused this picture to be taken in the open air. The women have just finished baiting a long line. Lining was an autumn and winter occupation, and it was the women who were responsible for skaning (shelling) mussels and baiting the lines while the men were at sea. Because of the cold weather these activities were carried on indoors, so homes were also workplaces. Skaning and baiting were mucky, smelly, laborious, repetitive and time-consuming tasks, but for at least six months in every year the women had to set to daily: 'and sometimes in winter the mussels were frozen and they cut your hands' – Mrs Maud Hind (1896-1976), Whitby.*

how many jars of bait would be needed for the lines. In other words, she estimated according to volume rather than number: 'You might need three mussels for one hook, but Tees mussels were big and plump and then you only needed one', said Mrs Hind. When a jar was full the mussels were tipped into a tin bath and cold water poured on them ('the colder the better') to make them swell and grow firm ready for baiting.

Skaning and baiting were done in the home: as remarked earlier, houses were workplaces as well as dwellings. When the cobles returned from the fishing grounds the women went down to the harbour to meet them, and carry the lines back home. Lines were coiled on oval-shaped, wickerwork skeps. The woman would hoist the skep onto her head, having first put on a circular object made of twisted cloth called variously a bun, raith or rowler.*

---

* At South Shields on the Durham coast it was called a 'weeze' (see Joe Robinson, *The Life and Times of Francie Nichol of South Shields*, London, 1975, p.18: 'the weeze was just a ring of straw wrapped with cloth, put in between your basket and your head'.)

FACING PAGE:

92 *Baiting a long line. Unopened mussels are in the basket on the table; skaned bait is in the bowl in front of the girl. Hanging on the wall to the right of the window is a 'bun'. Mussels became so scarce because of the great demand for them on the Yorkshire coast that they were imported from the Wash and from as far away as Hamburg in Germany and Harlingen in Holland. This photograph was taken c.1905 by F.M. Sutcliffe.*

Then back home to start caving and baiting.

Caving is clearing the line of old bait, seaweed, and other rubbish. First, the line is tipped off the skep onto the table. Then, the empty skep is placed to one side and the woman begins to coil the line onto it afresh. Occasionally, hooks are missing: some women could put hooks on themselves. 'Old Walter Corrie's wife, she used to do all his hooks. She used to whip all his hooks on for him', recalled Will Richardson. The coils are arranged at one end of the skep, and as each hook is baited it is laid out neatly at the other end. There must be no carelessness; a snagged hook as the line is being shot at sea could be time wasting and possibly dangerous.

In the meantime, the men would be mooring the cobles and seeing to the selling of the catch. Then they would go home, and, after something to eat, would work alongside the women at the caving and baiting.

By far the worst job was mucking the lines if the boats had not been able to go off. This happened when there was a storm, and, since the mussels would not stay fresh on the lines for more than a few days at a time after having been skaned, the women had to set to and remove the putrefying bait and start all over again.

The difficulty of keeping living rooms clean where skaning and baiting were being done can be imagined. In the Harland household, the blackleaded fireplace and brasses were covered up on a Monday morning and were not unveiled again until Saturday tea-time, when all was given a polish ready for Sunday. Maud saw to it that she and the younger children had eaten before their father and two older brothers came in from sea. After the men had had their dinners all was sided away and two tables pulled out into the middle of the room. At one table worked Maud and her father, and at the other her two brothers, all baiting lines with the mussels she and her aunt had skaned earlier in the day. When they had finished, and before going to bed, everything had to be left ready for the next morning; and particularly father's clothes, sea boots and oilskins, lest the lifeboat should be called out during the night.[*]

As well as gathering bait, fetching and carrying, skaning and caving, women had many other tasks. To take but one example: Whitby harbour is protected by massive, sandstone piers. Whatever the state of the tide cobles could be left afloat. Scarborough and Bridlington have protected harbours, too (although, there being no rivers at these places, they tended to dry out almost completely at low water); but at Flamborough, Filey, Robin Hood's Bay, Runswick and Staithes there were only unprotected beaches, open to the sea. At the South Landing, Flamborough, the cobles were hauled up off the beach by horses

---

[*] Robert Harland was successively bow-man, second coxswain and then coxswain of the Whitby lifeboat.

93 *'The Brave Women of Runswick Bay'. On 15 April 1901, after the cobles had left for the fishing ground, a sudden storm blew up. At Runswick a scratch crew was got together, leaving no men to launch the lifeboat. Heroically, the women waded into the huge breakers and got the lifeboat away. Every man was saved.*

(and horses were used, too, at Filey for the same purpose); while at the North Landing a steam engine was employed. At Robin Hood's Bay the cobles were manhandled ashore with the aid of a wheeled under-carriage; and at Runswick the men simply dragged the boats up themselves. At Staithes, however, it was the women as much as the men who launched the cobles up and down.

That the women's contribution was recognised to be indispensable there is no doubt: 'None work so hard as Filey women', Munby was told by the Filey fishermen. Yet that very day, because of a rough sea, the men were ashore and 'laakin' about the street in crowds, playing at 'pickaback, etc.', while the women were indoors mending nets ('They find work at that when we have none', said the men).

This division of labour was also noticed at about the same time by a Filey Methodist minister. Writing about the women, he described them as 'a very hardworking and industrious class'; 'the men', he continued, 'have only to catch the fish, their labour, as a rule, being over as soon as the boat touches the sand'.[5] It was this attitude which clearly shocked a visitor to Staithes in 1904:

> The men were for the most part watching their womenfolk at work. They were also to an astonishing extent mere spectators in the arduous work of hauling the cobles one by one onto the steep banks of shingle. A tackle hooked to one of the baulks of timber forming the staith was being hauled

94 *At Staithes the women helped the men to launch the cobles and carry the lines and gear aboard ...*

95 *... and they were there waiting to unload the catch when the men returned from the fishing.*

at by five women and two men! Two others were in a listless fashion leaning their shoulders against the boat itself. With the last 'heave-ho!' at the shortened tackle the women laid hold of the nets, and with casual male assistance laid them out on the shingle, removed any fragments of fish, and generally prepared them for stowing in the boat again.[6]

Looking back on those days, John Verrill remarked, 'It was a crime if those women weren't there when they landed'; and, at the time, women had what today seems like a somewhat perverse apprehension of their rôle: 'A woman 'at weant work for a man is nea worth yan', was their maxim at Filey.

How should such sentiments be interpreted? To begin with, one should not be misled by phrases such as 'the men had only to catch the fish', for behind that 'only' lies a hazardous, tough occupation. Also, one must beware of attributing to the 19th and 20th centuries attitudes which perhaps belong more properly to an earlier age. For instance, Sherpa women, it seems, carry enormous loads leaving the men to make the actual climb; and on St Kilda women were responsible for doing the most burdensome tasks, and especially those involving carrying, while the men reserved for themselves the dangerous, skilled, and 'male' tasks of scaling sheer cliffs to catch birds and gather eggs. Could this mean, then, that in primitive or 'non-civilised' communities there was a tendency to differentiate male and female work-rôles not according to the arduousness of the task, but according to the degree of danger and skill involved? And if this were so, did the distinction rest simply upon some notion of male hegemony over the female; or could it be that in primitive communities women were shielded from dangerous activity, but not from heavy, 'non-dangerous' labour, because of the biological circumstance that it is the woman who is the procreator and therefore the perpetuation of the community depends more upon her than upon the man in the event of tragedy in the course of dangerous activity? Put simply (and no doubt crudely), if most of the men of an isolated community were lost at sea in a terrible storm would the chances of that community's recovering be better than if it had been most of the women and girls who had perished in some awful tragedy? The answers to such questions lie, presumably, more in the realms of anthropology than in recent social history; but one is left with a niggling suspicion that the male/female relationship in the inshore fishing communities derived from something more complex and deep-seated than the unfair and unequal conventions of Victorian and Edwardian society alone.

Be that as it may, only one case has come to light of women engaging in the fishing itself, and that, it must be emphasised, was a type of fishing which was exceptionally wearisome, relatively unskilled, and did not require the use of a boat. It was shrimping, an activity carried on by women at Redcar, but already, in 1868, on the decline and, according to Munby, 'the first I ever saw in England'. Since this is a unique instance, it is worth citing the entry in full:

> One was a tall stalwart sunburnt woman of fifty, the other ten years younger; and a lad with them. They wore old hood bonnets, tattered bed gowns and skirts, and stockings without feet, and old shoes. Their baskets, full of shrimps, were slung round them; and they carried on their shoulders their shrimp nets, which were smaller than those of Boulogne. They had been fishing at Teesmouth, five miles from home: Most folks go there for shrimps [they told Munby]: the sand and mud is so broad you may wade through it for near two hours before you come to water at low tide. We wade up to our waists often, said they, fishing for shrimps: there's many dangerous holes, but pushing the net before you is a guide, like. Some women shrimp at Redcar itself: fifteen or twenty years ago, there were as many as forty nets at once, all women; and women still do what shrimping there is; but girls don't take to

it as they did; they go out to service more, the demand for servants being so much greater now.[7]

The cumulative effects of the life lived by fisherwomen were frequently ill-health and premature death. For on top of the irregular hours, exposure to bitter weather, the standing, lifting and carrying of heavy burdens, there was the grind of housework and the dangers attached to frequent pregnancies: all took their toll on the woman's constitution. It was a style of life accepted sometimes consciously and by choice, but often fatalistically and with a sense of inevitability. The observer from outside the fishing community, as Sutcliffe noted, viewed fisherwomen's activity more often than not only superficially: it was 'quaint', 'picturesque', a sentimentalised image with the toil only dimly recognised. In reality, a fisherwoman's life, although not devoid of joy by any means, was too often, to paraphrase Dame Laura Knight, dedicated to toil and tragedy.

'The attendance has gone down the last two days', the head teacher of Staithes school entered ruefully in the log book for Friday, 15 June 1883, 'partly owing to a coal ship which anchored on Thursday and *girls* [emphasis added] have been kept at home to carry coals.' (See Plate 84.) Coal figures, too, in Mrs Martha Boddington's recollection of an event which occurred during her girlhood (she was born in 1901). Her mother had gone on Whitby scaur gathering sea coal, fragments of coal which had drifted ashore with the tide:

My mother had been on the scaur and she'd been up to the waist in water. It was March, and she was coming along the sand and she felt ill. And she just dropped down on t'sand and this baby was born. She was between four-and-a-half month and five-month pregnant. She delivered herself of this baby and she put it in her skirt (they always wore their skirt and their aprons fastened round them with a big pin). And she carried it, right up. She had forty or fifty steps to climb, right from the sands nearly into Henrietta Street. And across the street, and just dropped the basket of coal in the yard. She says to me, 'Get me some dry clothes, honey; and go and ask Mrs Noble to come, I want her'. I got my mother dry clothes and I got Mrs Noble. And then I went for my Uncle Dick's wife. She came, and she sent for the doctor. The doctor said she was a lucky person that she was alive, because, he said, it was the intense cold and the weight on her head that had caused her to have the miscarriage.

Ten

'MAKING ENDS MEET'

96 *Gathering driftwood for fuel, Runswick Bay, 1908.*

UNTIL comparatively recently, fishermen sold their catches themselves, without the intervention of a salesman, using a method akin to a Dutch auction. The procedure adopted at Hastings in the fore part of the 19th century was typical of scenes all round the coasts of England. The catch was sorted into heaps on the beach according to species, and then the fisherman would stand behind one of the heaps holding a pebble in his hand. When the potential buyers had assembled, he shouted out a price which, as everyone knew, was more than the fish were worth. So, progressively lowering the price, he simultaneously lowered his arm until someone among the crowd accepted the price named, whereupon the fisherman dropped the pebble and the sale was concluded.[1] It was the custom on the north-east coast for the buyer at this point in the proceedings to cry out 'Het!', which is believed to be a contraction of 'I'll have it', or, as it would be pronounced in those districts, 'I'll hev it'. It was an expression used at Hartlepool, north of the Tees; and at Flamborough, as this extract from an old poem describing the scene at North Landing demonstrates:

> And then I saw the fish market begun,
> Numbers of fishing boats on shore had run;
> Large fish they threw in scores upon the beach,
> Spread on the sand, and where the waves can't reach.
> One values it, if that he cannot get,
> He lowers it – the buyer calls out 'Het'.[2]

At Whitby as late as 1870 there was a system still in operation which combined the Dutch auction practice of lowering prices with the now more conventional rising scale of bids. By this time, as the following account also shows, the professional buyer, no doubt soon to become the salesman, too, has with his 'book' made an appearance on the quay-side:

As the cobles near shore, after their day's or night's work, the men begin to take the fish from the 'crib' ... and toss it over to the stern for display. The skate goes first, then the haddock, ling, and whatever else they may have. Sometimes they have a preponderance of what is locally known as 'coal-fish', an inferior kind of cod, or hake, worth only three-pence each. On the wharf expectant stand the buyers, as each coble comes up in its turn. The fishermen and the buyers are old acquaintances. 'Well, Jack, what have you got?' cries out one of the latter. 'Score and a half cod, three score skate, four score haddock, ling, halibut' &c., replies Jack.* 'What's t'price' inquires the buyer. 'Two pound', says Jack, promptly. The answer is received in silence so prolonged, that Jack at last calls out, 'Is none of you goin' to bid?' 'I'll gie a pound,' says another of the buyers, who in the interval has been trying to take stock of the fish. 'Pound's boden!' roars Jack. ''Nother shillin', calls another buyer, and so on, bidders rising their price, and, if need be, Jack dropping his until a satisfactory bargain is come to. Then Jack hangs up an instrument which is called a klep-hook by the side of his craft, to denote that his stock is sold; the buyer enters the name of the boat and its owner, and the price of its purchase, in his book, though he does not pay until Saturday, and Jack pushes off to land his fish lower down the wharf, and to make way for the next comer.³

The appearance of the fish salesman as intermediary between producer and retailer seems, on the evidence just quoted, to have been a comparatively late development. The salesman would no doubt have justified his rôle on the grounds that, given the emergence of railways, the evolution of regional and national markets, the use of the post and, later, of telegraph and telephone, his was a vital service to both the fisherman and to the public, in that it facilitated the speedy sale and distribution of a highly perishable commodity and was, therefore, to everyone's advantage. And there is some force behind this argument, especially when it is applied to the small, family, fishing enterprise which was facing intense competition from the heavily capitalised, deep-sea trawling fleets. But, as time passed, individual salesmen became companies; and in some of the smaller ports and villages these companies found themselves eventually in situations of complete or near monopoly. The commissions charged tended to rise, and accumulated capital was often invested in new craft (with varying degrees of 'owner' participation) so that, in the end, the sales company's economic hold on the producer, however benign, became very strong indeed. If, as occasionally happened, the fish-selling company was also the principal buyer on a particular market, its influence within the fishing community could become even more pronounced.

In this respect, the individualism so characteristic of inshore fishermen in other aspects of their existence may have been a handicap in the economic sphere. Certainly, unlike in Scotland, there has been no tendency towards co-operation, and many fishermen have said that, although such a marketing organisation might have been to their advantage, so suspicious were they of each other where prices were concerned that it would never have worked. One Whitby skipper went so far as to suggest that some fishermen even welcomed a degree of economic dependency in return for the paternalism

---

* Quantities and prices in this passage are, presumably, notional.

exercised over them by a company. Be that as it may, the disadvantageous terms accorded to fishermen in the past have been remarked upon frequently. Edgar March's strictures on the counting and sale of herring have been cited in an earlier chapter. There were other critics, too.

The system employed in the sale of white fish was, it seems, from the fisherman's point of view, little better. Mary Linskell, the Whitby novelist, mentions a commission being paid by the fisherman of one shilling and six pence in the pound (i.e. 7½ per cent), with six pence being returned to the purchaser of the fish, six pence going to pay harbour dues, and the remaining six pence belonging to the auctioneer. 'The arrangement', she wrote, 'seems somewhat primitive.'[4] Of course, if the purchaser happened also to be the auctioneer then his discount doubled to 5 per cent.

Such overheads apart, the fisherman, who took by far the greatest risks in the enterprise, received little enough for his labours. From the mid-1870s cheap grain began to flood the country from overseas, while technological innovations such as canning and refrigeration brought cheap, good quality foreign meat to the masses. The price of fish fell. To make matters worse, industrial economies went into a cycle of boom and slump until eventually, in the decade preceding 1914, real wages became depressed and purchasing power declined accordingly. It was these factors, together with competition from trawling fleets, which dealt a very hard knock to the inshore fishermen.

97 *Apart from shelter, another prerequisite for the founding of a fishing village was the presence of fresh water. Usually, as here at Staithes, this meant one of the becks which tumble down to the sea from the peaty moors. The girl in the picture is drawing water with a metal pail; but the traditional utensil was a 'skeel', a container made of oak, with iron hoops, and wider at the bottom than at the top. When piped water was laid on in the last century some old Staithes people complained, saying 'We always did drink the beck'.*

Many villages – Staithes, Runswick, Filey – never fully recovered from the blow received then. James Cole, when he was well past ninety, reflected on those times: 'You had to catch a lot of fish in them days for very little money. Before the First World War ... when we had the two cribs full and we got £3, we thought we'd got a good day.' If a three-man crew together earned £100 clear in a herring season they were well satisfied.

Dr Paul Thompson cites figures which show that in 1913-14 the average annual earnings of occupied men and women of all classes were £80, with an unskilled, male manual worker receiving £79 and his female counterpart only £35.[5] As remarked earlier, whatever the skills deployed by a man at the fishing, his status in the shore-based labour market was that of unskilled manual worker, and, indeed, so far as can be estimated from scant evidence, the fisherman's average weekly income, as earned by fishing, was at that time in the region of thirty shillings a week. However, it must be stressed that the inshore fisherman had no wage as such. 'Fishermen had no income', exclaimed Jinny Hutchinson, 'it couldn't be income, for t'weather.' What she meant, of course, was that fishermen had no regular, fixed, or predictable income. No matter how long or hard they worked, much depended upon the size of the catch. Yet, unlike in those occupations where high productivity meant more pay, fishermen were subject to a highly volatile market in which more fish did not necessarily mean more money. Big catches could just as likely lead to glut and low prices. Above all, there was the weather. Rough seas might keep cobles in harbour for weeks on end. No fish, no money. Hence, it is extremely difficult to compute a fisherman's 'average' income: 'No person knows what the yield will be till the last moment: it may be abundant, or it may be a total failure'.

So far as the individual inshore fisherman was concerned, a share, or dole, system was used to determine his earnings. Throughout the week fishbuyers or auctioneers recorded each boat's daily sales, and on the Saturday the net earnings of the boat (i.e. less commission and landing dues) were handed over to the skipper. Taking a three-man coble as the example, the lump sum would then be divided into four equal shares, one share for each member of the crew plus the boat's share. If, as was quite often the case, the boat was owned by one of the crew, then that man received two shares, but it was his responsibility to keep the coble in good repair and to bear any costs of maintenance. Moreover, should the boat be wrecked, the material loss was entirely his. However, so far as personal earnings were concerned, the working owner's return was exactly the same as those of his two crew mates. Similarly, when the lines were shot at sea (they were individually owned), the total catch from them went into the same crib and was sold subsequently in the name of the boat, and not according to which fish had been caught by whose line.

There were variations of the basic system, depending upon the composition of the crew and the type of gear being worked. Five-man boats had five share-men, one man who was paid half a share, and a lad who did, in fact, receive a small fixed wage. At Scarborough in 1849, the arrangements were:

> Of the five men who have shares, one is usually the owner of the boat; the other four, with himself, are joint proprietors of the fishing gear, *viz.* the cobles, lines, nets, &c. A new boat will cost about £600, or upwards; and the fishing gear necessary for a boat, may be valued at £100 more, or £20 for each man; the half-share man having no property in the gear. The proceeds of each fishing expedition are divided into six parts, or rather 6½: one share to each of the five men, and the half share to the sixth man. Consequently, if the owner is one of the five men, he has two shares, one for the boat, and one for himself as a fisherman.[6]

As the uneconomic five-man boats dropped out of use, their share system was transferred almost intact into the newer, cheaper yawls, so that, when James Cole first went to sea in 1895 as the 'little lad', things were much the same as they had been some fifty years earlier.

> *So many men found the gear* [he explained], *four men might find the gear. Well, there was four in the* Venus. *There was my grandfather, my father, and John Cole (his father was drownded in one of t'yawls), and Bill Verrill, he was a relation. Those four fund the gear in the* Venus. *And then Jimmy Tose, Dan Brown Harrison, and 'Old West' – Edward Verrill – he was nobbut a young lad but he always got 'Old West' – them was the three 'big lads'. And the young lad that was going, George Brown, he refused; so my father had to get me off school at the age of twelve to make the crew up. That's how I got there.*

James Cole experienced a slightly different system when he was a young man at Staithes. Then, during the herring season, the coble got one shilling in the pound after expenses had been met; while in winter her share was four shillings a week, irrespective of total earnings. A good week then was two pounds a man, and in a bad week 'nowt'.

The boat's total net earnings were paid out on Saturdays by the buyers or auctioneers. This often took place in a pub, but even if it did not, the men usually shared out amongst themselves there. It was a great temptation after a hard week's work to spend too much on drink, and it cannot be stressed too strongly that the well-being of fishing families depended to a very great degree upon the sobriety of husbands. No matter how good a manager the wife was, it availed little if the man overspent on drink. Robert Harland always shared out at home, nor did he drink, and his daughter, Maud, was

98 *Castle Hill dominates this busy scene at Scarborough harbourside. Its immense bulk provides shelter from the dreaded northerlies, which is why the fishing community settled at its foot, creating a maze of alleys and courtyards close by their boats moored in the harbour.*

The lassies in the picture are gipping herring. The vessels are mainly Scottish, but those on the right with white counter sterns are Scarborough yawls. The steam yacht is a portent of the future: the days of sail were numbered when this photograph was taken in about 1908. On the opposite pier are stacks of barrels into which the salted herring will be packed. The principal customers were Germany and Russia, but the war and 1917 revolution dealt a severe blow to the east-coast herring trade, and it was not until after the Second World War that there was any substantial recovery. Today, the Yorkshire herring fishery is virtually dead.

convinced that this, together with her mother's efforts, was the chief reason for the family's comparative well-being.

> I've seen my father never cross that harbour bar for a full week, but as long as they've got off on the Saturday we've had a nice dinner and a bit of cake for our Sunday's tea. But I can safely say I never went without anything … . My mother was a good manager, and my father wasn't one as went boozing; he never drank, you see.

Nonetheless, in the decade before 1914 it was a brutal fact that, no matter how sober the husband or capable the wife, the margin between sufficiency and want was so fine that few fisherfolk were able to put money by as an insurance against illness or bad weather. Hence the critical importance of other sources of income, or, to use a modern term, of secondary earnings.

It was the irregularity of income which troubled the fisherman most. Not that they were alone in this; other trades suffered, too. Building and construction workers were subjected to lay-offs in winter when frost and snow made brick-laying impossible. Day labourers in agriculture could go weeks without employment if the land was too wet to work. But the fisherman, while reckoning on bad weather in winter, suffered from storms at all seasons of the year. Another problem which fishermen had to contend with was noticed by a writer in 1838:

> In the case of meat or grain, the supply can be proportioned exactly to the demand; but the fisherman cannot direct his labours with the same regular results, and on the one day he toils in vain, while on the next he gluts a limited market. This does not, however, recompense him for ill success previous, and ... the price at length descends so low, that the farmer is enabled to buy a part of the fisherman's cargo for manure ... .[7]

99 & 100 *The guernsey is a practical garment, warm and close-fitting to keep out the wind and to minimise the risk of its getting snagged on anything and so causing an accident when working at sea. Yet the patterns are beautiful, and great skill goes into the making of them. Every fishing town and village had its own patterns.*
    Tom Clark of Bridlington is shown on the left; note the intricate pattern at the shoulder of his guernsey. On the right is 'Coo-ee' Gaskin of Whitby wearing a rope-patterned guernsey. Both men, as it happens, were shrimpers. Shrimps abounded in the sandy bays at Whitby and Bridlington.

101 *In those rare moments when they had nothing else to do, the women busied themselves knitting. Sometimes it was socks, or thick, thigh-length, sea-boot stockings. Or else they knitted guernseys on steel needles out of heavy, dark-blue, slightly oily wool. This photograph was taken at Scarborough in 1876. Note the length of the women's skirts: short by the standards of the day, but very sensible in view of the work they had to do.*

While this statement over-simplifies somewhat the difficulties faced by the farmer, it does not exaggerate the plight of the fisherman. Weather, the market, and the unpredictability of the catch all combined to make fishermen's income precarious; and it is this point which is emphasised over and over again in conversations with elderly fisherfolk. The question arises, then: if the weather would not allow them to earn, how did they manage?

Unlike, say, the carpenter who worked for an employer by day and did a few jobs on the side in his own time, the fisherman, when prevented from fishing, had no special skill which he could sell. Short of the dreaded 'Parish', the fisherman and his family had to go hungry and cope as best they could. It was a hard struggle at times which demanded great resourcefulness. Somehow, they recall, 'you had to mak' ends meet'. The rest of this chapter is an account, told chiefly in their own words, of how they coped.

*　　*　　*

At the time when James Cole first went to sea, the off-shore fishing began in February and went on until about the end of July, when the yawls were laid up and the ploshers launched in readiness for the annual herring fishery. When that ended (on the North Yorkshire coast, about the end of September or early October), the ploshers were hauled up out of the water and the winter line-fishing began. The yawls carried two cobles on deck for the off-

102 *Unloading ice from a Norwegian schooner, Scarborough. Yawls put to sea on the Monday and returned to port only on Friday or Saturday. To keep the catch fresh, ice was carried. Until a way was found to make ice artificially, most of that used in the Yorkshire ports came from Scandinavia. Blocks of ice were sawn out of glaciers, packed in the holds of schooners, and brought to England to be stored in 'ice houses'. Towards the end of the 1870s, 30,000 tons of ice were being imported annually from Norway into Hull alone.*

shore line fishing, and the herring ploshers, of which there were more than there were yawls, carried up to four men, or four men and a lad. The winter cobles, however, had crews of only three men; and, thus, from October to February there was a surplus of men to boats, chiefly boys and young men. Most did as James Cole:

> I worked in the shipyards, labouring. I worked in the shipyards at Crag and Taylor's at Thornaby, and William Gray's at Hartlepool. We had to go anywhere where you could. There was no signing on the dotted line in them days … . If you didn't arn a shilling by then, you didn't get one. When the season was finished, the herring season, you couldn't walk about. You had to get away: Either find a job ashore, or go in the Merchant Navy.
>
> In Britannia [Works] there was about thirty of us in what we called the 'sailor gang'.[8] And there was twenty-odd on 'em, Staithes and Whitby. They did all the erecting and high rigging, stack building and shed building, and all that. That was what they called 'the sailor gang'. And we were the top-paid sailor gang on the Tees side: we had 22 shillings a week! We had a good gaffer. He was a Staithes chap was the charge-man, Tommy Shippey. And he allus said that he'd try to get us two pound a week. He always had something for all the men to turn out of a Sunday, to get two days. He allus had that scheme somehow or other. In 1899, when the Boer War broke out, I was working in Middlesbrough then … .

In the early years of the 20th century, with prices low and the fishing in decline at places such as Staithes, many fishermen left the sea for good. Some moved with their families to Teesside and found industrial occupations; while others at Runswick and Staithes stayed in their native villages, but worked full-time in the nearby ironstone mines, or in the steelworks at Skinningrove. Some, however, saw the shore job as being simply a seasonal stop-gap. Edward Verrill's father was a member of the crew of the *Venus* when James Cole first went to sea:

> *Aye, my father was a fisherman all his life. Why, maybe odd times when fishing was slack, scarce, maybe get jobs in t'shipyards: Middlesbrough, Teesside, Hartlepool. 'Cos I've heard my mother say, many a time he's maybe sent a pound home, my father, he's sent it with old James (he was young Jimmy then!). Aye, things was bad i' them days. Yes …. . I once heard my father say: they were herringing, they had ploshers then … . Oh, they went weeks and weeks and nivver got a penny piece. Apparently, they'd left t'yards to come fishing. So, they went weeks and weeks and got nothing; so they all went back again. And I've heard them say: not long after, t'herring come on then, t'herring come on, then they all left [the yards] and come back to t'ploshers again!*

Edward Verrill left school when he was fourteen. That was in 1921, a bad time in the fishing and a bad time generally. As part of the government's measures to relieve unemployment, a small harbour was built at Staithes using local labour. Between 1921 and 1924 Edward worked on this and, later, at Boulby ironstone mine, before moving to Whitby to go fishing at the age of seventeen. His recollection of these years, as well as showing how fisherfolk would turn their hand to anything in order to earn, also implicitly contrasts

103 *Fish buyer and carrier, Bridlington. All along the coast, the carrier with his horse and cart was a familiar sight. He was employed mainly in transporting fish from the waterside to the railway station; but sometimes he carried small quantities to the inland villages for sale there.*

104 *Fish market, Coffee House End, Whitby. Until salesmen gained a monopoly in the latter part of the 19th century, fishermen auctioned their own catches. The novelist Mary Linskell's comment on the new system was: 'His* [the salesman's] *payment is deducted from the sales — one shilling and sixpence in the pound being kept back from the fishermen. Of this sixpence is returned to the purchaser, sixpence goes to the payment of harbour dues; and the other sixpence is the reward of the auctioneer. The arrangement seems somewhat primitive.'*

Fish was laid out for inspection according to the boat which had caught it and according to species. The fish in the photograph is chiefly cod. In those days, the catch was sold ungutted.

the daily life of the fisherman, its routine determined by seasons and weather, with the regular regime of the mine's buzzer:

> *When I was sixteen, I got a bit of a job when they built Staithes harbour. We got a job, young lads, shifting stones … . You got a few stamps on. Then after that, when that job finished, I got a little job at Boulby — you know where t'potash* [mine] *is now? — ironstone mine. We worked on top, on t'belt. Used to get up at five o'clock of a morning, and we had to walk right up there … . Started at six o'clock o' t'morning. Sometimes you'd take a bit of lunch with you, in a tin, pack up. A tin of cold tea already made; and you used to take it down to t'weighman's cab and he used to warm it. And you nivver had your backs up, nivver had your backs up! 'Cos it* [the iron ore] *was all pulled out with an electric rope: sets of tubs, and that. As the tubs come to the top, there was some men and lads … it come down like a chute and onto a blooming git belt. We were on there shovelling and picking and sorting, getting all t'rubbish out … then it went straight down into t'railway trucks. Then the buzzer went at six minutes past three, … knocking-off time. You would get about half an hour for your grub, half an hour for your bait. It just depends when the sets was coming out of t'pit. Sometimes you were getting it by half past nine, sometimes ten o'clock, sometimes nine o'clock — half an hour. And at six minutes past three, that's when you finished. Then you had to walk all t'way home again. About eleven shillings a week!*

An alternative to getting a shore job, as James Cole mentioned, was to sign on for a voyage in the Merchant Navy as a deckhand. This was Laurence Murfield's experience:

After I left school at fourteen years of age, I messed about in the cobles ... . Well, you couldn't go to sea before you were sixteen, and things was that bad in the fishing line, I thought 'Well, I'm going to have a go.' We had no money nor nothing – really I would have liked to have gone to the secondary school ... . So, when I got to just under sixteen ... I told old Bland (he was the chap that ran Harrowing's shipping office). 'Well,' he says, 'do you want to go to sea, like?' I says, 'Yes, I'd like to try it. There's nothing here.' And I joined the SS Ethelwulf, 11th of December 1925. And I went from Whitby, with an old pillowcase on my back, through to Hull, Alexandra Dock ... . Never been before, and I went by myself ... . Found the ship and went aboard her.

The first trip we did we went from Hull to Newcastle. Loaded general [cargo] at Newcastle, went over to t'Continent, Rotterdam. Came back to Hull, reloaded with beet sugar. First cargo to leave the country – they had a big ceremony on the quay afore we left. We went to Danzig … it was all ice and snow. We came from there, after we'd discharged, to the Tyne. We loaded up at t'Tyne, went from t'Tyne down the coast, along the Channel, 'cross the Bay of Biscay, through the Mediterranean, Port Said, Red Sea, across the Indian Ocean to Karachi. We went from Karachi to Bombay to Marmagoa … . Then we boarded across to t'other side and come right across the Pacific and came to Seattle. And after Seattle we came through the Panama; then back from the Panama to Barry. Barry to Hull, and then back from Hull to Sunderland. Eleven months and seventeen days … . That was the first trip I did. Do you know how much I paid off with? Four pound. *Four pound. You had twenty-one shillings a week, and [out of that] you had fourteen shillings compulsory allotment for your home. And that's what it left you with. Well, by the time there was odd things you had to buy, you had nothing to come back with. If we'd gone back to Hull and paid off in Hull, I'd have had my train fare to pay home … . But with staying on and going round to Sunderland, and coming to a neutral port, they paid my bus fare. And then I did another trip in her; and then another in t'* Ethelfreda. *And when I reckoned it up – it was in two years – I couldn't see me going ahead nowhere. I thought, 'Well, I'm back to square one where I set off.' So I went back to fishing.*

Laurence Murfield's experience was not unique. John William Storry first went to sea in the Merchant Navy in 1910 when he was 17 years old:

I got three pound a month. I was out to Valparaiso, round Cape Horn and t'west coast of America to Iquique: fetched saltpetre back to Hamburg, and three pound a month for five or six months. Next trip I went I got £3. 15s., from Cardiff. Next voyage I got £4. 7s. 6d., at South Shields. Then I joined a ship at Hull; I got £4.10s. And all during the war I was on His Majesty's Service in transports, and that. Never had any more than eight pound a month. Some got nine pound a month.

It was not just money that drew men into the Merchant Navy, as Mr Storry, who knew great want as a child, explained:

That's what I went to sea for, for grub. Only had three pound a month, you know. We got a breakfast, dinner, and tea … hard biscuits for supper. But that's what men went to sea for in them days. For t'grub. We only used to get paid off eight or nine pound. I remember doing ten months – River Plate. And the few bits o' things I wanted, like slippers and dungarees that I got out of t'slop chest off t'steward – I was only paid off with six pound. Then there was thirty shillings for my train fare home. That's only like four pound ten … . Why, I could have sitten and cried when I thowt about it.

Whitby boys still go to sea in the merchant service, but few of them come from fishing families. Today a fisherman who decides to give up the sea may get a job at the new Boulby potash mine, or go to Teesside. The aftermath

105 *Unloading herring onto the sands at Scarborough.*

of both world wars witnessed an exodus of many former fishermen from Whitby and its neighbouring coastal villages to the heavy industry of Middlesbrough, Stockton or Hartlepool in search of regular hours and regular wages. After the First World War they went to the shipyards and steel mills, and after the Second it was to the rapidly growing chemicals industry centred on Billingham and Wilton. Some fishermen still adopt a pattern not unlike that described by James Cole: they fish, or go 'partying' (taking parties of visiting anglers to sea) in summer, then, if they are lucky, find jobs as general labourers or scaffolders on Teesside in winter, travelling 30 miles in each direction daily by bus.

The shipyards, the mines, or the Merchant Navy offered extended periods of employment. In the case of the mines and the shipyards, it was seasonal; in the case of the Merchant Navy, it could be for several years. While the job lasted, these employments were permanent and for a winter or a voyage a man ceased to be a fisherman. To that extent, a secondary source of income became in practice the primary source.

At Whitby the physical obstacle which loomed largest in the fears of fisherfolk, and which exemplified the impossibility of earning a regular income, was the dreaded Bar. In a northerly or easterly gale it is still one of the most dangerous hazards on the east coast, even though the channel is nowadays dredged regularly and efficiently by the local council. In the early 1900s, however, it was silted up to such an extent that, 'We used to row in – maybe an hour's flood – and we used to touch the sand with our oars'. For the fishermen in their cobles, and for their families on shore, the Bar came to dominate their lives:

> In them days there was no Extensions,* there was only the lighthouses, the two piers, and it was all open sea. It was allus the danger zone, was between the piers ... . Because the seas used to break. And that was the danger zone. They never bothered if they got ower t'Bar. They allus called it: 'I wish they were ower t'Bar'. Ower there, and then they were all right, because it used to break and swamp them.

The anxiety and fear captured in Miss Jane Jameson's recollections (she was born on the Cragg and lived her entire life there) are echoed time and again. Tommy White's comment will serve: 'Weather was the worst. I've seen times when you couldn't get over that Bar for ten weeks in winter.' Ten weeks may have been exceptional, but periods of two or three weeks when the Bar was impassable were not uncommon. When this happened, the consequences could be harsh indeed. As Jinny Hutchinson put it, 'If fishermen got thirty bob that was a good week for them, when I was a child [c.1910]. And if there was bad weather you got no dole, no nowt. You had to do without. They've gone about, some of them, with no shoes on, no fire on, no nothing. They couldn't help it.' That phrase, 'they couldn't help it', needs emphasising. No doubt there were improvident families amongst fisherfolk, as in any occupational group; but fishermen in the fore part of this century were operating always on the margin of subsistence. Some families coped better than others, yet, as mentioned earlier, even where the wife was a good manager and the husband a successful fisherman, loss of gear or boat, injury or illness, a prolonged spell of bad weather, could all result in hardship and hunger. As a last resort there was 'charity' (itself a form of secondary income); but, except for the aged, who often had no alternative, few availed themselves of

---

* Extensions – breakwaters added to the piers in 1914. They made entry safer, but the Outer Bar remained treacherous.

FACING PAGE:

106 *Old age and sickness were the twin dreads in the days before the introduction of social security by the state. People helped each other as much as they could; but this rarely ran to financial support: fishing in those days was not an affluent occupation. Consequently, the elderly, in the face of charity and the hated workhouse, strove to maintain their independence as long as possible. This old woman, 'Pal' Arnold of Whitby, used to hammer lumps of pale-coloured sandstone rock out of the cliff (see her basket) and then hawk them at a ha'penny or penny apiece around the big houses on the West Cliff as 'donkey stone' for sanding doorsteps and flagstones.*

this source unless absolutely desperate. For old people, explained Will
Richardson:

> *There was nothing else to get; because they couldn't go to t'Social Security. When they*
> *went ... we used to call it t' 'Parish' then, they only used to get half a crown. And*
> *it wasn't in money, it was in ticket form. For a week. It was only, like, a half-crown*
> *ticket they used to get. They used to have to go to one of t'grocers' shops ... and get*
> *groceries. You couldn't get no money then.*

With the impassable Bar, on the one hand, and the Parish, on the other,
the fisherman was glad to 'arn a shilling' wherever he could. Many would walk
the scaur as the tide went out in search of jet, sea coal, firewood, or anything
washed up by the sea which could be converted into money. At Whitby this
activity was called simply 'beachcombing', but at Runswick and Staithes it was
known as 'ploagin'. Here are two examples.

The raw material for the Whitby jet industry came mainly from inland in
the Cleveland Hills, but some came from 'fishermen, who, due to bad weather,
cannot ply their trade'. Others who sought jet on the shore were ironstone
miners on shift work, and 'jetties', men who searched for jet more or less full
time. The method was the same:

> [They spent] most of their time watching for falls of cliff, and scratching
> amongst the debris for any stray pieces of jet, or waiting for the tide ebbing,
> on the lookout for washed jet of rounded shapes, caused by the action of
> the sea scouring it amongst the sand and shingle of the shore. Some very
> useful pieces came their way; the skin* was generally worn off by the ceaseless
> swirl, making it an easier piece to block out [chop roughly to the required
> shape] and work than if the skin was there. These men could always find a
> ready market in selling the odd bits to the small masters in the trade – who
> were only too pleased to get it – no matter how little they had managed to
> accumulate in their daily wanderings about the rocky scaur.[9]

In stormy weather, apart from jet, sea coal was often driven ashore. Sometimes
there were sizeable lumps, especially if they came from coal-burning ships
which had foundered and whose bunkers gradually washed up. But more
often it was small stuff which could only be scraped up and taken home in
bags. This was called brash. Wood, either beck sticks brought down the Esk,

---

* 'skin' – pieces of jet with a coating of shale, quartz, or other rock. Jet with this 'skin' still attached
is known as 'blueskin'.

FACING PAGE:

107 *At Filey, this old man, Robert Maulson, as the embroidery on his guernsey proclaims, earned a little in
the season by guiding visitors along the Brigg, the natural promontory which juts out into the sea*

108 *Scarborough lifeboat. The North Sea can change from tranquillity to storm very quickly; and the Yorkshire lifeboat stations have a proud record of saving life in atrocious conditions. Crews consisted mainly of fishermen.*

or timber, perhaps washed off the deck cargo of a passing steamer, was also gathered up. All this was used to fuel domestic fires, which, in those days, served not only to heat homes but also for cooking and doing the washing.

Shipwreck afforded other ways of augmenting family incomes; and since one of the main north-south shipping lanes from Tyne, Wear and Tees passes close to Whitby wrecks occurred frequently. Lifeboat service on the Yorkshire coast has a noble history and some of the rescues performed are by now almost legendary. No one could ever doubt the valour of the lifeboat crews, in past time or now. Up to 1958 the lifeboats were all pulling boats, and launching them over the sands into stormy breakers was a cold, wet, miserable task. Yet, when life was at risk, the utmost energies of every man were bent towards making a rescue; and this it is important to keep in mind.

Launchers were paid a very small sum for assisting in getting the lifeboat afloat. They had to haul the heavy craft over an open beach, at Whitby for several hundred yards if the tide was low, on a huge wheeled undercarriage. The boat had then to be manhandled through the surf until it floated and got away on service. The launchers, often wet through after being up to their chests in the breakers, then waited, sometimes for many hours, until the lifeboat returned. It was then hauled back to its shed. For all this, each launcher received 3s. 6d.

No fisherman could ever have as his chief priority anything other than the saving of life at sea. Yet so great was the need, so desperate were fishermen in times of prolonged bad weather to earn a few shillings, that they would scramble amongst themselves to get a launcher's token.

Ann Lowis's father, Thomas Welham, was a coxswain of Whitby lifeboat. When a call came:

Folks used to come here [to the house]: '*Welham, can you give us a ticket? You know, we have nowt.*' *Well, my Dad says to me, '*We only have so many. I can't give*

109 *Fishermen were intensely competitive in their everyday work and would do their utmost to keep a good fishing ground secret or to get to market first in order to secure the best price for their catch. But in many other respects they were extremely co-operative; and this spirit is best exemplified by lifeboat service. This sequence of four photographs shows a practice launch at Robin Hood's Bay. As the tide is out, the boat is being dragged across the scaur and into deep water. Fortunately for the launchers, on this occasion the sea is dead calm.*

110 *Twelve of the 13-man crew of the Whitby lifeboat perished in the dreadful disaster of 1861, leaving 10 widows and 44 fatherless children. At the fishing, tragedy struck all too frequently; and there was only charity to support the bereaved families.*

In 1821 the Port of Hull Society was established, and its Sailors' Orphan Home (for which fisherfolk's children were eligible) was set up in 1863. Here, children were 'carefully instructed in the truths of Christianity, without the use of any catechism or religious formulary' and received 'a sound elementary education by a certificated master'. When the children left the Home (the boys at fourteen, the girls at fifteen), each was presented with a copy of the Scriptures and 'a suitable outfit, the Committee endeavouring to provide situations for them'. The Society served the coast from King's Lynn to Hartlepool, and it undoubtedly relieved much distress at a time when support from the state was non-existent.

> 'em to all, and if you give to one I'm offending the other.' So, they used to give 'em like a penny. And he said, 'T'best way when they come: I'll be down at t'lifeboat house and I'll throw 'em up [the tokens] and them that gets 'em, they get 'em.' Three and sixpence!

Maud Hind's father, Robert Harland, was also a distinguished coxswain of Whitby lifeboat:

> They hadn't the motor lifeboat then, and they used to launch her down. And when there was a launching day, my Dad used to give so many tickets out, and they only used to get three shillings. And they used to come knocking on t'door: 'Will your Dad save us a ticket'. Well, you daresn't do anything .... They'd have done anything for a three-shilling ticket.

Occasionally, especially in foggy weather, steamers would run onto the rocks. If saving life was involved, it had first claim on the fishermen's attention.

But sometimes this was not the case (fog is often accompanied by calm conditions), and then competition to be first to the stranded ship was intense. A coble or lifeboat which could persuade the captain to let the smaller boat run out a kedge anchor, to be used at the next high tide to enable the vessel to pull herself off the rocks into deeper water, stood to receive what, by fishermen's standards, was a substantial sum of money from the ship's insurers. As J.S. Johnson writes: 'Under these conditions the lifeboats could be launched with maximum speed, with all working like beavers, because at the back of their minds was the thought of salvage money, this being the only real pay a lifeboatman could earn.' He adds, 'I'm afraid the skippers [of the stranded vessels] did not know until later that they had had the last of the pirate races aboard; almost anything was classed as a prize ... .' Clocks and compasses were apparently held in high esteem, and would be stuffed up the fishermen's jerseys.[10]

On such occasions, when no danger to life was imminent, the coxswain had no inhibitions about putting family first:

> When there used to be what we called a 'rocker', it used to be: 'Go on! Knock so-and-so up' – knock all your relations up to go to the rocker ... . I've been roused out of bed: 'Go and knock so-and-so up, go and knock so-and-so' ... I had to go and knock 'em up, and my Dad'd get t'lifeboat ready.

James Noble once (about 1937 or 1938) received £150 as his share of salvage money; and, to take but one of many other instances, £450 was paid out to 36 Staithes men in gold sovereigns in 1907 for assisting in the refloating of the steamer *Whitewood* which had run aground on Cowbar Steel, just to the north of the village. With a new coble costing only one pound a foot in the early 1900s, these were large sums of money.

Apart from the cash which a rocker brought in, there were goods, too. Steamers would discharge part of their bunkers to lighten ship in order to refloat and most fisherfolk recall removing coble-loads of fuel, enough very often to keep fires burning a whole winter:

> And when the wrecks used to come on t'scaur, maybe full of coal, people used to go on. And I used to have to go and mind the coal – frightened anybody took it – until my Dad brought it off. And he always thought about old people that had nothing. He would say: 'Well, I'll go and take them a bag or two.'

This last remark, by Mrs Lowis, reveals a characteristic of the old fishing community. Intensely competitive, individualistic, and even on occasions 'piratical', they would at the same time share good fortune with those among them worse off than themselves.

Apart from coal, saleable goods could sometimes be salvaged from wrecks and rockers. One memorable occasion was the wreck of the SS *Princess Clementine* which ran aground between Runswick and Staithes on 19 November 1924, in a south-easterly gale. The crew was rescued by the Runswick lifeboat, but her master stayed aboard for another eight days before being taken off by the same lifeboat just as the vessel started to break up.[11] The aftermath was remembered vividly by Edward Verrill, then a 17-year-old lad living at Staithes:

> *She* [the *Princess Clementine*] *all broke up. She had all general cargo aboard: bricks and coke, and goodness knows what she had … . Coals and all that washed up. But she was loaded mainly with cinders, coke – very hard. By … our fingers was red raw – we used to bring it ashore in t'cobles. She broke up in t'finish. And things we could have had a lot of, we never bothered with! She had all these cow hides aboard. Well, we got about half a dozen, and t'older men was playing up war, 'cos we were getting these (they thowt they were no good). Blow me down, we got a pound or thirty bob apiece for t'skins. Aye, a firm bought them. If we'd had a hundred of them, we'd have been … . By … ! And she had all these bricks, loaded with bricks, maybe for lining furnaces out. And they were all rough. Maybe got so much a hundred for them. Didn't get much.*

So, if a man was lucky, a rocker could mean a lump sum from the insurers, saleable salvage, and, at the very least, fuel of one kind or another for the winter fire. Little wonder that children on this coast concluded their nightly prayers with the supplication 'And, please God, send a rocker'!

Families could not, however, rely on there being a rocker whenever times were hard, and during a prolonged spell of bad weather when the boats could not get off any opportunity to earn money that offered itself was seized with alacrity. Jim Cole and Tom Welham once went 'bush beating', as they called it, walking several miles up Eskdale to beat for a shooting party. Evidently this was an old stand-by, for in the log-book of Staithes school there is an entry dated 1 November 1896, which reads: 'The attendance this morning is very low. The general excuses for absence from school are "game-driving", "baitin" and potato gathering.'[12]

Clearing snow for the county council or for the railway company were other temporary employments in bad winters, and, very occasionally, fishermen helped local farmers at harvest time. Said Edward Verrill,

> *I can only remember once, things was very bad, and my father went after a job at Skinningrove. Didn't get a job, and he was coming back* [to Staithes]*, walking somewheres about Easington, and a farmer come. He says: 'Would you like a day's threshing?' 'Aye,' my father says, and he went.*

It was a typical example of a readiness to take any chance to work that presented itself.

111 *Ashore near Robin Hood's Bay. The SS* Hermiston, *on passage from Antwerp to Newcastle, went aground on 19 May 1910, half a mile to the north of Bay Ness; but was refloated on 11 June with the aid of four tugs and powerful pumps.*

Dense fog is a serious hazard on the Yorkshire coast, and is especially prevalent in autumn and spring. It is usually accompanied by calm, still weather. Because, it is said, of the ironstone deposits on shore, ships' compasses often became defective and vessels ran aground frequently. They were known as 'rockers'. With the sea calm and no lives at risk, but with ship and cargo to save, it became every man for himself, and fishermen raced each other in their cobles to the stranded vessel in order to be engaged for salvage operations. For this they were paid by the insurance company. 'Please, God, send a rocker!' was a plea included in many a child's prayer, and Christmas was often more cheerful because of the timely payment of November's 'rocker money'. A typical case was the share-out of £250 amongst some Whitby fishermen in May 1878 for salvaging the SS Kenley *which went aground on the Rock in dense fog.*

Some of the sources of secondary income described, such as the merchant service, involved prolonged spells of regular work. At the opposite extreme were sporadic, short-term or accidental opportunities to earn money. A third category of subsidiary income, although in the main seasonal, was predictable and fairly reliable: namely the various activities which may be grouped under the label 'gathering'.

Just as autumn offered the fruits of hedgerow and field to country people,[13] so it did to fisherfolk. North of Whitby, and to the south as far as Ravenscar, are disused quarries, legacies of the 18th- and 19th-century alum industry, long overgrown with brambles. In September and early October these were a useful source of supplementary income for fisherpeople. Mothers, children, and the elderly went brambling; men, too, if the weather happened to be stormy. Just how important the few shillings earned by selling to local greengrocers could be is made clear by Jane Jameson's account:

> *Sin' I knowed, if a man hadn't been doing much* [at sea] *and it's brambling time, they've walked i' t'country, maybe to Sandsend or Robin Hood's Bay where there is plenty. And arned a shilling, or maybe two. They could get a lot with that, two shillings. They could get a quarter of tea for 4½d., in t'old days. And they could get a loaf or a quarter of a stone of flour maybe for sixpence, and yeast. Sugar, two pounds for 2½d. You know, they could do a lot with two shilling, to get a little bit. But they were always thankful ... . But if they weren't off* [at sea], *or anything like that, they couldn't get a penny anywhere. They must have been hungry.*

Income did not necessarily have to be translatable into cash; kind would do just as well. For example, when the trees were bare, villagers at Runswick and Staithes looked forward to 'stick day'. This was a day when local landowners (notably Sir Charles Mark Palmer, MP, at Staithes, and the Marquis of Normanby at Runswick) gave permission for local people to go into the woods and take away as many sticks as they could carry. It was a not altogether altruistic favour on the part of the landowners (as J.S. Johnson points out), but a welcome opportunity to obtain fuel free nonetheless:

> Stick day was really as much benefit to the Marquis as it was to us. If we had not been allowed to go into his woods to collect the dead timber he would have had to use his own men to clear these dead trees and so keep his wood clear and free from fire danger, but by giving our villagers one day to help themselves, they worked harder than any paid help would have done, and he got done in one day what would have taken his men weeks.[14]

Again, this was a task undertaken by women, children, and the elderly, joined by the men only if they could be spared from the fishing or if storm-bound. At Staithes, according to Edward Verrill:

> *Women went ... or maybe schools had a day's holiday for sticking. I suppose it'd be to clear t'woods out, and that. Used to go maybe four or five times a day, right down Dale House ... Palmer's and Major Turton's woods. T'women used ti go with the rowlers on, and baskets. Get long pieces, bundle 'em up, and put 'em on their heads. Aye, they always gave a free day.*

The Marquis's land provided another source of secondary income, in this case illegal, poaching game, an activity engaged in by some Whitby fishermen:

> *When I used to come home on leave just after the* [1939-45] *war, I'd hardly be in the house before G——y* [another fisherman] *would be knocking at t'door, to go shutting* [shooting]. *We used to go on past Kettleness to Kell Green after bods — game, pheasants. Used to shut 'em out of t'trees with a twelve bore. Cartridges were*

scarce, and dear anyway, so we'd try to line up two in the same tree (they sit close to t'bark, you know, up in t'branches). You had to be very quiet: hadn't to tread on a dry stick, and never talk to each other. When you'd got 'em lined up, crack! and down they tummelled. Pull their necks, and into t'bag.

Four cracks around one spot and then you'd walk on maybe two or three miles. Then a few more cracks. I've seen us finish up on Egton Moor side. But we always came back over t'golf links. Because that way, if t'police were waiting, you could bury t'bods in t'sand. Down on t'beach, lapped in a bit of dry bagging: sand doesn't harm, it's clean.

I had a licence to carry a gun and cartridges, and permission to shoot rabbits on t'golf course, but not pheasants! We used to sell 'em, to butchers. You only kept a few around Christmas. You had to get a dinner somehow in wintertime, when things were bad.

A legitimate activity which was a reliable stand-by in late autumn and early winter was potato-picking. In practically every conversation with elderly fisherfolk 'tatie-picking' has been mentioned as a source of both money and food. For Will Richardson, going into the countryside was something he looked forward to:

When I was ten year old [c.1916] I used to go to t'spuds field, with my mother, when t'boats wasn't off, tatie-picking. Sixpence a day; my mother had ninepence. Until you could put t'taties in the cart yourself you only got sixpence, and then you got same as them. If you couldn't put t'taties in the cart you only got sixpence a day. Oh, I've gone miles and miles – nearly eight or nine miles up t'dale. It used to be a good thing … . I was maybe three or four times off school a week, going potato-picking. I enjoyed myself.

Others mention being paid between 1s. 6d. and half-a-crown a day, but there was also some payment in kind, as Laurence Murfield's recollections show:

*There was no dole. At the back end – mostly September, after we'd been salmoning in the summer time – we used to go tatie-picking. Oh, aye, you had ti do … . On your knees, and as he ploughed 'em up, you were picking t'taties into a bucket, and then after you got so far up t'row you'd empty them into a sack. And you were all day bent, like that. You used to get 1s. 9d., from eight o'clock till five o'clock; but you used to get a ten o'clock, and you used to get a meal which was more than you ever got at home. A **real** meal, dinner, a real, hot dinner: pie, meat, anything you wanted – roasted spuds and everything. And then, at three o'clock you got hot apple pie, home-made. Then you used to get a cup of tea and a slice of bread and butter and a bit of cheese at five o'clock. And then as many taties as you could carry … . And you used to fetch half a bag, carry 'em over our shoulders.*

Now, that half a bag would last us … . What my mother used to do: peel 'em and boil 'em, and milk was cheap enough, and margarine (there was no butter – tons

*of butter, but you couldn't buy it, it was only 1s. 2d. a pound). Then she used to mash
'em up like that, with an old swede turnip. Fry it all up, and that was a meal for you.*

There was one other form of gathering which, although it lacked the
additional benefits that potato harvesting conferred, was at least a reliable
stand-by, in that it could be resorted to at any season of the year. That was
'cuvvining'. 'Cuvvin' is the local dialect word for the edible winkle (at Staithes
they are called 'checkers'). These were gathered on the rocky scaur and sold
to local shellfish dealers for forwarding to Billingsgate by rail. It was often a
cold, wet job; and, as stocks at Whitby became exhausted, people would walk
as far as Robin Hood's Bay and Ravenscar, pick cuvvins, and carry them back
to Whitby in bags on their heads. John William Storry's recollections of
cuvvin-picking, round about 1905, show just how crucial this source of income
could be:

> *I remember one Christmas Eve, me and my father* [Will Storry's mother had died
> when he was an infant], *we had nothing like, and he says, 'Is tha wakken, lad?'
> I says, 'Aye. What for?' 'Well,' he says, 'we'll have to go to t'scaur this morning to get
> us our Christmas'. That was at five o'clock. And he says, 'It's a lovely morning' —
> it was all white over with frost. And he says, 'Do you think poor old Joe' — my father's
> uncle — 'will come with us?' 'Well,' I says, 'I'll go and see. So, when I goes up I knocks
> at the door. He says, 'Whae's that?' I says, 'It's me, Joe. My father says, will you go
> with us to Hawsker Bottoms? We're going for cuvvins'. He says, 'Aye, I'll go'. He'd
> had no break'us, you know. But he'd putten a spoon in his pocket, a teaspoon. That
> was for a turnip, to scrape it.*
>
> *We gets to the top of the road, and there's the Hawsker coastguard coming up. He
> had a little lamp in his hand with a candle in, and about ten hooks on a wire trat,[*]
> with a spragg* [a medium-sized cod] *... and a dog. The dog come up first. When
> he popped up with his old white whiskers, Joe says, 'By God, you've given us a fright
> this morning! We never expected you down here'. 'Well,' the coastguard says, 'I thought
> I'd put this trat down. I wanted a fish for my Christmas dinner.' Joe says, 'Christmas
> dinner, be buggered! I'd have thought a man like you would have had a duck or a
> goose'. 'Oh no,' he says, 'I get plenty of fowl through the week' — he had a hen-run.
> We had a few words, and then we went. It was a lovely fish. We went up the road,
> and Joe says, 'What do you think of a bugger like that?! And us hungered to death'.*
>
> *Well, when we gets down* [the cliff onto the scaur], *we picks our cuvvins. And,
> coming up, we'd getten a turnip apiece in our pockets, little turnips* [pinched from
> a farmer's field]. *We sat on the grass. T'knives came out, and we peels the turnips,
> and Joe pulls his spoon out of his pocket and starts scraping. My Dad says, 'By God,
> Joe, tha's fetched thi spoon?' 'Aye,' he says, 'I have nae bloody teeth' — he was getting
> old — 'That's t'reason I've fetched t'spoon,' he says.*
>
> *Well, we gets home — it was a Monday — and on the Sunday me and the old man
> had had some soup. And he says, 'While thoo's up selling t'cuvvins, I'll get t'fire on*

---

[*] 'trat' – a line set at low tide and cleared at the next low tide (not a commercial mode of fishing).

and warm t'drop of soup'. So, I goes up, and I gets half-a-crown for t'cuvvins. So he [father] *went to the little drawer ... . He opens it, gets the rent book out, puts fifteen pence in out of the half-crown (that was the rent for the week, only fifteen pence). Threepence for an ounce of bacca, and I got a penny ... . And there was a tanner left, and we got two necks of mutton for a tanner for our Christmas dinners!*

Then he says, 'Do you think Joe would like a can of this soup?' – I thinks about it every time I sups soup. 'Well,' I says, 'I'll go and see.' He says, 'Reach me that can out of t'cupboard' – a break'us can,* with a lid on.

I knocked at the door and said, 'Are you there, Joe?' 'Aye.' My father says, will you have a can of this soup? He came with both hands. He had ya [one] *clog on, and in his bare feet with t'other. I heard him coming along t'floor, ya git iron clog on. I says 'Hey, Joe, you ain't gitten your clog on!' He says, 'Oh, wait till I get this soup'. And he sat down and got it, with his wet stockings on, he was that hungry. 'Aye,' he says, 'I'll get that one off when I get this down me.'*

Sociological analysis of this kind of experience would be superfluous. True, the various recollections tell something about diet, prices, class perceptions, conditions of work, and so on. But, reduced to their essence, what they show is that people were poor, hard-working, and following a calling which was dangerous and economically precarious. After talking with these elderly people, one is left with a feeling of awe and profound respect for the ways in which they tried to surmount these obstacles. Sadly, however, the obstacles were sometimes too great.

One Thursday morning in November 1909, at about nine o'clock, the coble *Providence* sailed out of Whitby harbour to haul its lines, which were shot off Sandsend Ness. In the coble were Thomas Hutchinson, his 17-year-old son, Joseph, and another lad of about the same age, David Forden. As they were hauling, the line snapped, and this delayed their return to harbour. At four o'clock in the afternoon a gale sprang up, and Tom Hutchinson, knowing he could not make Whitby, decided to run for Runswick Bay. But the wind and sea were too strong, and the coble was blown towards Skinningrove. It was dark by this time, rain was falling 'in torrents', and the sea was breaking over the coble. Tom Hutchinson was bailing out, while his son kept watch. Around midnight, however, the boy became incoherent and delirious. Telling David Forden to keep on talking to Joseph, Tom Hutchinson carried on bailing.

The gale began to abate somewhat, and at eight o'clock the next morning a coble was spotted off Staithes sailing south towards Whitby. Hoping that it was the boat for which the Whitby lifeboat had searched in vain the night before, a message was telegraphed to Whitby. At about nine o'clock a coble

---

* 'break'us can' – breakfast can, an enamelled can with a lid such as was used by miners, railway-men, etc.

could be seen heading towards Whitby beach under sail. As it approached the shore, Tom Hutchinson signalled for a doctor, and when the coble grounded two doctors were amongst those who carried the three men ashore. They had been at sea in an open coble in a terrible storm for 25 hours.

Joseph was unconscious. The doctors applied artificial respiration, stimulants, and hot cloths. Two and a half hours later, at about noon, the lad died.

At the inquest Thomas Hutchinson gave his evidence. The *Whitby Gazette* reported it thus:

> They had no food of any kind aboard the boat, nor any water. They had no food to take if they had wanted to take it – they went off without having had any food. Deceased had only a drink of tea before going, and witness had less than deceased, who had had his tea the night previous, which witness had not. They would have had food aboard if they had had any. Times had been very hard lately, and they had had only three weeks herring fishing – during which time they did well, though they had another boat to buy, their old one having given them up. That was how the money went. They did their best.[15]

Jinny Hutchinson was four years old when her brother perished. Her mother died at the age of 46, and she, not marrying, looked after her father, Thomas Hutchinson, until his death at the age of ninety-one. Miss Hutchinson had a newspaper cutting giving the inquest's verdict on her brother's death: 'due to heart failure, consequent upon exhaustion, due to exposure and want of food'.

Eleven

ASPECTS OF COMMUNITY

112 *Runswick, c.1905 – childhood did not last long if you were a fisherlass.*

LIFE WAS NOT all labour and sadness by any means; although there was no disguising the sombre reality, the endless struggle to survive. When Harold Knight, the artist, and his future wife, Laura, first settled in Staithes in 1896 they instantly recognised the fisherfolk there to be men and women 'dedicated to toil of the hardest ... and knowing tragedy at first hand'. When they left 14 years later to live at Newlyn in Cornwall it was because, said Harold, 'I can't stand constant tragedy any more'.[1] However, as well as in the moments of private joy which sprinkled their lives, fisherfolk found comfort and diversion in various kinds of collective activity. Two examples, one secular and the other spiritual, may suffice to make the point.

No one knew when Staithes Fair was first held, but everyone was certain that it was many centuries ago. Beginning on the Saturday after Corpus Christi, it was a time of jollification lasting a whole week. It was a general holiday in the village and careful preparations were made for the festivities. It marked, too, the change-over to summer fishing, so winter cobles were laid up, and tackle was brought ashore to be tanned, dried and stored away. New gear and different boats were brought out, and all the menfolk were busy painting and repairing.

Women and children were busy, too. 'Attendance not very good', wrote the long-suffering Staithes schoolmaster in his log on Monday, 15 May 1882, 'many [children] kept at home to fetch water, and help otherwise in the cleaning which always precedes Staithes Fair.'[2] Joints of beef and ham were roasted, for it was a time of reunion and open house. When the appointed day arrived at last, everyone donned their best clothes. Men no doubt kept a special guernsey for such occasions, while their wives and daughters, in Ord's phrase, 'exhibit a natural emulation; bright yellow and flaming scarlet being the favourite ornaments of attire'.[3]

Prodigious quantities of food were prepared, and consumed, a special Fair favourite being 'Kiss-me-quick' cake. Perhaps this is the confection mentioned in Dame Laura Knight's vivid description:

> For weeks women had been rushing to the bakehouse, laden with tins of speckled dough; they came back trailing a rich smell. Sometimes as much as a whole pound would be spent on the ingredients of one of these big black sweet cakes, too important to be cooked in cottage ovens. When we arrived the table was spread with every delicacy for which Yorkshire is famous: jams, gingerbread, spice-loaf, curd cakes and in the centre, the black sweet cake.

We had to have some of each; the pile on our plates was crowned by an enormous slab of black cake, containing in itself enough nourishment for a meal. The tea was strong and thick with cream and sugar; at the bottom of the white cup, a little shamrock pattern showed in gold outline.[4]

Outside, the narrow streets were noisy and crowded. The throng, in later years swollen by 'large masses of navvies and ironstone miners, some from a considerable distance',[5] pressed round the booths and stalls or tried their aim at the shooting galleries. Hucksters called their wares, for it was a time, too, for exchanging presents or fairings.

But, as well as the feasting and merry-making, Staithes Fair had its serious purpose. Being one of the few times of year when everyone was on shore together, now it was that crews were re-arranged, family differences patched up, half-yearly accounts settled, quarrels resolved, and matrimonial matches made.[6] As well as celebration, it was a kind of reaffirmation and renewal of the spirit of community. And if that sounds too pretentious, then perhaps the proof lies in the fact that as the fishing declined at Staithes so did the fair. As early as 1872 it was being described as a 'scene of great drunkenness',[7] and the court column of the *Whitby Gazette* testifies to the accuracy of that

113 *Club Walk, Staithes, 1904. In some villages there were thriving Shepherds' Clubs – friendly societies which afforded relief to regular contributors in times of sickness. At Staithes the annual 'club walk' was an occasion for colour, ceremony, thanksgiving and celebration.*

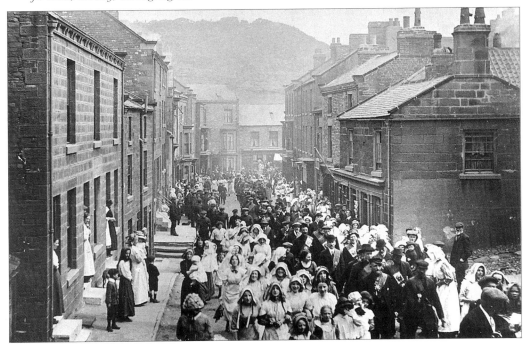

description. Eventually, it degenerated into little more than an annual fun-fair, but by then the fishing had practically ended anyway.

The main point, however, is that Staithes Fair was an occasion, closely identified with the fisherfolk, which afforded the opportunity annually to express the spirit of community in a more or less uninhibited fashion. However, as well as this once-a-year, secular event, there were other, more constant means of maintaining a sense of identity; and ones, moreover, which drew the isolated fishing communities into a broader fellowship and thus to some extent widened their cultural and social horizons. The means, of course, were organised religion, especially Primitive Methodism.

The point has been well made that Non-Conformity had had a good seed bed prepared for it amongst fisherfolk on the Yorkshire coast. As early as 1651 George Fox had visited Staithes and noted in his journal: 'A priest did much oppress the people with tithes ... . For if these people went one hundred miles fishing, he would make them pay the tithe money though they caught the fish at some distance and carried the fish to Yarmouth to sell.'[8] Elsewhere, at a later date, parsons were renowned for their prowess as huntsmen rather than for their piety. Some, it is said, would announce the times of meets along with the banns of marriage at Sunday services. Be that true or false, it was certainly the case that, in general, the established church was seen by the poor to have very little in common with themselves, and a great deal to do with the rich and powerful, from which classes the clergy were largely drawn. Hence one of the great appeals of Methodism: the message of spiritual comfort aimed at the poor and needy. Nor was the message exclusively spiritual. Wesley and his followers 'went right to the bottom of society, and lifted many whom they found there right up to the top', so that some, 'by industry and a favouring providence, rose from menials to masters'.[9]

Filey, however, 'long noted for wickedness of every description', remained impervious to the message. There, it seems, drunkenness, sabbath breaking, swearing, cockfighting, card-playing and 'similar evils' were endemic. Indeed, so hostile were the inhabitants to attempts to introduce Methodism that the preachers who spoke in the streets, barns, and sheds of the town were shouted down, mobbed, pelted with dried fish and other missiles, and on one occasion had pigs driven in amongst their congregation.[10]

As late as 1823 the Wesleyan Society at Filey numbered only 15 members, but then a sudden revival occurred. According to a contemporary:

FACING PAGE:

114 & 115 *Henrietta Street, Whitby, c.1905. Homes were often small and families large, so children played out of doors a great deal. Because mothers were so busy, older sisters or brothers looked after younger (top). Notice in the bottom picture the hurdy-gurdy in the background.*

It pleased the Lord to pour out his Spirit in a most remarkable manner. A young female was powerfully affected; her convictions were so deep, and her distress of mind so great that she could not rest for many days. Her relatives began to be alarmed lest she should lose her reason. A prayer-meeting was held … and she there found peace, and went home rejoicing. The change was so great, that all who knew her were constrained to acknowledge that the work was of God. Two of her sisters soon began to seek the Lord, and were made happy. The blessed word spread amongst the inhabitants of the place; prayer-meetings were held every night during the week, and continued at times until two o'clock in the morning. For some time all work ceased, whole families were brought under the influence of God's Spirit; night and day the voice of prayer was heard to ascend from the dwellings of the people; the fishermen held prayer-meetings on board their vessels, while anchored in the bay, and even the sea resounded with the praises of the Most High.[11]

The quasi-miraculous element in this account is very significant. A similar aura surrounds a number of events which occurred amongst fisherfolk, and also around one of the great figures of Primitive Methodism in Yorkshire, John Oxtoby.

Born in the wolds village of Little Givendale in 1726, the son of a small farmer who failed, Oxtoby grew up to become a farm labourer. As one source puts it, 'he spent thirty-seven years in sin' until, becoming a Wesleyan, 'he obtained peace … and soon began to save his fellow villagers'. In 1818, at Hull, he met William Clowes, one of the founders of Primitive Methodism, and soon after left the Wesleyans to join the Primitive connection. By then 52 years old, he was, according to the historian of Primitive Methodism on the Yorkshire Wolds writing in 1889,

of middle height; had a well-knit frame, brown eyes, and light-brown hair. He dressed quaintly, wore a chocolate coloured neckerchief, a broad-brimmed hat, a flitch of bacon coat, small clothes [knee breeches], hob-nailed boots, his hair was combed down almost to his eye-brows, was in fact the type of a village farmer of seventy years ago.[12]

This was the man who, in the early 1820s, set out to spread the message of Primitive Methodism in Filey. On the way there he met an acquaintance, who asked him:

'Where are you going?'
'To Filey,' replied Oxtoby.
'What to do there?'
'To save the people.'
'It's a forlorn hope,' said the man, 'and you had better go back.'[13]

Undismayed, Oxtoby carried on to Filey where his piety, determination and oratorical gifts soon began to impress.

Just as important in winning converts were the healing powers attributed to him. The Rev. George Shaw, writing not too long after the events in question, in 1867, remarks that, 'The stories told of the effects of his ministry approached the miraculous'. On one occasion Oxtoby went to a house to preach and 'had his sympathies awakened by the sight of a child, who by some unaccountable affliction had been unable to walk or stand'. Oxtoby prayed for the child who, the next day, 'got off its bed, walked to the fire-place without assistance, and continued to play about the house'. The analogy with the miracle described in the Gospel according to St Matthew (9, i-viii) is too obvious to require further comment, apart from mentioning that fisherfolk were unusually receptive to seemingly miraculous phenomena, given their notorious superstitiousness.

So much has been written about fisherfolk's superstitions that it is unnecessary to dwell upon it further, beyond noting that much of the success in converting fisherfolk from their 'wickedness' to godliness depended upon their response to incidents verging upon the miraculous. A case in point was the change-over from fishing seven days a week to Sunday observance. Sometimes this is explained simply as a conscious, reasoned reluctance to violate the Lord's day; yet just as frequently it is associated with the risk of incurring 'bad luck' by working on the Sabbath. In the case of Filey the two explanations intertwine so that Sunday observance (religious belief) and luck (superstition) become virtually synonymous.

Before the advent of Primitive Methodism at Filey 'Sabbath-breaking was general and shamefully open-faced'. Indeed, refusal to work on Sundays became the mark of the convert, and in one case three fishermen (T. Cowling, J. Jenkinson, J. Shippey) went so far as to buy a small three-man yawl from Whitby so that, independent of other owners and crew men, they could unilaterally give up Sunday fishing. Encouraged by their example, Jenkinson's sons, William, John and George, also got a boat of their own and named it *Three Brothers*. The Rev. Shaw tells what happened:

> When [the brothers'] determination not to fish on Sunday was generally known, it was almost universally derided. Among other things it was said, 'They cannot make a living', 'They will sean come to nowt', 'They will have their vessel to sell', &c. Considerable anxiety was felt by the Society [of Methodists] lest these predictions should be fulfilled, and earnest prayer was offered for their success, that 'their religion should not be disgraced'. This anxiety reached its height one Sunday, when two Scarborough boats which had gone out on the Saturday night, came in with about two-and-a-half last

(25,000 herring) each. Great was the rejoicing of the Anti-Sabbatarians, who challenged the *Three Brothers* 'to git hauf as mich'. This challenge was accepted in the firm persuasion that 'God would vindicate the right'. Monday arrived, the brothers sailed, and on Tuesday morning came in with three last. Neither of the other boats 'put in an appearance'. On Wednesday, the little yawl arrived with three last again, but nothing was seen of the rivals. Thursday came, and to the astonishment of the whole place the brothers arrived with *five* last, in all eleven last, or 110,000 fish. When the others came in, they had toiled hard and caught *nothing*. From that time, Sunday fishing was doomed.[14]

This story has been quoted in full partly in order to show how it bears all the characteristics of the classic folk-tale, with suspense building up until the 'good', 'little' yawl and its crew triumph over the bigger, 'bad' boats; and also because it typifies the quasi-miraculous happenings which abound in the missionary literature of the period.

Shaw's *Our Filey Fishermen*, from which the foregoing account is taken, appeared in 1867. In 1882 T.C. Garland published a description of his missionary work in the port of London. He tells of the captain of a sailing merchantman who, despite a favourable wind, refused orders to sail on a Sunday tide, and yet arrived at his destination ahead of skippers who had obeyed the owners' instructions.[15] Four years later, in 1886, E.J. Mather, founder of the Mission to Deep-Sea Fishermen, recounted in his book *Nor'ard of the Dogger* a similar incident which happened in a North Sea trawler fleet. It seems that the skippers in this fleet were all anxious to keep the sabbath and so sent a message ashore petitioning the owner to make that concession. It was refused. Nevertheless, all but one skipper agreed 'we ought to serve God rather than man', and so subsequent Sundays found only the sole dissentient working his gear. No reprisal from the owner was forthcoming, but it was not until Christmas that the puzzle was unravelled. Then, it was the custom for the owner to read aloud to the assembled crews the list of the different vessels' annual earnings.

116 *By the turn of the century a visit to the seaside was within the pocket of an ever-growing number of people; and, along with ice creams and donkey rides, a sail in the bay was an indispensable part of the fun. The fishermen touting for business by the harbour at Bridlington are unmistakable in their caps, dark-blue guernseys and serge trousers. The cobles used for pleasure boating at Bridlington were bigger than elsewhere. Most were half-decked and carried a bowsprit, while the untanned, white sails were intended to give the boats a less workaday appearance.*

At last he stopped and put down the paper:
'Oh, but, sir,' exclaimed several skippers, 'you haven't read what so-and-so made' [the skipper who had fished seven days a week].
'Why, what is that to you? I've read what *you've* made; doesn't that satisfy you?'
'Why, no, sir; 'cause don't you see he's fished every Sunday while we've kept our trawls aboard.'
'Well, well,' muttered the owner, 'I suppose it's sure to come out, so I may as well tell you. He's at the bottom of the list.'[16]

Such stories are legion, and identical in form and outcome. Moreover (and this circumstance is left to speak for itself), economic advantage is always on the side of the God-fearing, so that profit and religious observance are ever in accord; a cunning tactic, the sceptic might say, on the part of these Victorian evangelists, while the faithful can happily see in these stories proof of divine intervention. But even cynics should recognise the practical, beneficial consequences which followed upon religious revival.

First, there was a decline in drunkenness; and, while the dogmatic and often sanctimonious teetotalism of the newly-converted might have been too stern, there is little doubt that another consequence was that many families were rescued from the misery and brutality which prevailed in drunken households. And, second, sabbath-keeping had the effect of giving fisherfolk a weekly day of rest from their hard physical labours. This was particularly important for those men working in the nightmare conditions which prevailed in the deep-sea fleets; but even the inshore men, dominated increasingly by the market, also benefited once Sunday fishing fell into disfavour. Thus, even though the routine of a Victorian or Edwardian Sunday may now seem drear and sombre, it should be remembered that the tranquillity, calm and inactivity were in marked contrast to the weekdays' heavy toil.

As in so many other ways, religious practice at Staithes was very similar to that at Filey. There was the same juxtaposition of superstition and religious belief, the same preference for Non-Conformity. Religion, in fact, at both places was a strong cement binding together the fabric of community and giving point to much social activity. Symbolic of this at Staithes was the practice on fine Sunday evenings of holding a half-hour's communal hymn-singing on the staithe before everyone marched up the street, still singing, with congregations peeling off into the three chapels as each was reached. Such regular ecumenical acts, it is remembered, did much to generate and reinforce feelings of warmth and neighbourliness in the village.[17]

Non-Conformity was strong, too, at Scarborough, as Munby noticed in 1865. As he walked on Sundays along Quay Street he could hear coming from

117 *Most fisherfolk on the Yorkshire coast were Methodists belonging especially to the Primitive connection. At Filey and Staithes they were particularly devout and would not put to sea on the Sabbath. At Whitby, the Seamen's Mission was popular, and many children went to its Sunday school.*

inside some cottages 'lads and girls ... singing plaintive hymn tunes sweetly'. The girls were in Sunday dress, '*viz*: neat longish stuff gowns, much like other folk, but plain and no crinoline'. At six o'clock the young people all went into the Primitive Methodist chapel where a fisherman preached, 'rudely but earnestly', and the congregation consisted 'chiefly of fisherfolk'.[18]

Whitby was another place where Primitive Methodism had put down strong roots, especially among the town poor and shipyard workers. But the Mission to Seamen, founded in the port in 1875, was also held in high regard and successive missioners, by all accounts, worked hard to ease the lot of local fisherfolk. Choirs and Sunday schools flourished, uniformed youth groups were set up, children's treats organised, permissions arranged for fishermen to cut hazels for making crab pots, charitable gifts of food, clothing and fuel were distributed, and comfort was ever at hand when, as was too often the case, tragedy struck at sea. All of this, of course, was in the tradition of Victorian 'good works'. Reforming zeal was absent; which is perhaps why the Anglican church was not in those days much favoured by fisherfolk (except that at Whitby the ancient St Mary's parish church, standing high above Haggerlythe, was held in special warm regard).

The established church's identification with Conservatism was no doubt another reason why fisherfolk tended to prefer Non-Conformity. Methodism generally had inclined towards Liberalism, and this was particularly the case amongst Primitive Methodists. As well as its concern for people's souls, it saw also to their material well-being and individual self-respect. Politics, it quickly perceived, could be a means to achieving such ends, and preachers never tired of reminding the poor of their moral entitlement to participate in civic life. Primitive Methodism seized upon statements such as the one alleged to have been made by an Anglican prelate: 'The poor have nothing whatever to do with the laws but to *obey* them'; and it characterised social relations according to the well-known formula: 'The land for the squirearchy; the army for the officers; the church for the parsons'.[19] For its part, Primitive Methodism espoused readily the Benthamite maxim that the real end of politics is to produce the greatest happiness for the greatest number. It is not surprising, therefore, that, following upon extension of the franchise, the 1886 election results showed that Primitive Methodist votes had gone overwhelmingly to Liberal candidates. Indeed, it was a triumphant boast that the Buckrose constituency of the East Riding (containing Filey, Flamborough and Bridlington), for 40 years a Conservative stronghold, had been turned into a 'Yellow Rose'.[20] Further north, at Scarborough, Whitby and Staithes, Radicalism was also strong amongst the predominantly non-conformist fisherfolk.[21]

The high degree of religious and political Non-Conformity must have had a dual effect: fisherfolk perceived themselves, *and* were perceived by others, as a distinct community in terms of occupation, language and custom; and religion and political affiliation were thus additional, public reinforcers of separateness. Occasionally, however, community degenerated into intolerant clannishness. Probably the worst instance of this occurred at Staithes in January 1910. Two girls belonging to a prosperous local seafaring family had been to Whitby to hear the result of the poll declared in the first of the two general elections held in that year. Delighted, no doubt, to learn that their party, the Conservatives, had held the seat with an increased majority, the girls returned by train to Staithes. There, at the station, they found a crowd of some two hundred people, many of them fisherwomen, waiting for them. As soon as they stepped down onto the platform a storm of booing erupted: 'Some sods and earth were thrown, and some filth in paper packets. One girl was nearly blinded, and the stuff was thrown on their dresses … . Some of the stuff stank … .' Both girls were roughly manhandled, and a fisherwoman held one girl by the throat and 'tore her blouse almost off her back'. This girl, as the *Whitby Gazette* later reported,[22] 'had now only about half the hair on her head which she had before. The crowd was calling on them [the fisher-women] to kill the girl, or cut her in two. Two young men got her away, to Captain Pinder's house. They thought the girl was dying. She was in the house about two hours, while the crowd was crying outside to kill them.' Eventually, the unfortunate girls were rescued by the police.

Yorkshire fisherfolk stuck by Liberalism stubbornly when the party's decline set in after the First World War, and even today Liberal candidates tend to poll well in the Yorkshire coastal constituencies. But where allegiances did change the tendency was for erstwhile Liberal supporters amongst the fisherfolk to transfer their loyalty to the Conservative Party. This was in contrast to the trend amongst working-class former Liberals who in the main favoured the rising Labour Party. In the absence of any firm evidence, one can only speculate as to why this was so. In times of emergency, crisis, death, ill-luck or ill-health fisherfolk displayed a strong community spirit; indeed, so much so that outsiders often saw them as being a class or group apart from the rest of society. Yet in their everyday working lives fisherfolk were intensely competitive, especially in the economic aspect of their existence. A prolific fishing ground

118 *'We made a lot of our own fun. You had to do, in those days.' These children are thought to be Storrs, a well-known Whitby fishing family. They are having a rollicking time in some wickerwork herring swills. This uninhibited photograph was taken with an early hand-held camera round about 1908.*

would be kept secret, subterfuges would be employed to get back to market first; and, for example, fights between crews were not unheard of if it was felt that one boat had usurped another's claim to a good trouting shot. Moreover, as mentioned earlier, every inshore fisherman was to some degree a capitalist. Perhaps, therefore, the collectivist ethic as embodied in socialist theory held little appeal to fisherfolk, and, notwithstanding the communality of their social life, in their economic existence fisherfolk preferred the individualism and free enterprise of Conservatism.

AFTERWORD

DESPITE modernisation, the fishing industry today is, in one important respect, still a primitive form of hunting and gathering. Albeit armed with the latest technological innovations, boats still set out for the fishing grounds not knowing whether they will have a bonanza haul, or empty nets. Yet, cumulatively, modern fishing methods have brought many fish stocks to the point of extinction.

Once vessels cost up to a million pounds to build and perhaps another half million or more to license and equip, there is a powerful economic imperative to maximise catches. But whereas in the last quarter of the 19th century the contest was between traditional small-boat fishermen employing lines and pots and the steam trawlers, today it is huge national fleets that range far and wide across the seas of the northern hemisphere. Worldwide, too, fleets are 'hoovering' up one species after another – as soon as one nears extinction, attention turns to another species, formerly considered unmarketable (for example, the decision by Unilever's Birdseye Foods to discontinue cod fish sticks – 'fish fingers' – and substitute Pacific pollack and New Zealand hoki under the generic label 'white fish').

Unfortunately, both governments and fishermen tend to blame everyone but themselves for this state of affairs: they will call for stringent quotas and conservation measures, while at the same time insisting upon freedom to exploit local stocks. Nor is it just technological advances that are placing such intolerable strain upon natural resources. Paradoxically, perhaps, today's consumers, increasingly health conscious, are buying ever greater quantities of fish. Similarly, the huge growth of holidays abroad has encouraged a taste for species of seafood that, in the past, were often neglected (for example, prawns, scallops and squid).

Research organisations are adamant that greater control over the exploitation of fish stocks is imperative if they are to be saved. According to British government figures (*The Times*, 8 October 2001), whereas in the 1970s cod stocks in the North Sea stood at about one million tonnes, now they amount to only 290,000 tonnes (within that figure, cod by volume decreased by 21 per cent in the year 1999/2000 alone; haddock was down by 29 per cent and plaice by ten per cent; not surprisingly, the value of catches increased, thus placing even greater strain on stocks (*Fishing News*, 7 September 2001).

Cod should live for up to twenty years, yet more than 90 per cent are caught before the age of four. Investigations in Denmark revealed that licensed catches of sandeels consisted of up to 21 per cent undersized haddock (*Fishing News*, 2 November 2001). At the other end of the scale, large quantities of highly saleable mature fish are often dumped back overboard – dead – because they happen not to fit the quota at that specific time.

So far, attempts by the European Union and some national governments – such as by making funds available for decommissioning vessels – may have had some very limited effects. But at best they seem to have prevented the situation from getting worse; there are few signs of substantial improvement (one possible exception to this generalisation is the North Sea herring fishery, which appears to have been brought back from the brink of extinction).

Some fishermen recognise the validity of conservation arguments; but many more are sceptical about them; while some are outright hostile. One possible glimmer of hope is consumer pressure. Not only is the public increasingly resistant to certain commodities because of fears of foot and mouth disease, CJD ('mad cow disease') and genetically modified foods, it is also more open to altruistic marine conservation arguments than used to be the case. Unilever's rebranding of one of its most popular products is perhaps an example of this trend; and the Marine Stewardship Council has accorded the British South-West mackerel hand-line fishery the status of 'sustainable fishery', since, it is suggested, 'growing numbers of consumers will only purchase products from fisheries that do not damage stocks or the marine environment' (*Fishing News*, 7 September 2001).

Many of these developments have had their impact upon the Yorkshire inshore fishing communities. But, again, one can discern both symptoms and cause side by side. Very large, costly vessels fish out of Scarborough and Whitby; many are owned by companies, rather than individual crews. The imperative is entirely towards maximising catches: bigger boats mean higher overhead costs. Smaller boats have also over the past twenty years or so adopted fishing technology that, while technically efficient, is environmentally harmful. One possible 'solution' that suggests itself is the revival of line fishing, which, with improved marketing, might secure a premium for the fishermen, since line-fishing is both conservation-friendly and provides better-quality fish. However, when the well-known television chef Rick Stein filmed a Flamborough coble shooting and hauling its long lines the catch amounted to just one codling!

To regret the demise of the old ways in the Yorkshire fishing communities would be misplaced. Fishing as a way of life in past times was hard, dangerous, often cruel, and largely unremunerative. On the other hand, it is difficult to see how present trends (worldwide, never mind in the North Sea) can be allowed to continue without imminent total collapse. The conservation-environmental argument is increasingly persuasive; what is lacking, however, is political will. At the international level, politicians are under pressure to maximise terms for their own individual countries; nationally, democratically elected politicians often seem to be more concerned with winning the next general election or an individual constituency seat, rather than in taking a longer-term view.

If those fishermen who gave evidence to the Sea Fisheries Commissioners in 1865 and 1879 could see the situation as it is now, there is much that they would recognise, for it was at around that time that many of today's problems had their genesis. In the 19th century, as we have seen, the Commissioners were dismissive of the fishermen's arguments. Today, science is much more precise and less easy to refute or ignore. In the end, it will be the public, the consumer, who will hold the fate of the fisheries in his or her hands. One can only hope that, by then, it will not be too late.

NOTES

Preface

1. George Ewart Evans, *The Horse in the Furrow*, London 1960.
2. W. MacQueen-Pope, *Twenty Shillings in the Pound*, London 1948, p.11.
3. For more information on this point, please see: Peter Frank, 'History and Photographs: Frank Meadow Sutcliffe of Whitby (1853-1941)' in *History Workshop*, No. 2 (Autumn, 1976), pp.93-5.

Chapter 1: The Fortunes of a North Country Port, pp.1-16

1. Gough's Camden's *Britannia* (2nd edn. in 4 vols), Vol. III, p.323; Rev. George Young, *A History of Whitby* (2 vols), Whitby 1817, Vol. II, p.820; Edward Baines, *History, Directory and Gazetteer of the County of York* (2 vols), Leeds, 1823, Vol. II, p.574; *Whitby Fishing Boat Registers* (at Custom House, Whitby), 1891-6, manuscript computation on inside back cover; Robert Tate Gaskin, *The Old Seaport of Whitby*, Whitby 1909, p.216.
2. Daniel Defoe, *A Tour Through the Whole Island of Great Britain* (1724-6), Everyman edition (2 vols), London 1962, Vol. II, p.247.
3. *Whitby Repository*, 1826, p.35.
4. Lionel Charlton, *The History of Whitby*, York 1779, p.358.
5. Young, *A History of Whitby*, II, pp.551-2.
6. Violet Barbour, 'Dutch and English Merchant Shipping in the Seventeenth Century', *The Economic History Review*, First Series, No. II, No. 2, p.280.
7. Ralph Davis, *The Rise of the English Shipping Industry in the Seventeenth and Eighteenth Centuries* (1962), Newton Abbot 1972. See especially chapters III and IV.
8. Davis, *Rise of the English Shipping Industry*, pp.61-2.
9. The foregoing account of the alum industry is based on Charlton, *The History of Whitby*, pp.305-8; Young, *A History of Whitby*, II, pp.806-17; J.U. Nef, *The Rise of the British Coal Industry* (2 vols), London 1966 (1932), Vol. I, pp.184-5, 209-10.
10. Charlton, *The History of Whitby*, pp.307-8.
11. Charlton, *The History of Whitby*, pp.358-9.
12. Richard Weatherill, *The Ancient Port of Whitby and its Shipping*, Whitby 1908, pp.18-19.
13. J.F.C. Harrison, *The Early Victorians, 1832-51* (1971), p.34 in the Panther Books edition, 1973.
14. For more detailed information on the Whitby-Pickering railway, see David Joy, *Whitby and Pickering Railway*, 2nd edn, Clapham 1971; and G.H.J. Daysh (ed.), *A Survey of Whitby and the Surrounding Area*, Windsor 1958, pp.67-8.
15. F.K. Robinson, *Whitby: Its Abbey and the Principal Parts of the Neighbourhood*, Whitby 1860, p.198.
16. Rev. George Young, *A Picture of Whitby and its Environs*, 2nd edn, Whitby 1840, p.220.
17. Cited from Bewick's *Iron-Stone Mining in Cleveland* (p. 30) in Rev. J.C. Atkinson, *The History of Cleveland Ancient and Modern* (3 vols.), Barrow in Furness 1874, Vol. II, p.208.
18. Samuel Jones, 'Whitby, A Poem' (1718) in Gaskin, *The Old Seaport of Whitby*, pp.442-3.
19. Joy, *Whitby and Pickering Railway*, p.20.
20. J. Davison, *Social Life in Whitby in the Nineteenth Century* (mimeographed), Whitby n.d. (1975?), p.10.
21. Introduction to 1969 edition of Lady Bell's *At the Works* (1907) by Frederick Alderson, no pagination.
22. Bewick, *Iron-Stone Mining in Cleveland*, p.29, in Atkinson, *History of Cleveland*.
23. Hugh P. Kendall, *The Story of Whitby Jet*, Whitby n.d. (1936?), no pagination.
24. E.J. Hobsbawn, *Industry and Empire* (1968), p.114 (footnote) in the 1974 Penguin Books edition.
25. Weatherill, *The Ancient Port of Whitby and its Shipping*, p.19.
26. Weatherill, *The Ancient Port of Whitby and its Shipping*, p.20.

Chapter 2: 'Harrowing the Sea', pp.17-38

1. Rev. George Young, *A History of Whitby* (2 vols.), Whitby 1817, p.820.
2. John Walker Ord, *The History and Antiquities of Cleveland*, Edinburgh and Stokesley 1846, pp.298-9.
3. F.K. Robinson, *Whitby: Its Abbey and the Principal Parts of the Neighbourhood*, Whitby 1860, p.309.
4. John Howard, *A History of Wesleyan Methodism in Staithes*, Guisborough n.d., p.24.
5. J.S. Johnson, *The Nagars of Runswick Bay*, Bakewell 1973, p.5.
6. *Whitby Gazette*, 12 November 1870.
7. *Encyclopaedia Britannica*, 9th edn, Edinburgh 1879, Vol. IX: See entry on FISHERIES, pp.243-68.
8. *Report by Frank Buckland, Esq., and Spencer Walpole, Esq., Inspectors of Fisheries for England and Wales and Commissions for Sea Fisheries on the Sea Fisheries of England and Wales*, London 1879, pp.116-17 [hereafter: *Sea Fisheries Report, 1879*].
9. *Encyclopaedia Britannica*, 9th edn, p.249.
10. *Encyclopaedia Britannica*, 9th edn, pp.249-50.
11. *Encyclopaedia Britannica*, 9th edn, pp.246-7.
12. *Report of the Commissioners appointed to enquire into the Sea Fisheries of the United Kingdom* (2 vols. and Appendix), London 1865 [hereafter: *Sea Fisheries Report, 1865*].
13. *Sea Fisheries Report, 1879*, p.83.
14. *Sea Fisheries Report, 1879*, p.81.
15. *Sea Fisheries Report, 1879*, p.75.
16. *Sea Fisheries Report, 1879*, p.133.
17. *Sea Fisheries Report, 1879* (Hull evidence, 25 October 1878).
18. *Fishing News*, 2 April 1976.
19. *Sea Fisheries Report, 1879*.
20. *The Penny Magazine*, 12 May 1838, p.184.
21. Jeremy Tunstall, *The Fishermen*, London 1962, p.21.
22. See E.J. Mather, *Nor'ard of the Dogger*, London 1887.
23. *Sea Fisheries Report, 1879*, p.112.
24. Oral testimony: Many sources, all agreeing on price.
25. *Sea Fisheries Report, 1879*, p.74.
26. *Sea Fisheries Report, 1879*, p.111.
27. *Scarborough Gazette*, 28 August 1873, cited by Arthur Godfrey, *Yorkshire Fishing Fleets*, Clapham 1974, p.23.
28. *Whitby Gazette*, 24 December 1880.
29. Godfrey, *Yorkshire Fishing Fleets*, p.29.
30. Godfrey, *Yorkshire Fishing Fleets*, p.31.
31. *Whitby Gazette*, 3 January 1885.
32. Computed from data in *Whitby Fishing Boat Registers*, Custom House, Whitby.
33. *Whitby Gazette*, 1 August 1885.
34. *Whitby Gazette*, 18 July 1885.
35. *Whitby Gazette*, 12 January 1900; 9 March 1900; 28 September 1900.
36. F.G. Aflalo, *The Sea-Fishing Industry of England and Wales*, London 1904, p.94.
37. *The Field*, 27 February 1909, reprinted in J.R. Bagshawe, *The Wooden Ships of Whitby*, Whitby 1933, p.23.
38. Johnson, *The Nagars of Runswick Bay*, p.188.
39. *Whitby Unemployed Occupational Centre: Annual Report 1936*.
40. *Whitby Gazette*, 31 January 1975.

Chapter 3: Havens and Homes, pp.39-54

1. Brown, *Whitby Gazette*, 14 March 1924.
2. Nelly Erichsen, 'A North Country Fishing Town' in *The English Illustrated Magazine*, No. 31 (April 1886) (pp. 462-69), pp.466-7.
3. *All the Year Round*, New Series, No. 88 (6 August 1870), pp.228-32.
4. *Whitby Gazette*, 12 January 1900.
5. Rev. George Young, *A History of Whitby* (2 vols.), Whitby 1817, Vol. II, p.649.
6. John Walker Ord, *The History and Antiquities of Cleveland*, London, Edinburgh and Stokesley 1846, p.303.

7. George Roberts, *Topography and Natural History of Lofthouse and its Neighbourhood, with the Diary of a Naturalist and Rural Notes*, London and Leeds 1882, pp.358-9.

8. Leo Walmsley, *Three Fevers*, London 1932 (p.10 in the 1947 Penguin edition).

9. J.S. Johnson, *The Nagars of Runswick Bay*, Bakewell 1973, pp.170-1.

10. Johnson, *The Nagars of Runswick Bay*, p.170.

11. Rev. George T. Coster, *Points from my Journal*, London 1908, p.91.

12. Walmsley, *Three Fevers*, p.10.

13. Erichsen, 'A North Country Fishing Town', p.467.

14. *Photographic Journal*, August 1942, cited by Michael Hiley in *Frank Sutcliffe. Photographer of Whitby*, London and Bedford 1974, p.138.

15. Munby Diaries (Munby 33).

16. Johnson, *The Nagars of Runswick Bay*, p.32.

17. Log Book, Staithes County Primary School, 1886.

Oral Testimony
Ned Wright, Alice Maud Hind.

Chapter 4: Fishing Craft, pp.55-82

1. John Walker Ord, *The History and Antiquities of Cleveland*, London, Edinburgh and Stokesley 1846, p.357, quoting a Cottonian MS.

2. Arthur Godfrey, *Yorkshire Fishing Fleets*, Clapham 1974, p.11.

3. Edgar J. March, *Inshore Craft of Great Britain in the Days of Sail and Oar* (2 vols.), Newton Abbot, London and Maine, USA 1970, Vol. I, p.93.

4. G.S. Laird Clowes, *British Fishing and Coastal Craft. Historical Review and Descriptive Catalogue*, London, Science Museum 1937, pp.11-12.

5. E.W. White, *British Fishing-Boats and Coastal Craft. Historic Survey and Catalogue of the Collection*, London, Science Museum 1973, p.13.

6. Frank G.G. Carr, *Vanishing Craft. British Coastal Types in the Last Days of Sail*, London 1934, p.45.

7. March, *Inshore Craft of Great Britain*, I, p.137. The reader seeking detailed specifications of sailing cobles, and other information on the Yorkshire fisheries, will find the whole of chapter 4 of March's book of great interest.

8. Information supplied by Mr John Hunter (b. 1900), Whitby, the noted builder of model fishing craft.

9. *Whitby Gazette*, 21 January 1871.

10. *Whitby Gazette*, 25 February 1871.

11. *Whitby Gazette*, 4 July 1885.

12. Rev. George Young, *A History of Whitby* (2 vols.), Whitby 1817, Vol. II, p.820.

13. *Fishing Boat Registers*, Custom House, Whitby. The registration of fishing boats began in 1869 as a consequence of the Sea Fisheries Act, 1868. The original registers (five in all, including the one in current use) are kept at H.M. Custom House, Whitby. These are referred to hereafter as *Whitby Registers*. The author is extremely grateful to the staff of H.M. Customs and Excise, Whitby, for their courteous assistance, and especially to Mrs Gladys Smith.

14. See White, *British Fishing-Boats and Coast Craft*, p.15.

15. Young, *History of Whitby*, II, p.820.

16. See, for example, Edgar J. March, *Sailing Drifters*, Newton Abbot 1969 (first published 1952), p.19.

17. George Ewart Evans, *The Days That We Have Seen*, London 1975, chapter 8.

18. *Captain Washington's Report on the Loss of Life, and on the Damage caused to Fishing Boats on the East Coast of Scotland, in the Gale of the 19th August 1848*. Ordered by the House of Commons, to be printed, 28 July 1849 (hereafter *Washington Report 1849*). See Appendix No. 22, pp.64-5.

19. *Washington Report 1849*, pp.64-5.

20. *Washington Report 1849*, p.65.

21. Unless cited otherwise much of what follows is based upon analysis of the *Whitby Registers*.

22. Dora M. Walker, *Whitby Fishing*, Whitby 1973, pp.2-3.

23. See, for instance, Figure 51 (facing p.222) in E. Keble Chatterton, *Fore and Aft*, London 1912.

24. Much of what follows concerning the Whitby fleet of modern keel boats is based on Gloria Wilson's

Scottish Fishing Craft (London 1965), which, in addition to the extensive information on Whitby-based boats built in Scotland, contains also a section on boatbuilding at Whitby; and also much other useful information.

25. Dora M. Walker, *They Labour Mightily*, London and Hull 1947, p.3.
26. Walker, *They Labour Mightily*, p.14.
27. Walker, *They Labour Mightily*, p.15.
28. Walker, *They Labour Mightily*, pp.55-6.
29. Wilson, *Scottish Fishing Craft*, p.67.
30. Wilson, *Scottish Fishing Craft*, p.104.
31. Evans, *The Days That We Have Seen*, p.27.

Oral Testimony

John William Storry, Gordon Clarkson, William Esplin (Bill) Clarkson, John Hunter, Alice Maud Hind, Thomas White, Robert William Richardson, James Grimes Cole, Anthony Goodall, James Noble.

Chapter 5: Long-Lining, pp.83-108

1. Edgar J. March, *Inshore Craft of Great Britain in the Days of Sail and Oar* (2 vols.), Newton Abbot 1970, Vol. I, pp.??.
2. Thomas Hinderwell, *The History and Antiquities of Scarborough*, York, 1798, pp.225-6.
3. *Shorter Oxford English Dictionary*, 3rd, revised edn, Oxford, 1959.
4. *Penny Magazine*, No. XVI, 1837, p.391.
5. Hinderwell, *History and Antiquities of Scarborough*, pp.225-6.
6. *Sea Fisheries Report*, 1865, p.123.
7. Hinderwell, *History and Antiquities of Scarborough*, p.229.
8. Lionel Charlton, *The History of Whitby*, York 1779, p.362.
9. The *Guardian*, 28 January 1975.

Oral Testimony

John William Storry, Matthew Hutchinson, James Grimes Cole, Thomas White, Will Richardson, John Verrill, John Hunter, James Noble, Jeffrey Waters.

Chapter 6: Trunking and Potting, pp.109-122

1. Rev. George Young, *A History of Whitby* (2 vols.), Whitby 1817, Vol. II, p.823.
2. *Sea Fisheries Report*, 1879, p.43.
3. *Sea Fisheries Report*, 1865, pp.149-52.
4. *Sea Fisheries Report*, 1879, p.50.
5. *Sea Fisheries Report*, 1865, p.152.
6. *Whitby Gazette*, 25 November 1876.
7. Edgar J. March, *Inshore Craft of Great Britain in the Days of Sail and Oar* (2 vols.), Newton Abbot 1970, Vol. I, p.149.
8. Penny Magazine, *19 May 1838*.
9. *Sea Fisheries Report*, 1879, p.41.
10. *Sea Fisheries Report*, 1879, p.47.
11. *Report of the Inquiry into the Crab and Lobster Fisheries*, 1876, p.45.
12. Captain Leng, 'With the inshore fishermen: methods in vogue on the Yorkshire coast', *Fishing News* (Aberdeen), 27 September 1924.

Oral Testimony

Will Richardson, James Grimes Cole, Edward Verrill, Laurence Murfield.

Chapter 7: Fixed Engines, Jazzing, Blashing and Driving, pp.123-130

1. F. Marian McNeil, *The Scots Kitchen. Its Traditions and Lore with Old-Time Recipes*, St Albans 1974, p.36 (first published in 1929).

2. Lionel Charlton, *The History of Whitby and of Whitby Abbey*, York 1779, p.362.
3. Rev. George Young, *A History of Whitby* (2 vols.), Whitby 1817, Vol. I, p.823.
4. Young, *A History of Whitby*, 1817, I, p.823.
5. Captain Leng, 'With the inshore fishermen: methods in vogue on the Yorkshire coast', *Fishing News* (Aberdeen), 27 September 1924.
6. *Whitby Gazette*, 1 September 1978.
7. *Fishing News*, 27 September 1924.

Oral Testimony

Robert Allen, Albert Hunter, George Frampton, Matthew Hutchinson, Louis Breckon.

The author is particularly grateful to skippers Matthew Hutchinson and Louis Breckon, who kindly had him aboard when salmon fishing and supplied a wealth of technical information.

Chapter 8: Herring – 'The Fisherman's Harvest', pp.131-154

1. Tobias Gentleman, *England's Way to Win Wealth and to Employ our Ships and Mariners*, London, 1614.
2. Rev. George Shaw, *Filey and its Fishermen*, London 1867, p.126.
3. Probably the most informative and comprehensive study is to be found in Edgar J. March's *Sailing Drifters* (Newton Abbot 1969; first published in 1952).
4. Sea Fisheries Report, 1879.
5. Rev. George Shaw, *Our Filey Fishermen*, London, 1867.
6. Edgar J. March, *Sailing Drifters* (1952), p.30 in the 1969 edition, Newton Abbot.
7. March, *Sailing Drifters*, 1969, pp.81-2.
8. F.W. Horne in *Whitby Gazette* (undated cuttings book, Whitby Museum).
9. *Whitby Gazette*, 18 July 1885.
10. J.R. Bagshaw, *The Wooden Ships of Whitby*, Whitby 1933, p.52.
11. Horne (see footnote 8).
12. *Whitby Gazette*, 1884.
13. Horne (see footnote 8).
14. *Whitby Gazette*, 29 August 1885.
15. *Whitby Gazette*, 5 September 1885.
16. G.H.J. Daysh (ed.), *A Survey of Whitby and the Surrounding Area*, Windsor 1958.

Oral Testimony

Thomas Peart, Thomas White, Will Richardson, James Grimes Cole, Maud Hind, Edward Verrill, Matthew Hutchinson.

Chapter 9: Women's Work, pp.155-172

1. An early version of this chapter was published as: Peter Frank, 'Women's work in the Yorkshire Inshore fishing industry', *Oral History*, Vol. 4, No. 1 (Spring 1976), pp.57-72.
2. *Sea Fisheries Report*, 1879, pp.100-1.
3. *Amateur Phtotographer*, 24 July 1896, quoted by Michael Hiley in *Frank Sutcliffe, Photographer of Whitby*, London and Bedford 1974, p.213.
4. Munby Diaries, 1865.
5. Rev. George Shaw, *Filey and Its Fishermen*, London, 1867.
6. Gordon Hume, *Yorkshire: Coast and Moorland Scenes*, London 1904, p.45.
7. Munby Diaries, 1868.

Oral Testimony

Alice Maud Hind, James Cole, Marion Cole, Will Richardson, John Verrill, Ellen Martha Boddington.

Chapter 10: 'Making Ends Meet', pp.173-202

1. *Penny Magazine*, 1837, pp.124-5.
2. Rev. George Shaw, *Filey and Its Fishermen*, London 1867, p.126.

3. *Penny Magazine*, 12 May 1838, p.184.
4. Mary Linskell, 'In and About Whitby', in Whitby cuttings file II, Whitby Museum.
5. Paul Thompson, *The Edwardians*, London 1975, p.311.
6. *Capt. Washington's Report on the Loss of Life ... in the Gale of the 19th August 1848*, London, 1849.
7. *Penny Magazine*, 1838.
8. Lady Bell in *At the Works* (1907), a study of the iron-workers on Teesside, mentions 'what is called the sailor fitter gang, practically odd men, some of whom have in reality been sailors, and do any rigging up of anything incidental that happens to be necessary' (p. 26 in the 1969 David & Charles reprint).
9. J.G. Lythe, *Whitby Jet*, Whitby, 1957, p.6; Hugh P. Kendall, *The Story of Whitby Jet*, Whitby, n.d. (1936?), p.5.
10. J.S. Johnson, *The Nagars of Runswick Bay*, Bakewell 1973.
11. For a detailed description of these epic rescues, see Johnson, *The Nagars of Runswick Bay*, pp.144-6.
12. Staithes School Log Book, 1 November 1896.
13. For an excellent discussion of this question with reference to rural dwellers, see: Raphael Samuel (ed.), *Village Life and Labour*, London 1975, pp.183-227.
14. Johnson, *Nagars of Runswick Bay*.
15. From the report of the coroner's inquest in the *Whitby Gazette*, 17 December 1909.

Oral Testimony

James Cole, Jinny Hutchinson, Bob Storm, Maud Hind, Edward Verrill, Laurence Murfield, John William Storry, James Jameson, Tommy White, Will Richardson, Ann Lowis, James Noble, Bob Marson.

Chapter 11: Aspects of Community, pp.203-216

1. Laura Knight, *The Magic of a Line*, London 1965, p.135.
2. Staithes School Log Book, 15 May 1882.
3. John Walker Ord, *The History and Antiquities of Cleveland*, London 1846, p.229.
4. Laura Knight, *Oil Paint and Grease Paint*, London, 1936, pp.89-90.
5. *Whitby Gazette*, 8 June 1872.
6. Ord, *History of Cleveland*, p.299; *Whitby Gazette*, 14 March 1924.
7. *Whitby Gazette*, 15 June 1872.
8. John Howard, *A History of Wesleyan Methodism in Staithes*, Guisborough, n.d. (1966?), p.5.
9. Rev. Henry Woodcock, *Primitive Methodism on the Yorkshire Wolds*, London 1889, p.17.
10. Rev. George Shaw, *Our Filey Fishermen: With sketches of their manners and customs, social habits and religious condition*, London 1867, pp.16, 44.
11. Shaw, *Our Filey Fishermen*, p.16.
12. Woodcock, *Primitive Methodism on the Yorkshire Wolds*, pp.37, 39.
13. Woodcock, *Primitive Methodism on the Yorkshire Wolds*, p.35.
14. Shaw, *Our Filey Fishermen*, pp.46-7.
15. T.C. Garland, *Leaves from my Log*, London 1882, pp.181-3.
16. E.J. Mather, *Nor'ard of the Dogger*, London 1922 (first published 1887), pp.8-9.
17. Oral testimony: John Verrill, Staithes.
18. Munby Diaries.
19. Woodcock, *Primitive Methodism on the Yorkshire Wolds*, p.264.
20. Woodcock, *Primitive Methodism on the Yorkshire Wolds*, p.264.
21. Henry Pelling, *Social Geography of British Elections 1885-1910*, London 1967, pp.311-13.
22. *Whitby Gazette*, 11 February 1910.

GLOSSARY

Andy Billy (Handy Billy) two blocks so arranged as to enable a **coble** to be sailed very close to the wind (see footnote on p.66).

bait band two cords held close together by a sliding knot (**snotter**) into which the bait is placed in crab pots and **trunks**.

bark; to bark a method used to preserve lines, nets and sails by steeping them in **cutch**.

basket lines lines (usually the heavier **over** lines) that are coiled in baskets, as distinct from on **skeps**.

baulk the main part of a **long-line** (see also **snood**).

beck a small stream or brook.

bed-place a cupboard-like recess for sleeping that can be enclosed when not in use.

berried lobster a lobster that is carrying spawn.

blashing a technique of fishing for salmon and sea trout in which a net is shot across the end of two **steels**, after which the fishermen, from the landward side, work towards the net, all the time shouting, banging and beating the water to frighten the fish into the net.

blebs jelly-fish; the blisters caused by jellyfish stings.

bow-bender a simple instrument for shaping the bows of a crab pot.

braiding (a crab pot) covering a crab pot with netting. See also **knitting**.

brash very small pieces of coal that wash ashore and were raked up to provide fuel in fisherfolk's cottages.

building ram a baulk of timber upon which a **coble** is built (not to be confused with a **ram plank**, which is an integral part of the vessel).

buss a type of Dutch vessel used in the 17th century in the great herring fishery.

carvel-built a method of boat construction where the planks are edge to edge; sometimes referred to as corker-built (compare with **clinker-built**).

caving (pronounced 'kee-aving'): cleaning a **long-line** of seaweed and bits of old bait prior to rebaiting.

checkers see **cuvvins**.

clench to fasten overlapping planks (**strakes**) with copper nails when building a **coble**. See also **dolly** and **clinker-built**.

clinker-built a method of boat construction where the planks overlap each other (compare with **carvel-built**).

coble the characteristic fishing craft of the north-east coast of England. It has a deep forefoot, flat bottom and a square stern. On the Yorkshire coast, 'coble' is pronounced with a short 'o' (cobble), whereas in Durham and Northumberland it is spoken with a long 'o' (co-bel).

crown the curved part of a fish hook. See also **shank**, **wither** and **flat**.

cutch a kind of tannin deriving originally from 'catechu', a substance extracted from the Acacia Catechu, a tree that grows in Malaysia, and used to **bark** lines, nets and sails.

cuvvins the edible periwinkle (known also at Staithes as 'checkers').

dead rise the steep sides of a boat; the **coble**, for example, has little dead rise, whereas with Viking ships it was very pronounced.

dillis a seaweed (Dilsea Cornosa) that was sometimes used to cover freshly-gathered bait to keep it fresh.

dolly an implement used by coble builders when **clenching** the **strakes** of a **coble**.

double-ender cobles and mules that have pointed (as distinct from square) sterns as well as pointed bows (sometimes referred to as 'double-bowed').

drafts strips of wood, not unlike the runners of a sledge, attached to the bottom of a **coble** in order to protect the hull when launching and landing (more conventionally known as 'skorvels').

driving drift-netting.

enders buoys that marked the end of a **long-line** or a net; known variously as 'bowls', 'bladders', 'bunches', 'starts', 'pellets', 'hummocks', 'mullucks' (or 'mollags').

fee-ak and **'ee-ak** a spacing of hooks on a **long-line**; other measures are hook and a miss; two fee-aks and an 'ee-ak; 'ee-ak and 'ee-ak: "ee-ak' is the dialect pronunciation of 'hook', while 'fee-ak' derives from a word in use up to the 17th century, 'fake', meaning a coil of a rope or line.

feeler see **tittler**.

fifie a type of fishing craft characteristic of the north-east coast of Scotland; as the herring season progressed they worked their way southwards, eventually, via Whitby and Scarborough, reaching Yarmouth in autumn.

five-men boat a larger type of fishing craft that persisted into the 19th century, the chief port of ownership for which was Staithes. Five-men boats fished offshore. Sometimes pronounced 'fahve-men' or 'farming boats', the term has nothing to do with farming, but, rather, with the number of men in the crew.

flat the flattened end of the **shank** of a hook that is whipped to the **snood**; see also **crown** and **wither**.

flithers limpets.

fluit, flyboat a type of 17th-century Dutch merchant vessel.

forefoot the bow of the **coble**; this is sharp and deep and, together with the long, projecting rudder, it helps to give stability in the absence of a keel.

fresh a flood of fresh water caused by rainfall on the upper reaches of a river or **beck**; sometimes also referred to as a spate.

ghaut a narrow alleyway, often leading from a street to the waterside (e.g. Tin Ghaut in Whitby).

gip to remove the insides of a herring, a task usually carried out by young women using 'gipping knives'.

gog; gog-stick a short length of hazel with a notch cut in one end and used as a disgorger when taking fish off a **long-line**.

grade (often pronounced 'grathe'): a grappling iron. See also **kess**.

grilse see **summercock; summerbod**.

guernsey a woollen jumper knitted on steel needles to traditional patterns that were handed down from generation to generation and often peculiar to a particular village.

haaf piece see **half-piece**.

hale to haul.

half-piece (more correctly 'haaf piece'): the term derives from the Swedish Norse word 'haaf', meaning 'the main sea'; it refers to the number of lengths that together make up a **long-line**; half-pieces varied in length and, confusingly, there could be as many as twelve 'half'-pieces to a line.

hard ground rocky, uneven sea bed (see also **soft ground**).

'hoss (horse) arses' the fishermen's slang term for the razor shell, which, especially at Flamborough, was often used as bait.

jazzing a type of fishing for salmon at Whitby when a net is shot across the pier ends (often illegally) to catch a run of salmon tempted to go upriver by a **fresh**.

jowl a jowly sea; when the surface of the sea is whipped into choppy waves by a fresh breeze.

keel-boats motorised fishing boats that succeeded **mules** and **ploshers**.

kelkin after attaching a hook by means of a **snood** to the **baulk** of a **long-line**, some 1½ to 2 inches of cord were left free; this was twisted round the main part of the **snood** and then knotted, thus forming a kind of loop. When a line was unbaited, the hooks could be hooked through this loop, the kelkin. A line thus secured was said at Staithes to be 'kidged'.

kess; kessen bowl a buoy (see **ender**) that was attached by a rope to an anchor and which was used to mark the location of a broken **long-line**; sometimes referred to, logically, as a 'guess-bowl', but in fact the term derives originally from the Old Norse 'kesta', meaning 'to cast', which in Middle English became 'casten'. See also **grade**.

kidged see **kelkin**.

klep a gaff; a length of hazel to one end of which is lashed a very big hook; used to gaff fish as they are hauled to the surface.

knitting (a crab pot) covering a crab pot with netting. See also **braiding**.

line-fishing see **long-lining**.

line-set a length of wood that corresponded to one or other of the spacings of hooks on a long-line (see **fee-ak** and **'ee-ak**).

long-lines stout lines to which are attached short lengths of cord bearing hooks; used to catch bottom-swimming fish, such as cod, haddock and skate.

Lowstermen (literally, Lowestoftmen): elegant sailing vessels from Lowestoft that came north each year to Scarborough and sometimes Whitby for the herring fishery.

lute stern the square stern of a **yawl** that inclines inwards.

mawn see **swill**.

miffy a crab that has lost its big claws.

muck sometimes it was not possible to put to sea for days on end, so, if a line had already been baited, the putrefying bait had to be removed, that is, 'mucked'.

mule a large double-ended **coble** used for herring fishing. See also **plosher**.

nab (Old Norse); ness: a headland.

nancy, nanycock see **ninty**

ness see **nab**

ninty an undersized (and, therefore, illegal) lobster, known also as a 'poke'; at Runswick and Staithes as a 'nanycock', and at Hartlepool as a 'nancy'.

otter trawl a trawl net, the mouth of which is kept open by wooden doors (otter boards). The term is thought to have originated with the invention of this device by the skipper of the Scarborough trawler *Otter*.

one-eye a crab pot with only one **smout**, instead of the usual two.

overing see **spring fishing**.

pap a kind of sea anemone used as bait; the word derives from the appearance of the anemone.

parlour pot a crab pot that has an additional compartment that can be entered by the crab or lobster only from within the pot itself.

pipe see **smout**.

ploagin beachcombing.

plosher a bigger version of the **coble** used mainly in the herring fishery. At Filey the plosher was known as a 'splasher'. Ploshers could be square-sterned (as at Staithes) or double-ended (as at Scarborough).

poke see **ninty**.

potting fishing for crabs and lobsters using crab pots.

pull to row.

queens; queenies scallops.

ram plank the **coble** has no keel; instead it is built on a ram plank, a solid baulk of wood that is like a knife on edge at the front (bow), but which gradually shades off to being flat at the rear (stern). Should not be confused with a **building ram**.

ring-netting a method of fishing for herring, pioneered by Scottish fishermen, where a pair of **keelboats** stretch a long net between them and then gradually come together, trapping the fish in the bag of the net.

rowler a doughnut-shaped, circular pad (see footnote on p.149).

sand fishing; fishing in t'sand fishing for salmon by shooting a net on the sandy side of the West Pier at Whitby.

sand stroke the plank (or **strake**) that is almost flat to the ground and upon which the **coble** rests when not afloat.

scaur, scarr smooth, rocky foreshore, usually shale, with scattered boulders.

shafts see **steels**.

shank the straight part of a hook (see also **wither**, **crown** and **flat**); may refer also to the straight part of an anchor.

share men a **coble** usually had a three-man crew, but sometimes two men and a lad (the **tratter** or **trat lad**); the proceeds of the boat's catch would be divided into four shares – one for each man, plus one for the boat (in the case of two men and a tratter, there would be three shares – one for each man and one for the boat, the trat lad keeping the proceeds from his own catch, but from a shorter line).

size, or sizeable, crab (also known as a 'tale' or 'tally' crab): a crab of full, legal, market size.

skane to remove the soft bait from mussels and limpets.

skeel a type of wooden bucket, wider at the base than at the rim.

skep (Old Danish): an oval, flat, wickerwork basket upon which **long-lines** were coiled; at Hartlepool on the Durham side of the Tees, skeps were known as 'rips'.

skorvels see **drafts**.

slack; slack water a short period between tides when the water is neither coming in nor going out.

smout the netted entrance to a crab pot through which a crab or lobster approaches the bait; known also as a 'spout' or a 'pipe'.

snood (pronounced in the Yorkshire dialect 'sneead'): a length of thin cord to which a hook is whipped at one end, while the other end is attached to the **baulk**.

snood board a board around which snood-cord was wound before cutting it to the required length.

snotter the sliding knot that holds bait in the **bait band** of a crab pot or **trunk**.

soft ground (sometimes referred to as 'mild' ground): sea bed consisting of mud, clay, sand or gravel (see also **hard ground**).

splasher see **plosher**.

spout see **smout**.

sprag a medium-sized cod.

spring fishing a type of fishing that involves catching young herring with drift nets and using them for baiting heavy long-lines to catch bottom-living fish such as cod, haddock, ling and skate; often referred to as 'overing'.

steam box a long box into which a plank is inserted and into which steam is pumped in order to make the plank more pliable when building and shaping a **coble**.

steels long fingers of hard rock extending seawards that may be exposed at low tide; also known as 'shafts'.

strake, stroke a plank, as used in the construction of a **coble**, for example.

summercock, summerbod a salmon under 8 lbs; usually a fish returning to the river from the sea for the first time. Also known as a 'grilse'.

swills baskets into which bait, usually limpets or mussels, were gathered (at Filey known as 'mawns').

tale, or **tally, crab** see **size crab**.

telpie hermit crab, the soft part of which was a favoured bait.

thoft seat (more conventionally referred to as a **thwart**).

thole-pins iron pins fitted to the top side of a rowing **coble** over which iron rings attached to the oars are placed; a kind of rowlock.

thosk the nereid worm, used as bait.

tittler a 'tickler'; a short line put down when fishing for dogfish to ascertain whether or not fish are present; sometimes called a 'feeler'.

tongs an implement used to hold planks (**strakes**) rigid while they are being **clenched** when constructing a **coble**.

trat; trat line a relatively short long-line that is anchored at both ends and set, baited, on the foreshore at low tide and the catch gathered at the next low tide; a type of small-scale fishing favoured by elderly fishermen or other non-fisherfolk members of the community mainly as a source of food for personal consumption (see also **tratter**).

tratter; trat lad the junior member of a **coble's** crew who has his own line (**trat**), usually shorter than those of the **share men**, the catch from which he keeps for himself.

trunk a net bag attached to an iron ring and baited to catch crabs and lobsters, used up to about the middle of the 19th century at Flamborough; this type of fishing was known as 'trunking'.

tumble-home where the sides of a **coble** incline inboard.

willock whelk.

wither the barbed point of a hook (see also **shank, crown** and **flat**).

wyke; wike (Old Swedish): a small coastal bay.

yager; herring yager Dutch vessels that, in the 17th century, carried barrels of salted herring from the fisheries off the northern coasts of Britain to the Baltic, returning to Holland with valuable commodities purchased there.

yawl large, off-shore fishing boat which engaged in drift-netting for herring that was then used as bait for **long-lines**; successor to the **five-men boats**.

yuck salmon nets when **sand-fishing** were usually shot at right angles to the shore; at the furthest seaward extremity the net would be turned to form a loop, the yuck.

zulu a fishing vessel characteristic of the far north-east coast of Scotland (in particular the Moray Firth) which, together with **fifies**, worked their way southwards to Yarmouth, via Whitby and Scarborough, following the herring.

BIBLIOGRAPHY

Aflalo, F.G., *The Sea-Fishing Industry of England and Wales*, London, 1904

Atkinson, J.C., *The History of Cleveland Ancient and Modern* (3 vols), Barrow in Furness, 1874

Bagshawe, J.R., *The Wooden Ships of Whitby*, Whitby, 1933

Baines, Edward, *History, Directory and Gazetteer of the County of York* (2 vols), Leeds, 1823

Bell, Lady, *At the Works* (1907)

Browne, H.B., *Chapters of Whitby History, 1823-1946*, Hull, 1946

Carr, Frank G.G., *Vanishing Craft. British Coastal Types in the Last Days of Sail*, London, 1934

Charlton, Lionel, *The History of Whitby*, York, 1779

Coster, Rev. George T., *Points from my Journal*, London, 1908

Crohan, Tomas O, *The Islandman*, London, 1929

Dangerfield, George, *The Strange Death of Liberal England*, London, 1935

Davis, Ralph, *The Rise of the English Shipping Industry in the Seventeenth and Eighteenth Centuries* (1962), Newton Abbot, 1972

Davison, J., *Social Life in Whitby in the Nineteenth Century* (mimeographed), Whitby, n.d. (1975?)

Daysh, G.H.J. (ed.), *A Survey of Whitby and the Surrounding Area*, Windsor, 1958

Defoe, Daniel, *A Tour Through the Whole Island of Great Britain* (1724-6), Everyman edition (2 vols), London, 1962

Encyclopaedia Britannica, 9th edn, Edinburgh, 1879

Evans, George Ewart, *The Days That We Have Seen*, London, 1975

Evans, George Ewart, *The Horse in the Furrow*, London, 1960

Garland, T.C., *Leaves from my Log*, London, 1882

Gaskin, Robert Tate, *The Old Seaport of Whitby*, Whitby, 1909

Gentleman, Tobias, *England's Way to Win Wealth and to Employ our Ships and Mariners*, London, 1614

Godfrey, Arthur, *Yorkshire Fishing Fleets*, Clapham, 1974

Gough's Camden's *Britannia* (2nd edn. in 4 vols),

Harrison, J.F.C., *The Early Victorians, 1832-51*, London, 1971

Hiley, Michael, *Frank Sutcliffe: Photographer of Whitby*, London and Bedford, 1974

Hinderwell, Thomas, *The History and Antiquities of Scarborough*, York, 1798

Hobsbawm, E.J., *Industry and Empire*, London, 1968

Howard, John, *A History of Wesleyan Methodism in Staithes*, Guisborough, no date

Hume, Gordon, *Yorkshire: Coast and Moorland Scenes*, London, 1904

Johnson, J.S., *The Nagars of Runswick Bay*, Bakewell, 1973

Joy, David, *Whitby and Pickering Railway*, 2nd edn, Clapham, 1971

Keble Chatterton, E., *Fore and Aft*, London, 1912

Kendall, Hugh P., *The Story of Whitby Jet*, Whitby, no date

Knight, Laura, *Oil Paint and Grease Paint*, London, 1936

Laird Clowes, G.S., *British Fishing and Coastal Craft. Historical Review and Descriptive Catalogue*, London, Science Museum, 1937

Lythe, J.G., *Whitby Jet*, Whitby, 1957

McNeill, F. Marian, *The Scots Kitchen. Its Traditions and Lore with Old-Time Recipes* (1929), St Albans, 1974

MacQueen-Pope, W., *Twenty Shillings in the Pound*, London, 1948

March, Edgar J., *Inshore Craft of Great Britain in the Days of Sail and Oar* (2 vols), Newton Abbot, 1970

March, Edgar J., *Sailing Drifters*, Newton Abbot, 1969

Mather, E.J., *Nor'ard of the Dogger*, London, 1887

Nef, J.U., *The Rise of the British Coal Industry* (2 vols) (1932), London, 1966

Ord, John Walker, *The History and Antiquities of Cleveland*, Edinburgh and Stokesley, 1846

Pelling, Henry, *Social Geography of British Elections 1885-1910*, London, 1967

Report of the Inquiry into the Crab and Lobster Fisheries, London, 1876

Roberts, George, *Topography and Natural History of Lofthouse and its Neighbourhood, with the Diary of a Naturalist and Rural Notes*, London and Leeds, 1882

Robinson, F.K., *Whitby: Its Abbey and the Principal Parts of the Neighbourhood*, Whitby, 1860

Robinson, Joe, *The Life and Times of Francie Nichol of South Shields*, London, 1975

Samuel, R. (ed.), *Village Life and Labour*, London, 1975

Sea Fisheries Report, 1865

Sea Fisheries Report, 1879

Shaw, Rev. George, *Filey and Its Fishermen*, London, 1867

Shaw, Rev. George, *Our Filey Fishermen*, London, 1867

Thompson, Paul, *The Edwardians*, London 1975

Tunstall, Jeremy, *The Fishermen*, London, 1962

Walker, Dora M., *They Labour Mightily*, London and Hull, 1947

Walker, Dora M., *Whitby Fishing*, Whitby, 1973

Walmsley, Leo, *Three Fevers*, London, 1932

Washington, Captain, *Captain Washington's Report on the Loss of Life, and on the Damage caused to Fishing Boats on the East Coast of Scotland, in the Gale of the 19th August 1848*, London, 1849

Weatherill, Richard, *The Ancient Port of Whitby and its Shipping*, Whitby, 1908

Whitby Unemployed Occupational Centre: *Annual Report*, 1936

White, E.W., *British Fishing-Boats and Coastal Craft. Historic Survey and Catalogue of the Collection*, London, Science Museum, 1973

Wilson, Gloria, *Scottish Fishing Craft*, London, 1965

Woodcock, Rev. Henry, *Primitive Methodism on the Yorkshire Wolds*, London, 1889

Young, Rev. George, *A History of Whitby* (2 vols), Whitby, 1817

Young, Rev. George, *A Picture of Whitby and Its Environs*, 2nd edn., Whitby, 1840

Barbour, Violet, 'Dutch and English Merchant Shipping in the Seventeenth Century', *The Economic History Review*, First Series, Vol. II, No. 2, p.280

Erichsen, Nelly, 'A North Country Fishing Town', *The English Illustrated Magazine*, No. 31 (April 1886), pp.466-7

Frank, Peter, 'History and Photographs: Frank Meadow Sutcliffe of Whitby (1853-1941)', *History Workshop*, No. 2 (Autumn 1976), pp.93-5

Frank, Peter, 'Women's Work in the Yorkshire Inshore Fishing Industry', *Oral History*, Vol.z 4, No. 1 (Spring 1976), pp.57-72

Leng, Captain, 'With the inshore fishermen: methods in vogue on the Yorkshire coast', *Fishing News* (Aberdeen), 27 September 1924

All The Year Round
Guardian
Penny Magazine
Whitby Gazette
Whitby Repository

Munby Diaries (Trinity College, Cambridge)
Staithes School Log Book
Whitby Fishing Boat Registers (Custom House, Whitby)

INDEX

Note: Page numbers in *italics* refer to illustrations